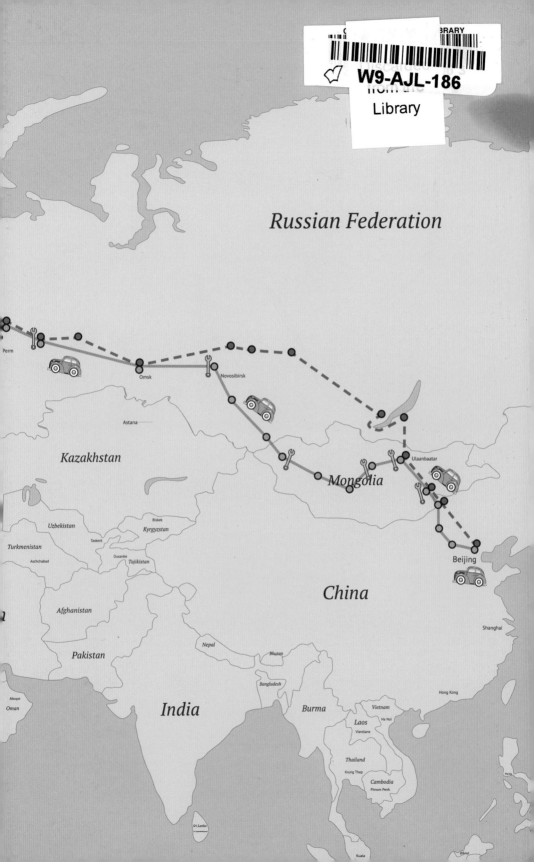

Russian Federation

Perm

Omsk

Novosibirsk

Astana

Kazakhstan

Mongolia

Ulaanbaatar

Uzbekistan

Biskek

Kyrgyzstan

Taskent

Turkmenistan

Aschchabad

Dusanbe

Tajikistan

China

Beijing

Afghanistan

Pakistan

Nepal

Bhutan

Shanghai

India

Bangladesh

Burma

Hong Kong

Masqat

Oman

Vietnam

Laos

Ha Noi

Vientiane

Thailand

Krung Thep

Cambodia

Phnom Penh

Hanila

Sri Lanka

Kuala

Bynai

Peking *to* Paris

Peking to Paris

*Life and Love on a
Short Drive Around
Half the World*

DINA BENNETT

Skyhorse Publishing

Skyhorse Publishing books may be purchased in bulk at special discounts
for sales promotion, corporate gifts, fund-raising, or educational purposes.
Special editions can also be created to specifications. For details, contact the
Special Sales Department, Skyhorse Publishing, 307 West 36th Street,
11th Floor, New York, NY 10018 or info@skyhorsepublishing.com.

Skyhorse® and Skyhorse Publishing® are registered trademarks of Skyhorse
Publishing, Inc.®, a Delaware corporation.

Visit our website at www.skyhorsepublishing.com.

10 9 8 7 6 5 4 3 2 1

This book relies on my memory of events leading up to and during my
participation in the 2007 Peking to Paris Motor Challenge. As such it is a
purely personal recounting, reflecting my opinions and recollections. I did
change some names and identifying details of individuals to protect the
privacy of those who are now friends.

Library of Congress Cataloging-in-Publication Data is available on file.

ISBN: 978-1-62087-800-2

Printed in China

*"The mere sight of a good map
fills me with a certain madness."*

—Freya Stark

To Bernard—the driving force in my life—with love

Table of Contents

Preface: Flirting with Disaster

I would like to say that I am a brave, adventurous person. But if I did, this would be a work of fiction. In truth, I have always had a love-hate relationship with adventure. My ambivalence goes back to my earliest memory. Actually, it's not a memory at all, just fondly recounted family lore. It concerns how I took my first steps, holding onto a recording of Artur Rubenstein performing Chopin nocturnes. Apparently, the feel of something solid in my hands offered me just enough illusion of security that I was able to stand and walk. Briefly. It took only two wobbly steps for me to realize the nasty trick that record was playing on me. I was holding *it* up, not vice versa. Lucky for me that when I pitched forward I had the presence of mind to fling the record out of harm's way. Otherwise I would have shattered it in the fall—not to mention deprived my mother, a gifted pianist, of a favorite recording. But when I fell and didn't break the record, my mother and her friends all applauded. And I didn't cry. I beamed. In that instant I learned a brief but powerful lesson: that imagination could take me further than common sense.

For every positive there's a negative, though. Ever since that record's betrayal I've tended to imagine the worst. Always, always, I'm accompanied by worries. If I'm swimming near shore where it's shallow enough for my feet to touch the bottom, I see myself pummeled by a wave, drowning with my mouth full of salt water and sand. The presence of snow conjures images of an avalanche, and I feel the agonizing claustrophobia of an icy coffin with my arms pinned by snow set as hard as concrete, gasping as I suffocate. My progress through life has been a bizarre cha cha cha, as my desire to experience everything pulls me forward, while my nameless dreads yank me back.

I have another memory from my childhood. In it I'm lying on the TV room couch under a white comforter printed with sprays of pale pink and green flowers. This was the sick-day comforter, the one I was allowed to snuggle under as I watched daytime shows when home from elementary school with a sore throat or the flu. If I wasn't so sick that I was confined to bed, I'd establish a beach head on that couch and watch TV all day. I'd start with the strange calisthenics of *Jack LaLanne,* followed by the shrill silliness of *I Love Lucy* and the drunken cooking instruction of *The Galloping Gourmet,* who slurped slivovitz while handling sharp knives. After an appropriately soothing lunch of chicken soup with rice I'd return to the couch with my glass of ginger ale for the best show of all: *Let's Make A Deal.* I found Monty Hall's ritual for choosing contestants fascinating and humiliating. I knew that, even were I old enough to attend a *Let's Make A Deal* taping, I would not have had a purse large enough to carry the variety of items Monty might ask for, let alone the foresight to store a pair of underwear, a spatula, fifteen keys, and a hardboiled egg in it on the off-chance he'd request them. But once he yelled his trademark, "Come on dooowwwwn," to the overjoyed contestant, I was all in, rooting "Pick door number one. No, no, no. Stop. Take door number two!"

Let's Make A Deal made a peculiarly lasting impression on me. Which is why, as I do my awkward dance with worry, I'm also on the lookout for an opening, a possibility, a door that may be cracked just a fraction, enough for me to stick a toe through and push it open so I can see what's on the other side. This is the story of one such door and what occurred when I blindly decided to step through. Had you been in my shoes, I suspect it's a journey you could have accomplished as well as I did. Probably even better.

Beijing: Take One

It never occurred to me that I would spend so much time in a car—any car—and in places a GPS has to think twice about pinpointing. I'm just not suited to this. I get carsick. I live in a perpetual state of anxiety. And I hate not knowing what comes next. I've done a lot of things in life because I didn't think carefully enough beforehand, didn't know to turn tail and run. When I'm in trouble, I rue this major defect in my character. Once I'm out of trouble, I thank goodness for my ability to use fantasy to pull me into escapades for which I'm utterly unsuited. Without that ability, what follows could never have happened.

We've barely set foot in China, and already I'm feeling the familiar twinge of panic that I might get lost. Knowing how to find my way is a skill of more than ordinary importance to me. In a matter of days, we'll be idling at the Great Wall in a seventy-year-old vehicle and waiting for a checkered flag to wave downward, releasing us on a 7,800-mile car race to Place Vendôme in Paris. My husband Bernard will be driving. And for the next thirty-five days, I'll be telling him where to go.

At the moment, I am plowing my way through the crush of people jostling to meet arrivals at Beijing Capital International Airport. I walk as my mother taught me when, as a small girl, I struggled behind her, bucking the rush-hour crowds in New York's Grand Central Station. "Put your hands on your hips, darling," she said in her lilting French accent *"comme ça,"* her manicured hands placing mine properly, so my elbows stuck out. "When people are too close, just poke them," she told me, tossing her head

3

with laughter at her own daring. The trick worked for her, but I suspect it had nothing to do with arm placement and all to do with her glamour and perfume. I was five years old. My head barely reached the average commuter's waist. No one gave way for me, leaving me struggling to keep up, face reddening with panic, rubbing my bruised elbows.

Here in Beijing, my mother's crowd-tamer trick is once again deficient. Buffeted by hordes of happy greeters, I watch Bernard swiveling his hips through the mass of people like a retreating rumba dancer. So sure is he that he's breaking trail for me, helping me along, that he doesn't even glance back to see I'm falling further and further behind.

To keep my carry-on bag from sliding off my shoulder, I scrunch my neck to keep the strap in place. But my neck, already cocked at an odd angle from eighteen hours in a plane, refuses to maintain the position. The bag, loaded with maps, chargers, a handful of my favorite lemon Luna bars, and a Radio Shack-worth of spare batteries, slams to the floor. I stop to readjust, looking up just in time to make out Bernard as he dodges into a small taxi. By the time I duck in beside him, I'm a sweaty mess. I'm also a happy mess, ready for the relief offered by this safe, though sadly too temporary, mobile haven.

Despite being jet-lagged, with eyes shriveled to hard little raisins from too many hours on a plane, there's one thing I do notice: there are a *lot* of people here, more people in one square block than in the entire 2,400 square miles of my Colorado county, where the resident population barely breaks 1,400 souls on a day when everybody gets out of bed. Millions are going about their business as our taxi driver wends his way through traffic, stopping now and then to let a flood of pedestrians flow across the clogged streets. When a gap appears at the curb, new pedestrians swarm to fill it, backed by countless more. Peering through the window, I alternate between stunned gratitude that I'm here and a fretful anxiety at what this implies. Everywhere are street signs in Mandarin, a language I've been unable to learn. Since I'm stupefied with lack of sleep, I actually believe if I stare hard enough at them I'll learn the language by osmosis. If I don't, how will I ever understand signposts to get us out of the country once the race begins?

4

Our driver swerves around pedestrian obstacles in a marvel of brakeless daring, his body a universal symbol of diligence with hands clenching the steering wheel, back ramrod straight. As for me, normally so impatient I'd like to personally press a cab driver's foot on the gas pedal, I feel a distinct yearning for him to slow down. I'd be delighted to live in this cab forever, if it meant avoiding the moment when I have to don the mantle of navigator-in-chief to Bernard's role as driver. If someone were here to listen, I'd say, "This is all a big mistake." Yes, I know Bernard is next to me, but he's not in any position to understand my longing to flee. He's a man with limitless faith in himself. I don't mind a risk or two, but only if I can control the outcome. As surely as I know my long hair and deep-set eyes are brown, and that while I'm not plump I will never be skinny, I know the Peking to Paris Motor Challenge is a runaway horse charging downhill with the bit in its teeth. I've ridden such a horse so I can tell you: control is not one of the things you feel in that situation.

What perplexes me is how in the past 700-odd days I never found the courage to tell Bernard I don't really want to do this. Of course, that would have meant bucking the trend of our marriage. We're a couple who generally does everything together, accommodating each other's foibles in a way many people never manage. We created a successful software company together, built our dream home, turned our backs on it all, and took on the ranching life. Any one of those would have shredded a relationship more fragile than ours. Yet here we are, still married.

Let's be clear, though. This race is Bernard's dream, not mine. Cars for me are purely a functional means to reach a pleasant end, like a friend's house, a good restaurant, or my favorite nail salon. And then there's that other issue, that small matter of getting carsick. The nausea wells up as soon as I try to read in the car and it lasts for hours after I again set my feet on terra firma. Equally dire for any car-related enterprise, I can barely tell a car jack from a jackass. How could I have been so spineless as to agree to this enterprise or so deluded as to think it would go away on its own?

Giving up on learning Mandarin from the back of a cab, I rest my head on the nubby fabric of the back seat, a spot marked by so many resting heads that the gray upholstery is darkly stained with hair grease and scalp sweat. When I close my eyes, the lids become a screen for a movie trailer, an endless loop I've been rerunning for months now. It starts with clonking Chinese percussion, shrill violins, trilling flutes, then the booming bass voiceover: *"When their car collapses, stranding them in the Gobi, fun and fireworks erupt. Will they make it? Or will one of them walk home alone? Follow this manic duo as they feud their way through Siberia and beyond . . . ."* We're in the starring roles, and this sounds like a comedy preview, only none of it strikes me as humorous.

The whining din of those devil violins fades away as I drift back to a warm September afternoon on the courthouse lawn of my tiny ranching town. Sizzling elk burgers spatter their juices onto charcoal. Tantalizing riffles of meat- and fat-scented smoke drift into the heavy branches overhead, where robins twitter their fervent hope that they will not become bird-kebabs on that grill.

As days go, that one was benign and rustic in its charms. I saw no sign saying "Caution! Anguish and marital discord ahead," had no inkling I was about to descend into a realm of merciless travails with the swiftness of a barrel over Niagara Falls. All for one thing: to drive the Silk Route taken by Genghis Khan and race against 125 other teams, using a classic car most people would have left in their granddad's garden shed.

It's a day I'd reviewed in my mind countless times, wondering if that afternoon could have had a different ending.

Courthouse Revelations

Picture this: fifty exquisite classic cars parked haphazardly under the flickering shade of tall cottonwoods. They're the crème de la crème, the sort that make you gasp with admiration. I'm talking Shelby Cobra, Bentley, Lagonda, Aston Martin. Drivers and their navigators wander among plastic-clothed tables. They're sniffing, salivating, and waiting with good-natured impatience for the local Lion's Club to declare lunch ready.

This is the Colorado Grand classic car tour, a week in which the most beautiful old automobiles in the world are invited to drive through our state's small towns and breathtaking scenery. On this route, my beloved county is the smallest and poorest of all, a mere splash on the map, with only one town. That town is a ramshackle collection of buildings straddling the state highway, itself just a two-lane blacktop connecting Wyoming with ski resorts to the West and South. It's a place you'd drive through and wonder aloud who could possibly live in this cluster of lackluster clapboard houses. Look past those boarded-up buildings, and it all becomes clear. Our valley has wilderness areas on three sides as well as gold medal trout streams. Soaring over it all is that cerulean sky for which Colorado is famous. This is the place to drive through if you have an old car and want to use it. As these people do.

I wend my way through the crowd, pausing now and then to inspect a vehicle. I know even less about old cars than I do about new ones. Even if I had an iota of connoisseurship, I'd hardly dare touch the gleaming paint on any of these. Far be it from me to blemish a six-figure vehicle with a finger smudge.

When I finally spy Bernard, he's unconsciously bouncing up on his toes. His strong, five foot six frame is like a hot air balloon barely tethered to the ground. I grab his arm to prevent liftoff. Bernard's an effervescent man anyway, but now he's bubbling in a way I haven't seen in years. His green-blue eyes are framed by a mass of crinkles, his eyebrows are waggling, and his French accent is getting stronger, as it does when he's truly excited. "This is Matthieu and Amélie," he says, gesturing to a slender, sandy-haired gentleman with piercing blue eyes, his arm sweep including the classically groomed woman at the man's side. I take in their studied casualness, their creased khakis, no brand name visible. Around here the only time pants are pressed is when you wear them out of the store, the name Carrhart or Wrangler prominently displayed on your back pocket. With barely a pause for me to say, "Pleased to meet you," Bernard launches into the cause of his excitement. "Remember the book I have about the *Croisière Jaune*? Well, they've done something just like it, following the old Silk Route. It's a rally. For old cars." He spears me with a passionate stare. "There's another one in 2007."

Bernard takes barely a moment to swallow and catch his breath, but it's enough to give Matthieu an opening. This he fills with the most extraordinary information. "It's called the Peking to Paris Motor Challenge," he says in faintly accented, slightly off-kilter English, though whether his origins were Swiss, Dutch, or German I couldn't have said. He studies me in a professorial way, interested in me perhaps, but more interested in what he's about to tell us. "You know, this is a redoing of a car race organized by Italy's Prince Borghese a hundred years ago. So 2007 will be the centenary."

As he now recounts, in May 1907 five cars set out from Peking—as it was called then—to prove that man and machine could indeed go anywhere, that borders between countries were irrelevant. They left Peking with no passports; these had been confiscated by Chinese authorities on the pretext that the drivers were spies. The Chinese had no interest in seeing the success of the motorcar, having just invested in shares in the Trans-Siberian railway. On this first-ever endurance rally, there were no marshals or officials. Fuel was transported by camel. The person who went to Peking to drop the flag at the beginning of the race caught the ship back to Paris and arrived just in time to flag drivers across the finish line sixteen weeks later. Of the intrepid five, four made it to Paris, arriving to a tumultuous welcome and worldwide fame. The fifth, maneuvering an awkward motorcycle-automobile hybrid called a Contal cyclecar, bogged down in the Gobi desert. "The crew was lucky to be found alive by locals," Matthieu informs us. Arching an eyebrow, he continues ominously, "Their car was never found."

Wiping his hands on a clean rag and carefully closing the long hood of the exceedingly elegant car behind him, Matthieu offers a sop to calm the agitation that must be evident on my face. "Things are better organized these days, of course. But the Chinese still don't seem too happy to let us drive through their country." He doesn't appear to be someone's mechanic, so with my customary insightfulness I deduce that the vintage vehicle he's been working on belongs to him. It's massive, but, dare I say, artistic in its design; if it were a sculpture, it would be a Rodin, not a Calder. The vehicle itself seems unusually big, perhaps as long as our extended cab, full bed, one-ton Ford pickup. Its long, sloping front fenders bring to mind a springing cheetah. A steel-spoked spare wheel adorns each running board. The black convertible top is folded back, allowing the black leather seats to warm in the sun. "When I did a similar event in 1997," Matthieu continues, "we drove for thirty days. It was a completely different route. Quite difficult, very tiring. But fascinating."

"What did you drive?" I ask in a sociable, chatty way. It still hasn't dawned on me that someone with a car as splendid as that Mercedes would be willing to submit it to the rigors of Mongolian sands, Tibetan plateaus, or Siberian anything. If one had such a rare and beautiful vehicle, why would one court the possibility of smashing it on rocks, dredging it through rivers, or, even worse, flipping it over? I would like my expression to convey how intent I am on delving into the drama and the rigors of what he's done, but my line of questioning is halted by the need to fuss with stray strands of my hair, which the plucky breeze has just blown over my eyes and into my mouth.

Matthieu looks at me, tolerant and bemused. "This car, of course. Built in 1927. Runs very well." Then he exclaims, "Bernard, this is the thing for you! You will love it." It seems in the moments before my arrival he's discerned Bernard's love for remote places, his pleasure when in deep vehicular trouble, his intense knowledge of all things automotive. Matthieu has no idea that I get panicky at the thought of car breakdowns, that my automotive knowledge fits into the small vinyl pouch that holds my car's outdated first-aid kit. While I have long wished to be at ease in remote places, the truth is, not knowing if I'll reach safe shelter at the end of the day makes me intensely nervous. Why in the world would I want to subject myself to what he's described?

Then Matthieu drops the gauntlet.

"You must have an old car in order to go. Yes, the rally organizers allow only old vehicles to register. Prewar, if possible. Because, you see, they want to create an event that will use cars as close as possible to the originals." His eyes twinkle when he says this, relishing the fact that he clearly has the sort of car they're after. "Do you have one?"

Bernard and I look at each other, speechless. Do we have an old car? What on earth for? What we have are vehicles that can handle six months of winter snows, the deep powdery stuff others pay a fortune to ski in but that we have to drive through. Where we live, if you're waiting for a winter-time roadside rescue, you want a well-sealed, comfortable cab and a fanatically dedicated heater to keep you company during the cold hours it'll take for a tow truck to arrive. Two-seater convertibles with spoke wheels? Sedans with ribbed leather bucket seats and whitewall tires? These are not the conveyances that'll get us home from town in a blizzard.

The bird chatter seems to grow in urgency, while the buzz from the burger line dims into the background. I turn to Bernard and see him standing there, so eager he's almost vibrating. I think, "Well, if you're with him, how bad could it get?" "Bad," I answer myself.

"Go," my adventurous side pleads. "It'll be wild, a once-in-a-lifetime experience. Consider it this way: two years from now, would you rather be driving through amazing Mongolia, or fixing a barbed wire fence?"

"Forget about it," retorts the cringing side of me. "The entire concept is too far-fetched. It's everything you hate about travel. Too many people around. Too many unknowns. Stick with what you're good at . . . which is *not* reading in a moving car."

Matthieu is staring at us, a slight smile playing on his lips. If I could stop arguing with myself I'd have a chance to engage this gracious European in clever, meaningful repartee—that is if I could think of anything to say. Thankfully, Matthieu interrupts my baffled reverie, "But, you may not be able to register anyway. Because I think they are already full."

I look again to Bernard, see the wide, gleeful grin and his body tilted just a little bit forward, as if ready to go. I recall our vows nearly 25 years ago: to have and to hold, to love and to cherish. Who knows. Maybe there also was something in there about getting in a car together and going whither the road might lead. To drive and be driven. If there wasn't, who am I to say there shouldn't have been. Besides, to put a spin on Groucho Marx, if we can't get in, then the Peking to Paris 2007 Motor Challenge is clearly something we must do. Our eyes connect and I can't disappoint him. I nod.

"We don't have such a car," Bernard says. "But we can find one."

Why I Said Yes

We were a classic office romance. I was a recent MBA, hoping to get a foot in the door of a local word processing developer. When they offered a temp job subbing for a vacationing secretary over the Christmas holidays, I accepted. Bernard was a recently divorced Frenchman who'd just been transferred from Los Angeles to Boulder, Colorado, by the same company. It was love at first sight. I was smitten by Bernard's charm, his skill in things I knew nothing about, how the lines around his green eyes crinkled into rays when he laughed. He delighted in my sense of humor, fashionable clothes, and French cooking. When he peered over my shoulder at the office, sniffing Chanel, eying my shoulder tattoo, patiently explaining some new software, I knew he was *it*. At twenty-eight I'd looked long enough for the right man. That Bernard was a Catholic to my Jew, boundlessly brave to my innately cautious, French to my American, twice married to my never-been-hitched, made us complementary, not incompatible. I had no doubt he was the man for me.

On our first date, as he whisked me off to a glamorous hilltop restaurant in his sleek silver sports car, I knew one thing immediately: this man was a serious driver. He was self-assured, on intimate terms with the road. I found his elegantly fresh aftershave intoxicating. His hands on the steering wheel drew my eye: long competent fingers, neatly trimmed nails, his palms sheathed in supple, black kidskin gloves, the kind with holes over the knuckles and no fingertips. Part of that evening, the wine and luscious food, thrilled me. The other part, in which my fear of speeding filled the back of my throat as we careened through hairpin turns, did not.

I should have set the tone right then, told him plainly what my preferred car experience was. But it was our first date, and I thought that would spoil things. Besides, I wanted to impress him with my willingness to go where he went, at his speed. Keeping up seemed important. And then there was my belief that, "If there's a door in front of you, shove it open." In this case, I also wanted to shut that door behind me and live on the other side of it forever. With him.

Our relationship progressed rapidly. First a shared Christmas tree, next a communal kitten, then buying a house, and, within half a year, marriage in front of a priest and cantor, with a cross overhead and Bernard stamping on a wineglass in good Jewish tradition. In the months that followed, I exposed Bernard to quintessentially American endeavors: pumpkin carving, movies with candy *and* popcorn, the importance of heart-shaped gifts on Valentine's Day, why a campfire requires the roasting of marshmallows. Weekend mornings we lazed in bed while I read him *Winnie the Pooh* and *Charlotte's Web*, my answer to his *Asterix* and *Tin Tin*.

It was a fair trade, as Bernard showed me a world in which any difficulty could be overcome by staying calm and thinking carefully. His fearlessness inspired me, his continental courtesies made me nicer. He was effortlessly caring, putting three ice cubes in my ginger ale—just the way I like it—when I was sick, placing himself on the traffic side of the sidewalk to protect me with his life should a car jump the curb. He laughed at my puns, learned to waltz and two-step because I loved dancing, let me correct him when he charmingly pronounced English words in the French way, calling a Viking a "weeking" and Levi's jeans, "leh-wiss." He admired my knowledge of Mozart and Chopin, called me *"cherie adorée."*

Best of all, Bernard watched out for me, and that allowed me to be braver than I otherwise would have been. When the snow melted, we took to the hills on bicycles, Bernard pumping away in front, me drafting behind. Together we learned windsurfing and got our open water diving certificates. We went rollerblading, Bernard heading for an area that was all downhill. "I don't think I can do this, Bernard," I said.

"Yes, you can." He showed me how to brake, held my arm as we started, then stayed by my side as we picked up speed. I didn't fall.

Candles and flowers appeared just because. Without my even prompting, Bernard took care of washing the dishes. I figured that nicety would be cast aside before the ink dried on our marriage certificate, but he continued scrubbing pots and loading the dishwasher long after the wedding chimes were silent.

There was nothing Bernard couldn't figure out how to repair or rebuild. He drew plans, calculated supplies, while I, a natural helper, handed him tools or carted away trash. I also was highly attuned to the need for a hot chocolate with schnapps or a sustaining lunch. His seemingly innate ability to figure out how to do things impressed and thrilled me.

A year after our wedding, Bernard started his own business. It was the early 1980s, and a novelty item called a PC had appeared. Now, people around the world were whispering about how great it would be if software ran in their own language. Having worked for computer companies all his life, Bernard knew enough about language and software to smell a good opportunity. His business plan was this: "I am French, I know software; therefore, I can translate." He found a software developer who believed him, who gave him a translation contract just like that. I thought I could see the future, and it delighted me. He'd be his own boss, working a few months, taking plenty of time off to travel. I would pursue work as a free-lance writer. All would be well.

At last we're free, I thought.

Au contraire.

The first few years of business, as he scraped by on credit cards, showed just how out of focus my personal rose-colored glasses had been. Succumbing to the anxiety of looming bankruptcy, I ground my teeth at night as I dreamed about losing our home. Our attempt to maintain some semblance of a normal life meant that we tried a few short vacations. Our overworked credit card paid for those as well, which made those trips less than relaxing.

My dentist told me I should change my life or risk having my molars crack. "What are you suggesting I do?" I asked.

"Get rid of the stress," he advised. I would have hooted at his sense of humor if his fingers hadn't been pulling my lips open in an unsightly grimace. Get rid of the stress? Have Bernard give up after so much hard work? Unthinkable.

My anxiety built, to the point where after every meal I felt sick. I'd lie down, limp and pale, while Bernard paced, concerned I had a fatal illness. I feared admitting what I suspected. That my mounting worry about maxed-out credit cards was causing my stomach to go into acidic spasms. Instead, I decided to join him in the business, hoping my American forthrightness and PR experience would be the persuasive edge the company lacked.

Indeed, our talents complemented the other's perfectly. Though not good with technical things and fairly ignorant about the mechanics of what we did, I discovered a knack for convincing people who'd never met me to part with large sums of money to work with us. Whatever project I brought in, Bernard figured out how to accomplish. As the company grew, I continued to lose sleep, but now at least my nightmares were of the two of us going under together, rather than Bernard drowning and leaving me behind.

Success came, and it was great. And it also wasn't.

Beijing: Take Two

The smog in Beijing is a permanent thick blanket. It seems we are living in a dense cocoon of pollution, which coats my lungs, clings to my skin, and makes my eyes sting. Mornings we clamber up sections of the Great Wall, the steepness flexing my ankles to such a degree that the tendons start to shred. The next morning, my ankles are swollen and my first steps out of bed a painful hobble. I can't know it at the time, but this injury will be the gift that keeps on giving. Throughout the rally, my daily walk from parking area to hotel is a slow, mincing shuffle; a year later, the tendons are still so inflamed that I cannot even run.

Afternoons we wander past Mao's mausoleum in Tiananmen Square, craning our necks at the brownish-blue sky where a riot of boxy and serpentine kites battle it out, blue against yellow, red against orange. Kite handlers race about below somehow, magically, never colliding. Crossing the square, which is the length of nearly ten football fields, is a balancing act between two bad options. At first we circle around the oncoming throngs. Soon we tire of serpentining far out of our way and decide to wade through them instead. This is a total gamble, as there's equal likelihood we'll emerge on the other side as there is of being swept by the human current in their opposing direction. When we squeeze shoulder to shoulder with thousands of vacationing Chinese in the Forbidden City at the Square's north end, we realize the crowds near the mausoleum were meager.

One warm evening, we take a stroll along a canal behind our hotel. Above the constant hum of traffic I hear the strains of an orchestra, playing a Strauss waltz. It's tinny and faint, but so lovely and out-of-place in this rapidly modernizing city that our feet are drawn toward it. As we amble along under gracious old trees, we come upon a tiny park, with rusting, rickety workout equipment dispersed around a concrete slab. It's from decades ago, a Communist-era perk to spur public well-being. "Look Bernard, there's no one on any of these things," I say, so used to the masses at Beijing's tourist spots that I can't believe there's no queue for this stuff. Bernard does a few chin-ups and sit-ups, while I wobble along the balance beam. It's a balmy late-May night, and we're not the only ones out taking advantage of it. Some young couples, pudgy and round-shouldered, stand nearby. Their kids pedal tricycles in between the rings and the parallel bars. Everyone eyes us with unabashed curiosity, perhaps amazed to discover these sculptural relics have a use. Bernard hoists himself higher and I'm more acrobatic to please our audience.

Finished with our gymnastics, we allow the music to draw us onward, heading for a street lamp in the near distance whose weak glow pulls us through the gathering dark. Reaching it, we find a faintly illuminated plaza, where twenty or so couples twirl slowly to Strauss's "Blue Danube." Nobody's dressed up. They all seem to have hurriedly dried their hands on a dishtowel, perhaps leaving pots in the sink to come out to this open-air ballroom. A DJ manages a small boom box, its long power cord attached umbilically to the nearby street lamp. As he flips a CD and punches buttons for the right track, the dancers stand silent and respectful, as if frozen. He offers a polka, then a waltz, a foxtrot, and another polka. Since everyone's partnered up and knows the flow, it seems they must meet here for outdoor dancing on a regular basis. No one wastes time talking. It's all about the music, and if a woman doesn't have a male partner, she dances with another woman.

Bernard and I took ballroom dance lessons before our wedding, so we could waltz and foxtrot in style on our wedding day. Over the years, we'd wowed not a few old-timers with our jitterbug moves, had them clapping from their tables as we stomped the floor. This plaza, though, is small, and we don't want to offend anyone by knocking into them, or god forbid, stepping on their toes. So we stand arm in arm, hip to hip, on a patch of thin grass and watch.

With each new dance the couples adjust to the new rhythm, though their steps remain the same, a boxy, rigid movement without grace. It doesn't matter. I'm enchanted by what I see, because it's clear these plain, working class people in ill-fitting tops and shapeless dresses are here to do one thing only: dance. They're loving it, just as I do. We're about to leave when suddenly the lilting strains of "Vienna Woods" fill the Beijing night. Everyone on the dance floor nods and smiles in recognition of this beloved waltz, and they take off, whirling and dipping in three-four time.

Walking back to our hotel, arms wrapped around each other's waist, I think back to our euphoria on receiving confirmation that our entry application for the Peking to Paris had been accepted. It was July 2005, and everything those first few months was exhilarating. I ordered maps of each country the Rally would cross. Spreading them on the dining room table, Bernard and I pored over them, piecing together the tentative route the organizers sent with our acceptance packet.

We placed flags to mark the towns that would take us north from Beijing the 625 miles to Mongolia. From there we'd drive over 1,700 miles northwest across Mongolia and the Gobi Desert to a recently opened border post with Russia called Tsagaannuur, where we would enter Siberia. Through Siberia we would tackle the immensity of Russia, making our way nearly 3,400 miles along that country's southern edge to Moscow and then straight north to St. Petersburg. Once through Russia, we'd cross into Estonia, where we'd zip a seemingly minor 780 miles south through the Baltic countries of Latvia and Lithuania. Clearing the Baltic states would mean we had merely 1,325 miles left, driving west through Poland's Lake District, then southwest into the former East Germany. Within sniffing distance of Paris, we'd traverse the wine country of Germany's Moselle Valley and enter France from the east, near where fabled battles were fought in World Wars I and II. Then it would be a straight shot west, stopping for a sip of bubbly in Reims, the heart of champagne country, before crossing the finish line in Paris.

This epic adventure captured every corner of my imagination. In Mongolia we would be camping at night, in a set location where we would be met by fuel trucks. Such gas stations as Mongolia could offer would never have enough petrol to serve 125 cars at one time. There'd be a camp support team, hot showers, port-a-potties, chilled beer, and a hot dinner and breakfast for us each day. It sounded like a wonderful safari, absent the elephants and lions. In China and everywhere else, we'd be in hotels. In Siberia, though, some of the cities where we'd be sleeping were so off the tourist track that there weren't hotels large enough to accommodate the entire Rally; in those places as many as four hotels had been booked each night, with crews divided among them.

There were days I could see myself in an elegant, open-topped old car, chugging through quaint hamlets that time had passed by, my long white scarf fluttering behind me in the wind, à la Isadora Duncan. Only I never would be so careless as to let my scarf get caught in the wheel spokes and snap my neck as hers did. In my daydreams, we'd pull into a humble cafe, where we'd be able to sample whatever the regional cuisine had to offer. Villagers and kids would stop by and, drawn by our exotic car, sit down and chat with us. We'd learn about their lives, share details with them about ours. "I don't think we'll be able to stop for lunch," Bernard told me. "Normally on rallies you keep going till you reach your final control point for that day."

"Oh, that can't be possible, Bernard," I scoffed. "Why would anyone bother driving through these places if they couldn't ever stop?" I was busy creating the trip of a lifetime and didn't want to dwell on what he was saying.

On other days, I envisioned myself dressed in immaculate khaki pants, unpacking a brown embossed leather trunk with brass hinges, jaunty in my crisp white shirt with sleeves rolled to the elbow, a sporty, soft deerskin vest holding my navigator tools, whatever those might be. I'd be a Ralph Lauren model come to life, and I even toyed with the idea of asking Ralph Lauren if they'd care to sponsor us. Then it occurred to me that if they accepted, I'd be beholden to someone or something. For me, the appeal of the Peking to

Paris was that it would be Bernard and me against the elements, with no one looking over our shoulder, not even the 250 other competitors and 50-odd members of the support crew.

Through a contact at The Nature Conservancy, we asked to host three visiting Mongolian naturalists. They brought a book of photographs with them to show us their country. I was stunned how similar our landscape was to theirs, the deep forests, rushing rivers, and alpine flowers, and the eagles, marmots, and other wildlife that filled it. I loved the notion that two places a world apart could resemble each other so closely and thought myself the luckiest person in the world to be able soon to see it for myself.

At more practical times, I made secret plans to enroll in various auto mechanic and rally driving classes. "Don't worry about that," Bernard said. "I'll do the driving. And I can take care of the car." This was Bernard's gracious way of telling me I had never shown aptitude for auto mechanics, so why start now. A new dream began to recur, with me kneeling beside Bernard working on a repair, the two of us bent over an antique car, heads together, discussing what the problem could be with the engine. Bernard would look at me adoringly, flabbergasted by my new skills. Again we'd be equals. One day when I was showing him an off-road driving course I'd discovered, which I thought would give me the driving chops I lacked, he said, "But Dina, in a rally the driver stays as the driver throughout the race. You won't need to drive." Then he added, "Besides, as navigator, you'll have your own responsibilities." I would?

Grill That Beaver, Ride That Ditch

After a decade, it seemed that Bernard and I had given up our souls for the growth of our company, that all we did now was work. Gone were the joys of discovering shared passions. The jokes, the dancing, the laughter, all faded. *Pooh* gathered dust on a shelf. Bernard had become The Road Runner, zipping along in manic overdrive, gripped by a compulsion, which I couldn't fathom and no longer wanted much part of. I was Wile E. Coyote, panicked smile glued to my face, clinging to the crumbling cliff of our marriage with frantically scrabbling paws.

In the cartoon, Coyote plunges into the abyss, to be resurrected moments later battered and disheveled, but ready for another go. But this was real life, and I desperately didn't want to fall. So I hung on, feeling ever more frayed, sometimes despairing, but always convinced that if I could just manage a bit longer, I'd be able to pull myself—pull *us*—over the precipice and back to safety.

Several more years passed before things finally fell into place and our company sold. With funds and freedom firmly in our grasp, it was time to blow the lid off our pent-up travel urges. We trekked to remote Kanchenjunga in the eastern Himalayas. We cantered on horseback through the African bush. I even squelched my fear of avalanches to ski in the Canadian wilderness. Before each of these trips, I steeled myself to the anticipated rigors with a stern talking-to, shoring up my timid side with a bracing reminder that lesser mortals than I were able to do this. Not so Bernard. If anything, the impression he gave me was that the trips were pleasant, but, well, rather tame. Another sign I should have read, but ignored.

In between all this coming and going, we moved to a cattle and hay ranch high in the Colorado mountains. Acquiring land, having space, was Bernard's idea, but as usual I was happy to follow. Besides, I'd acquired a horse habit. This had started seven or eight years before, when I told Bernard, half in jest, that I wanted to be a well-rounded human being, one who, for instance, could handily saddle a horse and mount up should I be invited to Balmoral Castle by the Queen. For some reason, he didn't need to ask me which part of that statement was the joke.

On my next birthday, Bernard led a handsome bay gelding across the field in front of our house. Behind him trudged my father, nearly buried under a western saddle so large and heavy I could barely heave it onto the upstairs railing in our home, where it stayed as a decorative element for many years. The next morning, Bernard and I spent half an hour trying to figure out how to get a halter over my new horse's head. Things could only improve from there. I bought myself a lightweight English saddle, took riding lessons, and learned by personal experience how carefully one rises after falling off a fast-moving horse and how long it takes the purple to appear on ones butt when the bruise is bone-deep. We got a barn built and learned the difference between good and bad hay, as well as how much of the former a horse needs to eat. Terms like farrier, tack, and worming entered my consciousness. Bernard bought a horse, too. It was his only hope of ever seeing me again.

By the time the ranch came into view, I knew one thing for sure. I no longer wanted to be tied to home, throwing hay to horses each day. That the ranch came with eight additional horses was not a worry. There was so much pasture we could let the horses self-feed—locals called this 'grazing'—and still have plenty left for a few spare equines. Besides, we both wanted a radical change of lifestyle. On a ranch we'd be outdoors. I've read all the *Little House on the Prairie* books, so I knew what that meant: fixing fences, checking cows, tracking water through ditches, cutting and selling hay, bringing hot covered casseroles to neighborhood potlucks, helping those neighbors with branding. That our ranch was eighty miles and two hours of winding mountain roads from the nearest shoe store or pharmacy was put in the category of "minor inconvenience."

Though things didn't go perfectly our first summer on the ranch, we were hooked by our new life. Instead of being slaves to product release schedules, we now followed the seasons. Our concerns shifted from errors in a Japanese translation to whether it would rain. I abandoned hard drives and learned to drive a tractor pulling a baler over a back meadow. The first summer on the ranch I helped put up a thousand tons of hay. In the golden light of a setting summer sun, I watched red-tail hawks wheeling low, on the mouse hunt, as my baler compressed sweet smelling grass into a tight seventy-pound package bound with orange twine.

As for enlarging our horse herd, I went to the federal penitentiary in Cañon City, home to the BLM's wild horse adoption program, where I adopted a scrawny young mustang stallion newly culled from the wild herds that populate western Colorado and Utah. In my quest to become the ultimate horsewoman I rode alone over the ranch's dry bluffs and marshy willow cars. My horse sniffed the recent scat of a large elk herd and spooked six feet sideways when equally surprised mallards took flight from a beaver pond. I attended clinics on natural horsemanship, practiced the tricks back home, and picked sagebrush out of my hair every time I got bucked off. Bernard had time to indulge his passion for big equipment, amassing a collection of trucks and tractors, each one necessary for some ranch task. It seemed to me I should learn to use them, too. That doing so was an essential part of being a ranch woman. But then there was my penchant for daydreaming, for spacing out at critical moments. Bernard couldn't fathom how I never seemed able to remember how to turn any of them on, couldn't understand how what had become so obvious to him remained so obscure to me. Impatience burgeoned between us, and I left the equipment side of ranching to him. I'm keeping the peace, I told myself. And anyway, why would I need to use them myself, when Bernard could drive, use, and fix them all?

After a summer of putting up hay and tending to ranch chores, the sparkling days of fall were pure pleasure. With no more snow melt to fill it, the river outside our door shrank, and beavers built their dams in inconvenient places, creating ponds deep enough for moose to swim across. Six-point bull elk jousted in the meadow, keeping us up at night with their clacking antlers and strident, ringing calls.

Bernard accumulated an assassin's-worth of guns, one for every sort of bird or animal. Ever since his days as an artillery captain in the French army he'd been a crack shot, on friendly terms with the sort of precision rifles of which Carlos the Jackal would approve. He bought me a lightweight, century-old Winchester .22 repeating rifle. It had a long, slender barrel of some deeply tanned wood, black burnished steel fittings, and a manual scope. Recalling my childhood shooting a cap pistol around the backyard, terrorizing my sister as I chased her in my red cowboy hat while she fled screaming in her matching blue one, I was delirious to finally have the real thing. When my first shots came within inches of the bull's eye, we both were stunned. Secretly, I put another notch in my pioneer woman belt. Then I bought a handgun.

On cold, misty mornings, Bernard rose at four o'clock to hunt. Though I refused to hunt, I was happy to share in the bounty, insisting only that if he took an animal's life, we needed to make use of it. Cured elk skins carpeted the floor and beaver pelts covered the backs of chairs. With only an occasional glance at a cookbook, our diet changed from beef to elk. My culinary adventures began with a wild goose hung for so short a time that the roasted version was as tender as a basketball and as palatable as a rubber tire. The beaver tail I grilled made us grateful we weren't nineteenth century trappers, dependent on its dense white fat to keep us alive. My beaver haunch pot roast drew fairly favorable reviews, though the leftovers remained in the freezer for a year.

One day Bernard took his Unimog, a monster-size vehicle that's an adult equivalent of a Tonka truck, far into the mountains beyond our ranch. When he returned, hours late, he was covered with grime and flashing a smile as wide as the Mississippi. "I got stuck on a road in a really tight spot," he explained, beaming. "So I figured I'd wrap my winch around a tree, to pull myself to a spot where I could turn around." So far so good, I told myself. Nothing new here.

"Then, guess what? I heard a creaking, looked up, and," he held his head in his hands, shaking it back and forth as if he himself couldn't believe what he was about to say. "That tree was coming down on me. The winch pulled the tree over instead of pulling me up to it. I just barely managed to jump off the bed before it crashed down right over the hood of the Unimog. I can show you the dent . . ." I was no longer so happy. The Unimog's bed was eight feet high and I could too easily imagine Bernard breaking his leg in that unplanned leap.

"So there I was with a sixty-foot pine tree lying on my truck. Thank goodness I had my wood knife with me." He dug into his back pocket and pulled out the Japanese serrated knife with the six-inch blade he'd bought at a hardware store some years ago. "It took me hours." Eyes squeezed shut and head thrown back in utter joy at his escapade, he gasped and wheezed in the throes of a major laughing fit.

I offered a tentative chuckle of commiseration. I wanted to show him my appreciation for his accomplishment, but the truth was, what filled him with pleasure sent a surge of resentment through my gut. Bernard was euphoric with the ranching life, able finally to indulge his passion for the outdoors and all things mechanical. At that moment I knew that at heart I was a suburban girl. I was raised on *HMS Pinafore* and ski vacations. I had never gotten cozy with a wrench and had never thrilled to the delights of diesel engines.

Here I'd thought I had everything in balance. We were living in heaven, weren't we? Now I realized Bernard had far outdistanced me. He was fully involved in keeping everything running. He understood our water rights, knew our ditches, and, with repair people hours away, fixed anything that broke. After two decades of marriage, we'd grown nonchalant about our togetherness. We needed a new project, something that would pull us off our separate paths and merge us into a team again. The Peking to Paris seemed just the ticket. There was no way to know that the eighteen months of preparations would nearly undo us.

Car Troubles

For the year and a half after we are accepted into the Peking to Paris, I inhabit a hitherto unknown level of Dante's Inferno. It's the one where you're forced to repair a car engine over and over again. Even now I can't tell you what sins I committed to deserve such misery.

It's a sign, surely, that the most fun either of us have in the eighteen months prior to the actual race is perusing classic automobile websites for a suitable rally car. There are thousands from which to choose. Bernard, who's been tinkering with cars since babyhood, is in his element. To narrow the search, we agree our car has to be American-made. "And it has to be good-looking," I say. "Something we're proud to sit in." That doesn't narrow the search since, in my view, all pre-WWII cars are gorgeous. There are elegant Packards, the choice of Hollywood stars in the 1930s, fabulous Cadillacs favored by mobsters, and spindly Ford Model Ts that hauled migrants across the dust bowls during the Great Depression. An Hispano Suiza catches my eye, but it's out of our league, too expensive and so beautiful neither of us can imagine taking it on what's appearing to be an extraordinarily difficult drive.

One morning, Bernard calls me over, and I lean on his shoulder to peer at his computer screen. "What we need is this," he says, pointing to a car so voluptuous she seems ready to burst at the seams. "This is a beast of a car. But beautiful, don't you think? And fast," he says, rattling off various details about the engine, which go directly over my head.

The 1940 GM LaSalle two-door coupe that steals Bernard's heart has many things going for it, not least of which are a split front windshield, pontoon fenders, and a tall, handsome fountain-style grille in the front. On the open road, of which there should be plenty between Beijing and Paris, the car can easily do seventy miles an hour. It's helpful that she's new enough in an old way that we won't have too much trouble finding spares. Best of all, the brand is named for the French explorer, René-Robert Cavalier, Sieur de La Salle. Call it fate, good fortune, or karma, it's a perfect mirror to the nature of the drive we'll be doing and our own dual nationality. True, Bernard took the oath of US citizenship about thirteen years ago, but in his soul, his voice, and definitely his stomach, the man remains French.

The car payment has barely cleared the bank before Bernard is typing up what will be done to make the LaSalle rally-ready. My first rally-related job, if not meaningful, is helpful: to read his lists and check for typos. It's just like the earliest days of working together at our company, and just like then I'm soon looking around for something more compelling to do. "We have to give this car a name," I declare. "When you talk about *driving* from Beijing to Paris, you have to call your car something as epic as the trip. We can't just refer to it as 'car'." Bernard gives me a specific smile. It's small and sweet, signaling he doesn't understand me, but won't object.

Suggesting this is evidence of just how delusional I have become. I wasn't even able to name our last puppy. But I've convinced myself that my lack of car knowledge and my general carsickness will disappear because I will them to and that I will be transformed into Mother Courage when the need arise. Why not become good at names, too?

"Dudley? Jeeves? Godfrey?" I'm attracted to a British name, because this is a British rally.

"Too simpering. Too stiff. How about Momo? Or Lansky? I know: Scarface!" Bernard's been riffing on 1940s Las Vegas ever since discovering our LaSalle was used in the movie *Bugsy*.

I move on to literature, always a source of inspiration. "OK, there's Bilbo, you know, from *The Hobbit*?" Bernard doesn't know. "He was adventurous, an explorer, but also comfy. It all fits our car." Silence. I move on to literature Bernard will be more familiar with, like Shakespeare and the classics. "OK. How about Cyrano?"

He counters with "Quixote?"

"Too tall, and too hard to say when you're tired. D'Artagnan?" I offer, naming our favorite musketeer. "Daring. Loyal."

"Possible. But it doesn't really grab me. How about Homer? The greatest voyager of all times." We both shake our head.

"This is getting worse, not better. I like the name of Romeo, but it doesn't really suit, does it?"

To which Bernard has a reply. "Juliet?"

"Of course!" The LaSalle is curvy, voluptuous, a real stunner. She's not a gangster or a butler. She's a woman. "I think we're onto something here. But the car can't be Juliet. Juliet dies at the end. Kind of bad luck, don't you think?"

We email our cheering section to see if anyone is more creative than we are with car names. Weeks pass during which offerings dribble in. We try out the mouth feel of a slew of adventurers, explorers, and cutey-pies. There's the androgynous Hillary, conqueror of Everest or, conceivably, first female U.S. president, boldly going where no man or woman had gone before. And there's Baby, which strikes us both as not mature enough for the rigors ahead. One day I receive an email from the husband of one of Bernard's four sisters. "Consider Roxana," he writes. "The wife of Alexander the Great. In Persian, the name means 'luminous beauty,' and your car obviously is very beautiful. She also had the courage to accompany her husband into battle, and this is a quality you want from your car." I don't need anyone to tell me this is also a quality it'd be nice to have myself.

We have a winner.

Roxanne rolled off the General Motors assembly line in the summer of 1940. She was painted a discreet field mouse gray, though the quantity of chrome girdling her fenders was enough to blind an entire town. Inside were stiffly padded bench seats and crank windows. Her steering wheel was as wide as a wedding cake platter, her instruments round and easy to read. She seemed to cast a spell over her owners, who treated her like a coddled pet rather than a mode of transportation.

When Roxanne enters our lives in July 2005, sixty-five years on, she's been driven barely 29,000 miles. She is perfect as is, if all we plan to use her for are gentle jaunts. The Gobi, however, is no Sunday drive in the park. This grande dame has to be transformed into Lara Croft, Tomb Raider, beautiful, elegant, yet capable of surviving whatever's thrown at her.

Bernard has been fascinated by cars and car engines his whole life. As a young man with little money to spare, he rebuilt a Renault, called, in that fanciful way the French have, a Topolino. He followed that with a spell doing winter rallies in France, the sort where cars are driven for 24 hours straight, through blinding snow on icy roads. For fun. Even before Roxanne arrives, his mind is churning with what she'll need if she's to complete the Peking to Paris. Concepts like dual fuel pumps, special brake lines, extra-large fuel tank, and off-chassis rebuild enter our conversation. After Roxanne arrives, his list quickly grows to two pages, single-spaced.

Roxanne, with her white wall tires and glossy bordeaux paint job, reminds me of a vaudeville performer. Like any seasoned entertainer, she immediately becomes the apple of our eye. We show her off, take friends for drives, memorialize her in photogenic spots. We are smitten, in love with the idea that we own something so beautiful. Then there's the novelty of rebuilding her into a car capable of surviving thousands of miles of tough road, a project of greater scope than even Bernard has ever done. It's fresh, full of possibilities, with the drama of the Rally always looming there on the horizon.

We're suffused with excitement about the enterprise we're undertaking, and so is everyone else who signs on to help us. They're all specialists of one sort or another, skilled with brakes, wiring, fuel consumption, engines, gear boxes. Best of all, they all work in the same town, a place called Greeley on the edge of Colorado's eastern plains. There are pluses to Greeley. It's home not only to a branch of the state university, but to every sort of car repair or supply shop one could want when rebuilding an old car. But there are also minuses, one being that it is home to a huge, malodorous meat packing plant, the smell from which permeates the air. Here's the other unfortunate thing about Greeley: it's nearly three hours away from where we live. This gives us pause, but ultimately we agree that distance pales in comparison to the benefits of all the mechanics having their shops mere blocks from each other. Besides, we have no choice. There's only one auto repair shop in our town, and it has only a part-time mechanic, except during haying, when he doesn't come in at all.

While Bernard shepherds the mechanics into a semblance of a team, I study classic car magazines and subscribe to *Hemmings*, the bible of old car aficionados. I call elderly gentlemen with a passion for LaSalles and Cadillacs. One has a backyard full of original wheels from the 1930s and '40s. Another scavenges nothing but carburetors for those cars. Each is willing to talk to me for hours, and many go further, researching the Rally, remembering my name, taking a lively personal interest in Roxanne, a car that would soon be carrying their own set of carefully saved spark plugs into Mongolia and beyond. One man in particular, Bob Cooper, is a consistent savior. I need only phone Bob with the latest bit Bernard has told me we need, and, like a magician, he finds it somewhere in what must surely be a vast warehouse holding a lifetime's collection of LaSalle and Cadillac parts. Bob manages to locate everything from a dimmer switch, washers for the brake assembly, and an original LaSalle outside mirror to front wheel bearings and even a rear axle. Our UPS man delivers odd-shaped packages. We open one after another, marveling that a small part made over sixty years ago still exists on someone's dusty garage shelf. It is a time of thrills and satisfaction, as if we're children kneeling in front of a Christmas tree, ripping open presents year round.

Months slip by. We discover that the mechanics assigned to strip Roxanne to her chassis are more interested in drinking and dreaming than in rebuilding her. The beer-soaked planning chart shows the grim truth, at least what's still readable under the blotches of Budweiser smearing the deadline column. We begin to dread seeing each mechanic, steeling ourselves to hear that, again, the promised work has not been done. Like a summer romance, the glow has worn off our relationship with them. Bernard is perpetually exasperated, which he takes out on me in fits of anger centered mainly on the fact that I do not disrupt my life to go to

Greeley as often as he does. He's desperate for these mechanics to do their jobs, as we have no alternative, so he won't ever let on to them how frustrated he is. To them he's full of bonhomie, a hail-fellow-well-met comrade so familiar with Roxanne's needs that he can discuss her most intimate parts on equal terms with the best of them. Then he comes home and snaps, frowns, and picks at me, and in every other way makes clear just how unfair he feels it is that I'm at the ranch when he is not.

I, too, feel keenly the imbalance that has grown up around the car rebuild. Yet it seems to me I have little if anything to offer. My thoughts of learning auto mechanics faded as quickly as they arose. Now I have nothing material I can contribute to help solve the problem. The car has become Bernard's problem, while I stay at home and worry, a skill I've honed through my entire life. Tension builds between us until one day Bernard explodes. "You're not doing anything," he rages at me. "Why don't you do something, so I don't have to do it all!" He shoves me aside and storms out of the house. He's never been so furious at me, never said anything that could wound me so deeply. At the same time, I know he's right. What happened to the woman he married twenty years ago, the one who seized every opportunity to learn something new, no matter how foreign that something might be? I want a chance for Bernard to see that I'm not just the sum of my flaws. That, yes, they exist, but so do the parts of me that he first loved. More than anything, I want us to do the Rally together, to again have an epic project that we do side-by-side, and at which we succeed. So I tell him that, from now on, I'll be going with him to Greeley. By then, he's filled with remorse. "I'm sorry," he says. "You don't need to come. There's nothing for you to do there."

"I know that's what you think. That's what you've been saying for the past year and look where it's gotten us. I'm not helpless. I'm sure there are errands I can do, parts to pick up, things to bring to people, that'll free you up to do the things only you can do."

"No, no. Just stay home."

"Not any more. I'm coming with you. If I wind up sitting in a hotel room while you're out working on things, so be it. Though I doubt that'll happen." Thus we embark on the final phase of rebuilding Roxanne. Together again, if tentatively and politely so.

To display our good will, and, if need be, do the rebuild ourselves, we decide we have to leave the lovely green meadows and clear streams of our mountain ranch and move to the Greeley Holiday Inn Express, just ten minutes from where Roxanne is sitting on cinder blocks in a former bean warehouse. On Sunday evenings, we grit our teeth for the long drive to Greeley, where we stay for as many days as we can bear, before dashing back up the mountain for a literal breath of fresh air. Life has turned tense and sour, but it's too late to turn back now. We're in the race and we need a car to do it.

A bright spot is that we learn to love the Holiday Inn. My normally lean frame, accustomed to a more active life of horseback riding and outdoorsy-ness at the ranch, soon reflects an overly intimate relationship with their sugary warm cinnamon buns. The soft, dimpled, chemically chocolate chip cookies they offer each evening are just as alluring. We're assigned to the same room week after week. I look forward to the cordial greeting of the desk clerk, who barely raises her head from her college text book to greet us with "You again?" Our conversion to all things Holiday Inn is so complete that we even try to replace our mattress at home with their brand.

Through the months, we wheedle, pay extra, and otherwise twist arms to get work completed. It's like herding feral cats, trying to get each specialist to complete their part in time for the next specialist, who needs it to complete his part. "Please," we beg Bruce, the engine guru. "Could you install those new racing pistons in our engine? We have to have it to check if the radiator fits." "Please," we cajole the radiator shop. "Could you finish the radiator? We need it to check if the fan works." "Please," we plead with the powder coater. "Could you finish coating the chassis? We need it to mount the engine, radiator, and fan."

I find myself getting frantic, my natural impatience moving from simmer to hard boil. I want to kill every one of these likable, helpful mechanics whose main crime is that they have other jobs and no time to do ours. It's fortunate that Bernard is a born diplomat. Whenever I dent egos, he covers my caustic jabs with the soothing sounds of his French-accented words. Yet each morning, at the oatmeal-colored Formica Holiday Inn breakfast table, while I peel a banana and he spoons up strawberry yogurt, this calm man so adept at finding solutions seethes about the situation. He's a natural perfectionist, and now he's gripped in a fury over his inability to make things work the way they should, the way everyone has promised they would.

We no longer talk of esoteric ideas, local politics, or mundane ranch issues like whether to buy a new attachment for the tractor, but of where to find a spare sixty-year-old starter motor or who might redo the brake rotors. I cannot hold an intelligent discussion about cars, so mostly these are one-way conversations, with Bernard musing out loud and me nodding supportively. Still, I'm proud that I can mouth off correctly when I need to, even though it's about things I really don't understand. We reach the point where our only friends are auto parts clerks. They know everything about Roxanne, and we no longer need to look at their shirts before greeting them by name.

Six months later than planned, but still several months before the Rally's mandatory ship date, we bring Roxanne home. By then I've changed from the confident, assertive woman I usually am, the one who closed million dollar deals and built a successful company at my husband's side, to someone with pinched eyes and a grim face. In the years that it took us to build up our software translation company into an industry leader, I'd learned to work long hours. As the most senior sales executive in the company, I naturally took the lead in persuading new clients to sign with us. I also was the one called in to placate any client who was unhappy. All of our work, from proposal to job completion, was stressful and deadline driven. After seven years on the ranch, though, I'm no longer in shape for stress. I don't have the resilience to manage tension and uncertainty day in and day out. Battered by months of Roxanne-related disappointment, I'm drained, too easily distraught. Still, Roxanne's homecoming is undeniably a moment of euphoria. It coincides with the arrival of our passports, with visas for Russia and China in place. The Peking to Paris is again starting to seem a reality, and now, when I pass those maps on the dining room table, I'm again willing to look at them and dream, instead of turning my head.

Another thing that makes us giddy is the arrival of our special tent, an ingenious item that self-erects in two seconds, folding into a three-foot diameter, flat disc when not in use. The tent isn't sold in the States, because the fabric doesn't meet FDA fire retardant standards. We, however, have ignored that restriction and used a well-placed insider to secure one for us: Bernard's sister in Lyon, France. Our craftiness in securing the special tent leaves us both feeling smugly self-satisfied. We'll be camping all the way through Mongolia, which some people say will be the roughest part of the race. That we will be able to set up our tent in the dark whenever we arrive late is a reassuring notion. Few things make me happier than knowing I can get to sleep quickly.

The day it arrives we take it to the most obstruction-free zone in our house, the entry way, and remove it from its sheath. As claimed, it pops open in two seconds. It takes another hour for us to figure out how to twist, bend, and in other ways fold it back into a shape small and flat enough to fit back into its sack, and that's with directions and a video. "I think we better practice this," I tell Bernard, both of us wiping sweat off our foreheads. "Either that, or copy the directions and store them some-where we'll remember, so we can collapse this thing each morning."

"It's not difficult, cherie. I think I've figured out what the trick is," Bernard boasts, then pops it open again.

"No, not that way. This way."

"Read me the directions. What do I do at this point?" Bernard puffs. He's bent double, the tent squeezed between his knees while his arms hug the flexible rods that should have complied by folding into a circle.

"I think you're off course. It looks wrong," and I hold the instruction manual to his face, which is inches from the floor. Bernard falls to the floor, the tent flies into the air and, lands on top of him, a wonderful dome struc-ture that I am certain we'll be grateful to have somewhere in the Gobi. Our situation is absurd. How can we possibly believe we can finish a complicated car rebuild, when we can't even fold a tent? We agree to adjourn for a gin and tonic, leaving the popped-up tent in regal splendor in the entry way. Every day we each do a solo tour of duty figuring out how to fold it, until we both can get it flat and stuffable again within five minutes.

The tent is a perfect diversion from what any casual observer could have seen: the entire car project is cursed. To establish Roxanne's fuel consumption with her new double gas tanks, we take her for long, steady drives. The easiest route is the sixteen miles from the ranch to town. And back again. Over and over, past hay stacked in snowy fields, stands of naked willows, black cows exhaling jets of steam as they plod to their mineral lick. When the tank shows one quarter full, we fill up at the town pump, note the number of gallons and the miles covered, and repeat our short, steady circuit.

Even this one blessing, of living in a county crossed by empty two-lane highways that stretch to the horizon, proves useless. We drive Roxanne no more than a few hundred miles before her engine blows up. A day earlier, Bernard comments that the engine is acting strangely. When I stutter something uncertain about this not being a good thing, Bernard adjusts his blinders more snuggly in place. "Oh, it's probably just because it's still being broken in," he assures me. The next day the message comes clear. Instead of its normal purr, the engine alternates between a rheumy cough and a death rattle.

I place a frantic call to Bruce, our engine guru. On his instructions, I raise the hood, Bernard starts the engine, and I shake half a can of Bon Ami cleaning powder into the carburetor. The engine gurgles and splutters, as if to say, "Yummy. I like this stuff." I feel a glimmer of hope. "This seems to be helping. Maybe I should pour the rest in?" I shout to Bernard.

"Yes. No. Well, yes. OK, ummm, yeah, go for it." Hesitancy about a mechanical issue is not what I expect from Bernard, and that alone should have signaled me to hold off. We are both desperate. Nothing else has worked till now, so why not put our faith in a can of white powder? I dump the rest in, and for a second the engine comes back to life. Miracle. I peer around the hood to smile at Bernard just as the engine dies. For good.

It baffles me that such good mechanics could repeatedly fail to get our car in working order. Something else must be going on, but what? I'm a confirmed atheist, which leaves me no one to pray to when times get tough, and Bernard's a firmly lapsed Catholic, so he's no help in that department either. Still, there are times where things are so bleak that even I have to look elsewhere for help, and this is one of them.

Call it revelation, call it desperation, but what I decide is this: Roxanne, in whom we'd installed the finest parts money could buy, is sabotaging the work herself. I consider this to be a rational conclusion, because I believe she has good reason to do so. All her life she was a cosseted conveyance, never having done more than a sedate tour to the country club or around California's Central Coast vineyards. For months now she's listened to people talking about all the places she's supposed to drive. It's obvious that she's frightened out of her whitewalls about it. In despair, she's thrown every wrench she could into the works to sabotage the rebuild. If I were a car, I'd do the same thing. Even though I'm not a car, I *wish* I could do the same thing. Sabotage the trip, that is. Make it not happen. I mean, look at it from her point of view. Why in the world would we believe she could accomplish a trek as potentially torturous as the Peking to Paris? She had no choice. It's either injure herself severely enough that she's undriveable or wind up in places where she'll break down and, horrors, be left behind.

There's no time left to lose. I go to the service shop where Roxanne has been towed, nodding to the clerk up front and then heading through a side door directly into the back room. From there I weave my way past twenty or so car engines in various stages of deconstruction, inhaling the oily perfume of engine grease and solvents as I always do, hoping this time it won't make me gag. I hurry out the back door coughing. From there it's through the narrow, weedy concrete yard bounded by chain-link fence, pausing briefly to greet Buster, the guardian pit bull. His job is to look fearsome to the uninitiated, and he does it perfectly. Now he bounds over to me, tail wagging for his anticipated scratch. I'm not attracted to engines, but Buster I love.

Opening the door to a side building, it's time to brave ridicule. "Excuse me," I say to the three mechanics bent over Roxanne. "Could I have this space to myself for a moment, please?" How else could I say it? That Roxanne and I needed a little girl time? Predictably, they cast surreptitious looks at me, eyebrows furrowed as they stifle their collective desire to ask me why or to tell me not to mess with their work. I'm the owner and I don't need their approval. I just need them gone.

What does one do when trying to commune with a car? Pretend it's a dog. I wrap my arms around her hood and give a squeeze. Quietly stroking her fenders, I begin speaking in soothing tones. "Don't you worry," I murmur. "We won't abandon you." I pause and wait, nursing a faint hope that I'll receive a sign. Roxanne does not turn and poke a wet nose in my face to acknowledge the attention. Nor does she wag her trunk.

The whole situation is embarrassing to me even now. I observe myself and am not pleased with what I see. Despite my life on the ranch there's still much of the city girl in me. I have silk shirts and strappy sandals in my closet; I love opera; I take great pleasure in having a facial; I know the difference between regular and smoked paprika. What have things come to that I now find myself in a grease-spattered service bay, light filtering through the permanent fog of exhaust-clouded windows, muttering sweet nothings to an old car? Surely this can't be my destiny. I plow on, because for no rational reason, I feel what I'm doing is essential to our success. "Look at all we've done to make you strong. You can do this trip. And I swear we'll be with you every inch of the way." In a final bid to get her on my side, I say, "Trust me. I don't want you to break down anymore than you do. Because if you break down, I'll be stuck, and I *hate* getting stuck. So please," I plead. "Work with me on this. I promise you'll be OK."

There's no weird revelation when I stop talking. No mild exhaling of exhaust, or subtle sinking of tires to indicate vehicular relaxation. There's just the faint whir of the shop's overhead heater. Regardless, I have no doubt that, without ever lifting a wrench or dirtying my hands, I have fixed Roxanne. For on April 6, there she is, shiny new paint reflecting the snowy fields at our ranch headquarters, the white number 84 affixed to her doors next to the American flag, Bernard's name on the driver's side, mine on the passenger's side. She's packed, polished, and ready for shipment to China.

What I Learned

Car repairs didn't fill all my time in that year and a half. Several months after we received our acceptance packet from the Rally organizers, I decided it behooved me to know a bit more about what I would be doing between Beijing and Paris. I bought a pamphlet mentioned in the packet, which the organizers claimed would explain everything one needed to know about being a rally car navigator. The booklet that arrived was a slender sixteenth of an inch thick, small enough to fit in my purse. Its beige cover made it seem inconsequential. It was so modest in size, so rudimentary in its descriptions, that it gave me the impression there was little to know and even less for the navigator to do than I'd imagined. Here's what I gleaned from the book the first time around: the navigator is the person who sits in the passenger's seat of the rally car. Using the route book for reference, he or she describes the approaching road to the driver. "What's the big deal?" I thought. "The organizers will give me the route, I'll read it to Bernard. And that's that." I tossed the booklet on a corner of my desk, where soon it was buried under a stack of more pressing rally documents.

More than a year later, that slender, tan booklet resurfaced, just like one of those bloated Mob bodies come loose from their concrete mooring at the bottom of a murky lake. This time, with our departure for Beijing six weeks away, I opened it to the first page and read it with attention. I turned one page, then the next. Then I found Bernard and shook the booklet at him.

"They've got to be kidding," I said. "Did you know I'm supposed to track our time between intervals for the entire day, *plus* read maps, work a GPS, follow directions, and, lest we forget, know mileage to the hundredths?"

"Of course. I think I told you that a year ago."

"You mean that statement about the navigator having responsibilities? I thought that was just to make me feel good." I felt like sinking to the ground moaning before turning into the Road Runner, legs churning up a cloud of dust so fast would I be fleeing. "I know *you* know how to do all these things, but I can barely do one of those things at a time, and some I don't know how to do at all, like using a GPS and this Tripmeter thing. There's no way I'm ever going to do them all at once."

"We'll practice. How about we go out in the car with the GPS right now, and I'll show you what to do." Bernard's pragmatism jolted me with aggravation, which happens when he stays calm and I need to fret.

An hour of driving back and forth in front of the ranch and I had the basics covered. By the next morning, I'd forgotten it all. When we went out the next day I was too embarrassed to reveal to Bernard that he had to give me his explanations again, from scratch. This time I made notes to remind myself of what I needed to do. Reading the notes the following morning, I had no clue to what they referred.

"Do you want to go out again?" he asked.

"No. Don't worry about it," I lied. "I think I've got it." Despite so many years of marriage, I couldn't bear Bernard knowing my mind was such a sieve that I couldn't make sense of what I myself wrote 24 hours ago. I took the GPS to my office, planning to fiddle with it in private, notes in hand. Turning the GPS on, I stared at the screen, which remained stubbornly blank. Then it dawned on me that, since GPS stands for Global Positioning System, it only functioned outdoors, where it could scan for satellites. I stashed the offending gadget away, hiding my deficiency with it, nursing a vague hope that the instructions Bernard gave me would float to the surface of my brain, like a magic carpet, when I needed them most.

Perusing the pamphlet's pages until they became dog-eared, I picked up certain salient facts. For instance, I realized that a long-distance rally is a peculiar beast, part road race, part endurance event. And I accepted that, along with all competitors, we would be timed from the second we crossed the starting line in the morning till we crossed the finish line at the end of each day. In our case, that meant the clock would be ticking for 7,800 miles, a distance we were expected to complete in thirty days, with five rest days scattered in between in which to work on our car, relax, or sightsee. I had no qualms about the 250 miles or so that we were expected to cover each day. All it required would be maintaining an average speed of about 35 mph, the equivalent of a gentle cruise through a shopping mall parking lot.

I did not see this as posing a problem, because I willed my eyes to skip over the word "average." It was redolent of things mathematical, and I've always found math to be a bother. Word problems make me dizzy, and solving anything with an "*x*" in it gives me a headache. So, as a matter of convenience, I ignored the term. What I pictured in my mind was us driving along at a sedate but steady pace, as befit old cars. We'd be finished with a day's drive in seven hours. That seemed bearable to me, especially since going at a slow pace would give me that much more time to take in the scenery. It was all to the positive.

The Peking to Paris was organized by an English firm, which makes sense if you consider that the British are motoring enthusiasts, passionate about their cars and ardent about driving them. As I was to learn firsthand on the Rally, there's nothing an Englishman likes better than to take his grandfather's old Bentley out, wind up stuck on a rough road somewhere back of beyond, get filthy and exhausted getting himself out of trouble, and then laugh heartily with friends about it over beer or whisky that night. On the Peking to Paris Rally there were close to a hundred British crews (or, as some called them, teams); a smattering of other nationalities, plus nine American crews, rounded out the roster.

Though all the teams would be driving the same route, they would be doing so in vastly different cars, some nearly a hundred years old, others merely sixty years old, some with large, powerful twelve-cylinder engines, others with tiny four-cylinder engines. To create a level playing field, we were divided into car categories, pitting like against like. There was Prewar (for cars built before 1921), Vintageant (for cars from 1921 to 1940), and Classic (for cars from 1940 through the early 1960s). Each car was assigned a number, which also corresponded to the number of minutes post-departure of Car 1 that each subsequent competitor would be flagged off. We were given number 84, which meant our start time was always 84 minutes, or close to an hour and a half, after the first car would leave for the day. This, too, struck me as wonderful. I imagined we'd have time to sleep in and still visit the local village where we were staying.

Our organizers had been piecing together the details of our route since 2004, driving over every inch of it themselves and noting the distance between each reference point or landmark with two-decimal-point precision. I had thought the route was a starting point from which to explore on our own. Not so. The route book we'd be given was meant to be followed to the letter, plain and simple. I was disturbed to learn that for the entire 7,800 miles there'd be no deviating, no shortcutting, no self-determination. It's what makes a rally so quirky and appealing. To some. We are all making a gentleman's agreement that we'll go exactly where the organizers tell us and that we'll move at a pace and time of their choosing. Of course, there's great temptation to stray, which is why they set up points along the route where each car checks in with a course marshal during the day.

In a road rally, crews compete over a predetermined course against the clock, though not like NASCAR or Formula I, where the cars circle round and round the same track. In the morning, we would be flagged off from that day's starting point, called the main time control, at those one-minute intervals, so there would be no direct head-to-head racing. The pamphlet tells me that, if you're of the rally world, you call the starting point the MTC. I adopt this acronym immediately, which makes me feel sporty and in-the-know; I also make up one of my own, dumping the time-consuming, multi-syllabic Peking to Paris for P2P.

Once flagged off from the MTC, we'd be driving on normal roads, with each car having a set number of hours to cover the same distance between the MTC until the first time control and from there all subsequent time controls till we reached the finish time control at day's end. I figure out for myself that the "in" abbreviation for the day's end point must be FTC. At each time control there's a marshal whose job it is to check in each car. On arriving, I'm to hand my microchipped time card to the marshal, who scans the chip with a handheld gadget that logs in our car and its arrival time. The same is done when it's time to leave the time control and get back on the road. The marshals have a set of highly accurate synchronized clocks. At the end of each day, the number of minutes each car took to cover the day's distance would be tallied. Whoever wound up in Paris in the amount of minutes closest to what was specified, would win the overall gold medal. Within each car category there would be gold, silver, and bronze medals as well. Simple enough, until I learned there also were penalties.

As navigator, it was my job to make sure our watches matched the marshals' clock to the second. I also had to man the distance instruments in the car. I'd have a special computer that measures mileage to the hundredth of a mile, which I would have to set each morning and make sure its mileage matched exactly that in the route book. The route book itself seemed designed to give me a mental breakdown, crammed as it was with the minutiae of mileage and description, in numeric, verbal, and pictorial form, that I couldn't fathom how I'd ever grasp it all.

Our route would be divided into daily stages, or sections. To avoid any possibility of an enterprising soul checking out the route beforehand, we would be given the P2P route book in Beijing, two days before the start of the Rally. There would be no time to study it in advance, no time for me to learn what a route book looked like, nor to familiarize myself with the arcane symbology used to signify landmarks and directions.

There was a lot more riding on my ability and accuracy than I'd expected. Arrive too early and we'd get penalty points. Go off-route, arrive late, or miss a time control altogether, penalties again. If our car has mechanical problems, or we're distracted in a conversation and miss our check out time, more penalties. At the end of the day, all efforts would be for naught if I didn't present our time card to the marshal at the FTC before it closed. If we got lost, or had a bad breakdown en route, we'd drop further and further in the standings. We might even be out of the running for the gold or the silver altogether.

To further enliven our days, we would have time trials. The description of these terrified me. They were short stretches of road filled with tricky driving challenges like hairpin turns, sand or gravel patches, hills, and a multitude of other car handling tests. On these, the object is to drive as fast as possible and set the lowest possible time, which is tracked to the hundredth of a second. I knew that Bernard would have his foot on the gas pedal the whole way. What I didn't know is how I'd be able to give him instructions on what was coming up quickly enough, so he'd have time to react and deal with it, when we'd be moving at 60 mph. I could picture Roxanne flying over a ditch, ka-banging over stumps, doing a 360 when Bernard had to brake too late because of my delayed instruction, and coming to a halt in a swirling cloud of dust.

To bandage any competitor who crashed their car, whether in a time trial or elsewhere, a medical officer with a fully stocked ambulance was along for the entire Rally. This probably reassured many competitors. For me, the only "A" word in my medical vocabulary was Advil. It had not yet occurred to me that rallies were an activity where a crash of devastating proportions could occur. Why would anyone want to drive so recklessly as to smash a beautiful old car? Or to put this another way, if you were in such a car, wouldn't you drive carefully enough that you wouldn't ever crash? Pain of the sort requiring an ambulance was not part of my internal bargain about acceptable risks and when added to the list of Things I Do Not Possess, pushed me into a state of anxiety I hadn't known since discovering my wedding dress made me look like a crinoline-wrapped pear. I didn't sleep for days.

Then there were the five mechanics and their several mobile repair vans, whose job it was to patch up those smashed vehicles, or any vehicle for that matter, that could not handle the rigors of the road. Bernard was the best mechanic I knew and, given his intention to oversee the detailed preparations of our car himself, I doubted anything would go wrong with it. However, he couldn't change or build in just anything he wanted. Like all the others, our car would have to pass something called, in the arcane vocabulary of the rallying community, scrutineering. This task, in which each car would be checked to ensure no unauthorized modifications had been made, would be handled by a representative of FIVA, which is a French acronym for the International Federation of Vintage Automobiles. The P2P rules specified that every major component of a car must be as it was when the car was manufactured. If a car was built with rotor brakes, new ones could be put on, but they had to be rotor brakes, not disc brakes. If a car was built with an inline V-6 engine, that's what it had to race with. A few modifications for safety were allowed. A skid plate to protect a car's underbelly was permitted, as was rewiring for 12 volt electronics, necessary for running the trip computer. Anyone who wanted to install a roll bar could do so. "Yes to the roll bar," I told Bernard. And then I sank into gloom imagining that on the day before the race started, as we underwent scrutineering, the FIVA rep would take one look at Roxanne and send us back to the parking lot.

The myriad regulations, definitions, rules, and requirements didn't comfort me. They burdened me. I'd opened a Pandora's box of information, which revealed one thing: I was unfamiliar with every navigator's tool other than maps. Sitting in a passenger seat was something I knew how to do. But stick to Rally rules? How could I do that when I couldn't even remember them all? The mere thought of my elevated status as navigator, now of equal importance to Bernard's driver role, agitated me. I felt like a cornered animal, which made me panic, and when I panic, I do not get to work and solve the problem, the way Bernard does. I am overcome by deer-in-the-headlights syndrome: I stop in my tracks, petrified, and there I stay. If I could possibly veer off this path I'd gotten on and escape, I would have.

Unfortunately, by now we were not alone in our enterprise. A large set of family and friends had joined us, as excited about the Rally as I used to be. Actually, since they didn't have to do any of the work, I'd say they were more excited than we were. Whenever I thought about dodging what I saw as an inevitable bullet headed straight for me, I was stopped from doing so by them. My sister, her son, and her partner had already booked their flight to Paris. With the help of my two Parisian cousins, they were planning a "Welcome, conquering heroes" party for us, the day after we, in theory, reached Paris with Roxanne. All four of Bernard's sisters and their families were already Skyping and emailing about welcoming their adored brother. His son in Paris and his daughter in Geneva, plus his four grandchildren, would be on hand, with his son planning to film our approach to the finish line. My cousin from Israel was captivated by the event and promised to be there with his three children. Friends from England, Vienna, Switzerland, and the United States were coming with spouses and children, to fête our arrival. If I backed out now, my failure would be as public as a bride abandoned at the altar. The humiliation would be deep, and besides, I'd never be able to repay all those plane tickets.

Personal humiliation wasn't the worst of it, though. The matter of disappointing my coterie of supporters paled in comparison with that other minor obstacle: my carsickness. This had been a known fact about me since my childhood. My French mother and Austrian father, having spent their youth in the Alps, were passionate about the outdoors. Every weekend they took us on hikes in the Catskills, ski trips to Vermont, outings to the Long Island shore. Early in the morning we'd make sandwiches, using good butter, slices of cold meatloaf, steak, or chicken left over from last night's dinner, and plenty of crisp lettuce. Cucumbers, carrots, and sweet peppers would be sliced for crunchy bites. Apples were polished, cookies wrapped in foil. We were a family who loved our picnics. On the long drive to the slopes or the trailhead, my sister and I whiled away countless hours engrossed in silly car games. We'd chant hand-clapping rhymes like "The spades go two lips together, twilight forever, bring back my love to me!", try to divine the number of wheels on a big rig up ahead, search for out-of-state license plates, or challenge our parents with our favorite word games. On the way home, as night closed in, we lay on our backs with legs scrunched against each other, peering out our respective windows for satellites and shooting stars. We loved being in the back seat together. But when I tried to read, I went from good-humored to queasy. Word games, fine; books, not.

Some youthful ills we grow out of. This one stayed with me into adulthood, but wasn't ever more than a minor nuisance until I met Bernard. In our early years of marriage, he and I often carpooled the seven miles from our mountain home above Boulder, Colorado, down to our office in town. The first seven miles of that drive dropped steeply, winding around multiple hairpin curves to the junction with Boulder Canyon. We'd enter my car as a happily married couple setting off for work together. From there, things went downhill in all conceivable ways. First, he'd change my carefully adjusted seat so his hands could grasp the steering wheel like a Formula 1 race car driver: left hand at nine o'clock, right hand at three o'clock, arms comfortably flexed at the elbows. Feeling the thrum of the engine and the crunch of gravel as we began our 3,000-foot descent, Bernard handled the car as if he were driving a Ferrari.

On those drives to work I always had the best of intentions. "Relax," I willed myself silently. "Focus on the horizon." What with the horizon tilting at crazy angles, I had to wobble my head like a dashboard doll to follow it. My brain struggled to negotiate the conflict between what my eyes saw and what my body felt. It was a losing battle. Even though my inner ear was woefully out of balance, I still strove to remain level-headed and civil in the face of mounting nausea.

"Could you perhaps not swing quite so wildly around the curves?" I'd ask politely, wiping my sweating palms on the car seat.

"Don't worry, ma cherie. Your car can handle it."

It hadn't occurred to me to worry. That's because, despite my discomfort, even then I knew Bernard had an uncanny ability to gauge speed and distance with computer-like precision. Any man who could back up a car without ever turning his head clearly had the chops to handle that car going forward. Bile rising in my throat, I had to come to the point.

"I'm not worried. But I just may throw up. Now."

"What?!" Bernard would exclaim, expressing the doubt that only someone who's never had motion sickness can. "You're feeling sick?"

Filled with remorse, Bernard then handled the car so smoothly you'd think it was full of raw eggs. Yet he couldn't hide his chagrin that car motion, which filled him with such glee, made me nauseous. So the next day the drama repeated itself. I believe Bernard hoped that, if he involved me often enough in discomfort, he'd break me of the motion-sickness habit. It never worked.

When it was clear we were going to be driving 7,800 miles and I'd be the one holding the map and reading directions from the route book all day, we had to face the problem.

"What are we going to do about this?" Bernard would start out.

"You mean me, and cars, and how I get sick in them, and how if I read it'll be even worse?" I'd reply, doing a poor job of disguising how worried I was.

"What about those acupressure bands that people use on airplanes?"

"I tried those, remember? They didn't work."

"And scopalamine? You know, that skin patch that's supposed to suppress nausea?"

"I tried that, too, when we had to fly in a small plane six years ago. It made me sick for days, even using just a quarter of the patch." My recollection is that I felt worse with the Scop patch than I did just getting airsick.

"Hmmm," Bernard was running out of options. "Dramamine?"

"I could. But then I'd sleep through the whole Rally. What sort of navigator would I be if I dozed off all the time? Honestly, I think I've tried everything, and none of it's worked." Then we'd look at each other, both of us silent, both of us thinking the same thing: If I can't read in a moving car without getting sick, I can't do this race.

"I'll just deal with it. I guess. We'll just see what happens." I wasn't being brave, and I wasn't being foolish either. I was trying to be like Bernard, practical and positive.

Beijing: Take Three

In the couple of days we have left in Beijing before the Rally begins, there's rarely a minute that the upcoming race doesn't find a crack in my enjoyment through which to squeeze its large body and take over the view. The refrain "what if?" plays through my mind like a stuck record. I know from the past year and a half that if something's running fine it's simply an invitation for that something to break down. So even though I can say Roxanne runs fine I always have to append "for now."

Bernard comes down with a hacking cough. We blame it on air pollution. Beijing is the world's biggest boom town. Each day 1,200 new cars are added to the choking traffic on city streets. Everywhere, construction cranes like giant praying mantises scratch a turgid sky. The scaffolding of those partially built skyscrapers is an exoskeleton blurred by a brown blanket of smog. I thank goodness I've lived so long in Colorado, so I have a trunkful of memories of vivid blue sky to paste onto the beige facsimile I see here. That still leaves the local sun to deal with. It's a pale disk made white by the smoke of coal-fired power plants fueling the city's insatiable demands.

Discarding the air pollution excuse I decide the cough is his allergic reaction to my constant tension. He never gets sick, and it seems too far-fetched that he'd do so now. Besides, aspirin has done nothing for him. As for me, the extent to which the pollution makes me feel ill is a welcome distraction from the jittery anxiety that besets me once we drop our guide-book in the room and arrive at the formal Rally briefing, along with 250 other drivers and navigators. This is it. The main event is about to happen and it starts here, in this stuffy, windowless hotel ballroom with row upon row of hard chairs facing a low stage. The next three hours are my cram course in rallying. "Focus, Dina," I scold myself. "This is important stuff."

There's a problem, though. My mind is already chock full of imagined concerns. Actually, there are only three, but each one has so many permutations that anything factual will have to squeeze into the nook I prefer to reserve for essential information, like the time of my next pedicure appointment. There's the "We're hopelessly lost" worry, the "Our car's broken down" distress, and the "I have chronic diarrhea" horror. This last one is perhaps the worst of all, what with its attendant image of classic cars circling round while I squat, pants around ankles, unsheltered in the Gobi desert. Not only this, but I've seen that the organizers are all driving bright red, new Toyota trucks, which are four-wheel drive. They're air conditioned, too. I've started to wonder what they know about the route that we don't. I also can't stop the thought that perhaps I could persuade one of them to trade with me, on the grounds they'd have more fun than I riding in Roxanne.

The Rally medical officer takes the microphone first. He's not reassuring, divulging dire warnings in precise detail about all manner of health hazards on the road ahead. It's a small sop when he announces the hours we're allowed to crawl to his hotel room to plead for assistance or drugs. I reread the list of what's in our first-aid bag to console myself that the sheer vastness of its contents will keep me safe. It's stuffed with items for every possible malady I can think of, plus some I'd rather not dwell on. I have five variations on a theme of antibiotics, for everything from stomach ailments to eye and dental problems, plus skin diseases. I have packets of hydration salts in case we forget to drink during the day, along with muscle relaxants and narcotic-strength painkillers saved from various operations. I've even brought the morphine pills prescribed for my dog when he was succumbing to bone cancer. There's a supermarket aisle-worth of remedies for colds and cuts, including one of every type of analgesic and every size of Band-Aid, moleskin, and blister coverage, plus throat lozenges, oil of clove for toothaches, cough syrup, and cortisone anti-itch cream. And that's for the mild medical problems. For serious ones, I have a plethora of gauze pressure pads and tape to hold it in place, specialty tweezers and hemostats for drawing sutures, a canula, two bags of IV solution, and, thank goodness, a sterilized face mask in case I need to be attached to an oxygen tank. If I do get stuck in the Gobi, I can always set up a rural clinic.

What bothers me, though, are those tweezers, a constant reminder that I wince when I have to extract a splinter. Does this man sincerely expect me to insert a central line and begin stitching up the agonized victims of a major car crash? Thankfully he relieves me of heaping this on top of all my other worries. "If you're the first car on an accident scene, I'll need you to give me your medical kit as soon as I get there," he says. "So I have your supplies in addition to mine. I don't want to alarm you, but it's possible the smashed car would be in such a jumble it'd be impossible to find *their* medical kit. And, um, they might well be in no condition to tell me where it is."

"Well, what a relief," I think.

The mechanics, including Betty, a grandmotherly sort with short gray hair who's reputed to be the best of the bunch, explain the sign-up procedures for getting our car triaged when it falls apart. "We'll set up shop in the hotel parking lot each evening. When we're in Mongolia you'll find our van on the periphery of each camp. Just come over, tell us what the problem is, and we'll put you on the list. There's five of us, so we should be able to handle whatever you throw at us. Oh, but please don't actually throw things at us." Everyone titters nervously. "We hate that, especially when we've been up for 36 hours towing in bashed Rally cars." They've all assisted on rallies before and sound determined to be fair, given quantities of frazzled drivers clamoring for help. Novice that I am, I believe them. Only later do I learn how little of what I envisioned about the P2P bears any resemblance to reality.

Next, the course marshals give us an overview of time trials, time controls, and passage controls, as well as what to do at the FTC at day's end. They sound like my meager pamphlet; maybe they wrote it. Not to be outdone, the lead route surveyor illuminates just how unprepared I am, because while I have read the terms he uses, I've never actually collected them all at one time: "Bring your GPS to that table," he says, pointing toward the back door, "and we'll download waypoints and coordinates for the entire course. There are over two thousand of them, but if you bought the unit we recommended, they'll all fit." We didn't. We bought a different GPS, one with a large screen, as a sop to my near-sightedness. I've decided contact lenses are a recipe for an eye infection and glasses would only get dusty, smeared or, worse yet, broken. It's either read what's displayed with my naked, squinty eyes, or get lost. Now, though, my vision may not even be the main problem. "And don't forget your route book! They're full of tulip diagrams, all the controls are noted, and, of course, incrementing and decrementing mileage. We've also given you some extras, a bit of local history and such, what to see on your days off. Even a few of our favorite restaurants." All of these things are my responsibility. Here I was still vaguely hoping I was just along for the ride.

Not one of these presentations is about anything I'm familiar with. Our plans for practice rallies had gone up in the same smoke as our schedule for a six-month turnaround on Roxanne's rebuild. I am now two days away from the start of the Rally, and I have no idea what I'm supposed to do. I haven't had any practice, and I've never looked at a route book. Worst of all, I haven't had any room in my tired brain for thoughts of what this Rally will require. Sure, I understand the words "route" and "book." I learned those words from my Rally pamphlet. The dictionary definition of "medical kit" and "car problems" are clear. I don't need my advanced degree to know what those words mean. I feel like I've been playing a mental version of the card game Concentration for months. I turn over a card with a rally word I recognize, then search for the card that illustrates how that word relates to what we'll be doing. I've yet to figure out what a matching pair looks like.

All of this is terribly unsettling, and to make matters worse, I seem to be alone in my incompetence, because all around me people are nodding and some even dare to laugh, as if being explained something as elementary as a time trial is beneath them. When we first landed in Beijing, I didn't think anything could feel more foreign, but now it's as if I've transferred to Mars. I am so alien from those around me that I can't fathom how to walk or talk like them. It'd be humbling if it weren't so alarming.

We sit and fidget as a nattily dressed Frenchman approaches the mic. His air of incontrovertible authority is bolstered by a pale lavender silk handkerchief peeking from the breast pocket of his bespoke suit. This man is the arbiter of classic car authenticity, here to explain scrutineering. That's the pre-Rally inspection certifying that each car's components are indeed what they were originally intended to be when the car was built. The word scrutineer is so weirdly retro, especially when spoken by a haughty Frenchman, that I have to stifle a weak guffaw. I turn to Bernard and whisper, "Saying, 'We'll check your cars thoroughly' would do, don't you think?" Bernard shushes me. His own accent is such that this man has his natural sympathy. And then there's the small matter that if we don't pass scrutineering, we don't race.

All fidgeting ceases when a man with a pot belly and bandy legs heaves himself off his chair and walks with slightly crooked back to the microphone. His lank black hair is plastered to his head, his button-down shirt rumpled and spilling out of his trousers. This is the British organizer himself, veteran competitor of many a ruthless rally. Also veteran of too many crashes, as his stiff walk attests. His small eyes shrewdly scan the crowd for a long, silent minute before he says, "Each one of you must give thought to what you're doing here." He pauses for effect. "Are you going for a gold medal, and will you do all you can to make your start time every morning from here to Paris? If so, we salute you." His voice is pompous and aggressive. "Mind though. If a bronze is OK with you, there's nothing wrong with that. No shame there. That's why we made them!" He laughs loudly at his own joke and appears to hitch up his trousers, though perhaps he's rubbing his aching back. "We suggest you discuss this with your team mate. Be in agreement on how you're going to run, because the bronze means simply that you clocked out here in Beijing, clocked out again in St. Petersburg, and crossed the finish line in Paris. So talk it over. Make your decision now, not when you get in trouble down the road."

He sounds like he's scolding us. I feel a flush rising, expecting that at any moment the organizer will point to me. "You!" he'll shout, and haul me up on stage from where he'll reveal me as the imposter I know myself to be. I've had no time to become savvy about time trials and route books filled with instructions and symbols. I never learned enough about mechanics to be a full partner with Bernard on matters of engine difficulties. My understanding of the GPS is superficial at best, and as for everything else, I am a sailor cast overboard by a rogue wave, flailing in a deep ocean, hoping something, anything, will arrive to save me.

My mother used to say I was a good girl, that I did as I was told. She was wrong. I attribute that to the blindness of motherly love, rather than an unwillingness to acknowledge all the times I argued with her and pointedly did the opposite of what she asked. In truth, I've always found it weirdly satisfying to do the opposite of what's expected. I love bucking conventions. At a childhood party, when I realized my plastic spoon was flexible, I used it to slingshot chocolate ice cream in the birthday girl's face. In college, when everyone else was pulling an all-nighter after too many nights of partying, I happily went to bed at ten, my work done well ahead of time. Still, at this moment, the organizer's mandate to make a decision on how we'll do the Rally is an order I want to follow. It's the life line for which I've been casting about. I turn to Bernard and say, "Bronze." Before the word is even out of my mouth, Bernard says, "Gold." There it is in hard metallic terms. For me it's a journey, for Bernard, a race. I want to get through it. He wants to win.

In Which I Make Friends

Hoping to distract myself, I look around for some social interaction. After the big briefing in our hotel's mammoth conference hall, everyone seeks out others whom they know. They hail each other with high waves, two-arm hugs, loud hellos, and hearty backslapping. Like ground-level bird feeders, every coffee table has attracted its own drip-dry crowd, everyone dipping forward, pecking cheeks, their yellow plastic P2P tags on red lanyards dangling and clacking as they do. We don't know anyone in the Rally except Matthieu, though apart from a few emails since meeting in Colorado two years ago, we haven't had much contact. Still, I've used this slim thread of correspondence to weave a handy fiction that once we're in Beijing he'd take us under his wing, offering access to a ready-made circle of our own. Matthieu gives us a cordial greeting, then drifts over to his own huggy group. He's joined by five others; together, the six of them form a team of three cars. From the ease with which they move off, I surmise they're good friends. It doesn't escape me that no invitation to backslap with them has been issued.

Months back, feeling the P2P was all about Bernard's dreams and not about mine, I created a secret mission for myself. While Bernard would be doing the P2P to test his stamina and driving skills, I would use it as immersion therapy, surrounding myself with hundreds of people for over a month. Normally I'm a loner, though the sort who secretly longs to be the center of attention. If things went my way, I'd emerge from the P2P cured of my hermit-like tendencies, returning home a person who not only had covered 7,800 miles, but who would seek out crowds like a salmon seeks its home drainage. This to me seemed like a character rebuild worth achieving.

At the moment, though, I amble about, lonesomely superior, dodging the shrapnel of laughter from groups of which I'm not part. It's exactly how I used to feel at high school dances thirty-five years ago. Once I'm in its grip, the memory of that experience leaves me feeling just as vulnerable as if the dance had been yesterday. I can see myself leaning against the gym's stained white cinder block wall, staring at a nearby empty chair, hoping to convey telepathically to anyone who might notice me that I find the details of its construction truly fascinating. Then I occupy that chair and transfer my attention to the pleats of my skirt, as I whisper to myself, "Who'd want to dance with any of those losers anyway!"

"Baby steps," I say to encourage myself now. "You do have Bernard." He's walking beside me, fit and trim, his brown hair buzz cut to a military quarter-inch, the thick brush of a mustache he's sported ever since I've known him offsetting the lack of hair above. Both of us are the same height, five foot six, and our stride as we wander the mausoleum-like lobby easily matches step for step. We are alike in so many ways, but when it comes to looking for the support of others, Bernard and I are opposites, and I don't expect to get much succor from him on this matter. We head for the elevator and retire to our room.

One invigorating bubble-bath later, we wander into the starkly modern lounge on our hotel floor, in search of a reviving snack and some refreshment. Signing in, I notice the telltale P2P badges sported by several people sprawled on angular, pale yellow leather couches. They're engrossed in trading stories in that peculiarly British way in which one hair-raising tale is told in understated fashion, only to be topped by another, more mind-blowing adventure recounted in even more modest terms. These are my fellow competitors, in manageable numbers. I should say something. But what? "Hi, my name is Dina and I'm navigator for a LaSalle?" How inane is that? Instead, I sidle by them, eyes averted, as Bernard and I walk to the open bar.

"You lovely woman you!" booms a male voice in a clipped British accent. "Let me buy you a glass of champagne! Better yet, you buy me one!"

Spying an open bottle of champagne, I clutch it along with a few glasses and turn toward the sound of the voice. It appears to belong to a man about my age, whose pale wavy hair and somewhat fleshy features would be called pleasant, but not handsome. His arm is draped around a petite woman and he eyes me flirtatiously, then turns happily to the woman and gives her shoulder a squeeze. "Look Maddy, that wonderful woman is bringing me champagne," he says, gracing us both with an impish grin. We all start laughing. Drinks in this lounge are free.

I sit opposite them and fill the glasses. "Cheers," I say. "I'm Dina." I present my P2P badge to prove I know my name. "This is Bernard, my driver. And also my husband."

"Don't sit over there!" the man booms. I wonder whether this man ever speaks in anything other than exclamation points, but I say nothing, afraid my relief that anyone at all is talking to me, let alone someone who appears genuinely friendly, is so palpable that it may be off-putting. "Come sit by me . . . you don't mind, do you Bernard?" Before I have a chance to change seats, he grabs Bernard's hand instead, yanks him onto the couch by his side, and enfolds him in a one-armed bear hug. "You're Americans? I love Americans. What're ye drivin'?" doing his best John Wayne imitation.

"We have a 1940 LaSalle," Bernard begins, in his deep, warm, French-accented voice. The man interjects, now morphed into Maurice Chevalier. "Aaah, an American car, but 'LaSalle' is a French name. You say you are American, but from the way you speak I think you must be French. How clever. How confusing. I, too, have an American car in this Rally." Here he pauses for effect, then says, "A 1927 Chevrolet 75 roadster." He taps *his* P2P badge as proof.

Just like that, we have friends: Robert, like a bounding puppy, covering all comers with his loving slobbers. Maddy, his wife, though sometimes more like a proud owner, fondly tugging on the leash, but never too hard. Robert makes further introductions, pairing each person with their car. There's Ralph, a wiry coat-hanger of a man, seemingly composed solely of ligaments and tendons, whose brown eyes appraise me from behind Ben Franklin spectacles. Running his hand over his nearly bald head, he flashes me a smile revealing more bad teeth than I thought could fit in one jaw. "The organizer didn't want to let me in. Said my car rode too low to the ground. That the rough road would chew it up and I'd never make it. You'll see. I'm going to prove him wrong."

Then there's Nick and Sybil, both tall, he with a thatch of preternaturally white hair, she with an equally striking mop of black hair. And their friends, Carol and Robin, and Michael and Sophie. All of them have cars from the early 1930s, works of art with running boards, spoke wheels, and big tear-drop fenders. Everyone stands up and hugs me. It's as if someone's waved a magic wand and just like that I'm transformed from Cinderella sweeping ashes into a princess at the ball.

Robert is happy to share his claim to fame. In 1997 he was the British Airlines pilot for the flight that brought many of the first P2P competitors to Beijing. At that point, he swore he'd return to do the race himself. Now he has. "Bernard man," he says now, assessing that Bernard is shorter than doctor charts say is average for a man. "Do you ever plan to grow?" He laughs so heartily at this that no offense can be taken, especially since he himself would barely reach the nipples of an NBA player.

Conversation swirls away from me, as the others compare notes on where they'd each recently driven their spectacular cars. Talk quickly fills with "Remember when's," "Did you do's," and "Have you seen's." When it touches on vehicles, Bernard can jump right in, the language of cars and engines being universal. I listen, smile, nod, and practice feeling part of the group. This is ever so promising. From zero I suddenly know eight people to whom I can say, "So how has YOUR day been?" without having to introduce myself. I'm certain they'd return the favor and ask me the same. After all they're British, which means they're polite.

Maddy turns to me. "Have you looked through the route book?"

"No. Should I? We're not due to drive till day after tomorrow."

"Well, it helps to familiarize yourself with this Rally's style of instruction, make your notes . . ."

"Notes? What would I note? Isn't the book complete as is?"

"I'm sure at one point, early on, it was. By now there will be things on the route that have changed. The organizers send an advance car over the route 24 hours ahead of us. At the end of each day they send the Clerk of the Course, who's back with us, their route revisions. We get them the following morning. It's good to have a feeling of how the original route was intended, so you can easily assess how it's changed." Nothing was said about this at the briefing, which my stomach now assures me is cause for distress. It starts to squeeze itself into a tight ball, threatening to eject the array of delectable miniature hors d'oeuvres I've just wolfed down.

"Advance crew? I thought they were going ahead to check our hotel reservations."

Maddy starts to laugh, then catches herself. "Have you used a route book before? Or ever been on a rally?" she asks in the nicest possible way. There. At last my dirty little secret is out.

"Well, this is my first time, and I don't know what I'm doing," I tell her, feeling all blushing virgin. For a moment I'm silent. Then I decide this makes me out to be even more incompetent than I am. I blunder on. "I know. It sounds bad. We'd planned to do an easy rally before this. You know, for practice. I was also supposed to have time to work with the GPS. But . . ." and my voice trails off.

"Let's get together after dinner," Maddy says. "I'll take you through it. Don't worry!" she adds, giving me a pat on the arm that would have been motherly if we weren't the same age. "You'll get it. We all do."

"Dinner!" Maddy's Robert booms. "Peking duck anyone?"

We adjourn to a nearby restaurant favored by locals, where we sit around a ten-foot diameter table with an equally enormous lazy Susan in the middle. The others order Peking duck, with its accompaniment of duck soup and bronzed duck skin served on tiny crepe-like cushions smeared with salty, sweet Hoisin sauce. I order an item described as crispy duck parts. It sounds bizarre in an appealingly crunchy way. Platters mounded with glistening, succulent duck meat and slivers of jade green scallions are brought for the others. When my order arrives, it's a heap of deep-fried beaks and bones, golden and glistening with oil. Bernard wrinkles his nose. "You're not going to eat that, are you?" he asks.

"Why not? It's on the menu. Someone here must find it appetizing. Besides, if a bird's being slaughtered for *your* Peking duck, you wouldn't want the rest of it to go to waste, would you?" I survey the mound in front of me, happy in the knowledge that no one will ask to share. Anyway, I've had Peking duck before. Why not try something new?

Finding Roxanne

Lucky Roxanne. She's had three weeks of R&R snugged in a container crossing the Pacific, the car equivalent of a luxury cruise, followed by two weeks in a climate-controlled Beijing warehouse. Not so me. I've spent the intervening weeks since her shipment in a dither of anxiety. About what? For starters, everything. Because with Roxanne out of the picture, there's now nothing to prevent every other possible calamity from getting its fair share of my attention.

Yet even the most inveterate worrier knows she'll eventually have to get down to business. The day has come to collect Roxanne and, if the gods are willing, get her back to our hotel unscathed. That the organizers provide buses for the 45-minute shuttle to the warehouse is an act of kindness for which I'm abjectly grateful. I'd give anything to postpone having to direct Bernard back to the hotel, an endeavor sure to prove what I've been saying: that I have no navigational ability whatsoever. We're on the fourth bus to leave the hotel, which delays the inevitable for an extra hour. I'm test driving what will be my outfit for the next month: sand-colored eight-pocket cargo pants, fetchingly rolled up to capri length to expose my white cotton socks. I've put on my favorite lavender short-sleeve shirt, which has two more pockets. Sturdy shoes are on my feet, in case walking to Ulaan-baatar becomes a reality. The overall effect is one of baggy competence. It does not boost my vanity, but does make me feel efficient.

The moment has arrived to make something good out of our year and a half nightmare. Still, I feel shaky with uncertainty as we enter the vast, nearly vacant, Quonset warehouse. What if Roxanne's been damaged in shipment? What if she doesn't even start? Though I am a worrier, that doesn't mean I've forsaken rudimentary shrewdness. I know this is a perfect opportunity to evaluate the competition, or at least what's left of it. By the time we reach the warehouse, 75 percent of the cars have been collected. Still, I take my time, striding across the polished concrete floor, shoe soles squeaking, marveling at the beauty of the cars around me. It's like a museum, and the thought crosses my mind that, if only it were, I wouldn't have to get in one of those cars and guide it half way around the world. "Oh for god sake," I mutter to myself. "Get a grip." Then I see her, parked between two cars of similar vintage. I'm overjoyed and overcome. My heart races so hard I suddenly wish the medical kit sitting in the trunk included an atrial defibrillator. What if, after all this drama, we can't even drive her out of the warehouse and have to just ship her home? I'd be humiliated without even having done anything, or more precisely, humiliated because I *hadn't* been able to do anything.

Bernard reconnects the battery and in the immense echoing silence of the warehouse I can hear the click as he turns the ignition. A quick pump of the accelerator and Roxanne rumbles to life. He flashes me a brief smile, then cocks his head to listen to her engine. I want to run around shrieking and dancing with delight. Instead, I stifle my relief and walk to the passenger side. I wish I could have come up with something pithy, some words befitting the magnitude of the whole scene. A couple of months ago I wouldn't have bet my last bag of nuts and bolts that we'd be here, let alone about to drive through Beijing. Instead, I force myself to open my mouth, and out come words of utter banality. "So, I guess this is it," I say with feigned composure. "Time to hit the road, honey." That's the thing about extraordinary times. Sometimes all you want to do is diminish them to the ordinary, make them mundane so you don't have to come to grips with all the strange things that could happen next.

Roxanne rolls smoothly out the warehouse double-doors. "Make a left to the exit," I say with aplomb. This is my first direction of the Rally, so I throw in a broad smile for good luck. It comes out with calm certainty, as if directing a nearly seventy-year-old car onto Chinese pavement is something I do every day. Nothing in my voice betrays the ecstasy I feel. I have to gulp hard to stifle a shout of, "My first direction as a navigator and I got it right!" That would have been unseemly. I knew I couldn't be wrong because there's a warehouse worker standing outside the door pointing left. Beside him are the rest of the Chinese warehouse crew, in ill-fitting trousers and knockoff Nikes, grinning, waving, holding cell phones in front of their faces as they snap shots of one exotic car after another. They are so pleased for us that for the first time in many months I, too, relax and enjoy the moment.

Leaving the warehouse complex, we turn down a street of crumbling pavement lined with block after block of anonymous gray warehouses and shipping facilities. The neglected saplings planted on the divider look like they've run a marathon, too exhausted in their struggle against polluted air to do anything but slump. Within three blocks we pass one of the truly ancient Rally cars parked by the curb. A sense of foreboding blankets me. We don't yet know who's associated with which car, so all I can do is feel generally sorry for driver and navigator. They're standing next to their black four-square 1909 Model T Ford with its jaunty red-spoke wheels, faces engulfed in a cloud of steam rising from the raised hood, getting the first of what may be many a roadside spa treatment.

There's no chitchat going on in our car. Bernard is intensely focused. Everything from the trace of a squint in his eyes to the impassive expression on his face and the way he rolls his shoulders every few minutes tells me he's analyzing each burble and bang that Roxanne emits. At times like this, it's as if his hands are wire sensors, sensitive enough to detect everything about Roxanne's handling and transmit it from the steering wheel to his brain. His ears are data collection devices, able to discern an errant engine sound the way I, a classically trained pianist, can detect when a performer strikes one wrong note in a Beethoven sonata. I interrupt only to announce an upcoming turn.

The directions provided by the organizers note a gas station nearby, where we pull in behind three other Rally cars. Like all the other cars, Roxanne's gas tanks are pretty much dry, emptied before she was strapped into her private Sealand container for shipment across the Pacific. While attendants fill the fuel tank, drivers and navigators bustle, exuding purposefulness, checking engines, tugging straps that secure petrol cans to running boards. "Learn as you go," I tell myself, and begin extracting all manner of things from my shoulder bag, snapping giant red and yellow plastic clips onto the sunscreen to hold future toll slips and small currency, stashing extra pens in the door pocket, arranging maps in the glove compartment. Meanwhile, the gas station attendants are having a field day. They haven't sold this much fuel in ages, and none of them are lounging. Given the cars they're pouring that fuel into, they vie with each other for the honor of operating the pump. Service has never been so good.

One crew pulls out a thick stack of postcards and starts passing them out to the crowd of Chinese workers who seem to have materialized out of nowhere, as there are no shops or businesses apparent on this road. Arms stretch, eager hands grasp a card, turn it over and over. People point, and laugh. Some hand the card back for an autograph. Peering over someone's shoulder I see the crew has created a black and white image of their vintage car.

"Damn it, that's brilliant," I think, wishing I'd come up with the idea. They've printed easily a thousand cards, enough to hand out to everyone forever, delighting all ages. I, too, have gifts to give, little stuffed animals, bright plastic solar-charged calculators, and bulk pens, which I thought kids would enjoy. I felt clever when I bought them. Now I feel embarrassed. I had no notion we'd be mobbed. If the sheer number of people pressing around the cars at this first stop is any indication, my gift satchel will be empty within a few days. Worst of all, I didn't think about the adults and their pleasure in receiving something from my faraway home. All my giveaways were made in China.

Back on Beijing's ring road, each move I make smacks of huge accomplishment to me, whether it's getting into my seat again, rolling down the window, arranging my navigator nest, making sense of the directions back to the hotel. Even I can tell it borders on absurdity to be so hugely self-conscious, so I turn my attention to the several stuck Rally cars we pass.

After passing the Model T, I've had time to realize that, not only are we rolling along without mishap, but we have a trunkful of tools that these crews might need. I roll down the window and shout "Need help?" Then I'm instantly grateful for two things. One, that the window crank doesn't fall off in my hand, and two, that they all say no. Because while we could have maneuvered Roxanne through the zippy Beijing traffic to pull over, we'd have wound up a mile down the road before being able to do so. As it is, cars whiz by within inches of my door, and sticking my arm out to make a space for us to pass would result in it being smashed in seconds. I'm rattled by how fast everything moves, but I have sworn not to yelp, and I don't.

This is a major triumph. My small screeches while Bernard drives are emblematic of the biggest difference between Bernard and me, and why we are hopelessly inappropriate teammates. The Rally already is chipping away at my character, creating raw patches that wouldn't hurt so bad if I didn't feel they exposed the very essence of who I am. Of course we both can compromise. We are grown-ups, after all. But it's usually about little things, things like how to set the table, or when to get rid of the breadcrumbs on the cutting board, things where I can shrug and say, "Yeah, sure, I'll give you that one," because it doesn't really mean much. The bruising comes with the big stuff, like Bernard's near-obsessive desire to get things right, which clashes with my belief that good enough is, well, good enough. I arrive at decisions in a somewhat fanciful and circuitous way, whereas his conclusions rest on a solid foundation of rational building blocks. I like to leap to conclusions. If there's a problem, he wants to think it through. Thoroughly. My approach, of wondering about the best and worrying about the worst, gives him conniptions. His thoughtful, considered manner makes me twitchy with impatience. Probably the most dire aspect of our incompatibility is that Bernard is supremely self-confident, which is why he can thrive on uncertainty. I'm as opposite to this as lobster to lamb, which is why uncertainty makes my shoulders go stiff with tension and leads to unsightly skin breakouts. Though I always jump at the chance to try something new, I can only do so if I have a fairly good sense of what the future holds. I don't need to know all the details of what lies ahead, just enough to soothe me.

If anything's uncertain it's what is going to happen in the days to come. To even sign up for the P2P, I made up stories, because agreeing to do something that was one big unknown was less than thrilling to me. There was no way I could go forward with thirty-five days of 'what-ifs', unless I created my own scenarios of beauty and light, camaraderie and success. All our friends know that, when it comes to control versus lack thereof, Bernard and I do not get along. They have placed bets on the number of days we can remain civil in Roxanne's close quarters. They're only half joking, and I can't disagree with them. There have been times in my life when my desire to be Dina-in-charge, to change the predictable course of events, has almost overwhelmed me, especially on those repeated drives down the mountain to work. As we'd reach what I privately called "The Gauntlet of Nausea," I wanted to demand that Bernard stop the car *now*. I wanted to be done with dramatic swerving and braking. I wanted to get out and loco-mote to our office on my own. But I never did, because a greater rationality prevailed: it would ruin my shoes. With the Rally, shoes weren't the issue. Sheer unremitting isolation was, which gave me unhappy dreams that popped up even during the day. In them, I'd be standing outside the car, crying in frustration, fists clenched at my side. Around me was a hard-packed, gravel plain. Bernard sat in the car, grim-faced with frustration, too. He was not crying. Then he'd drive off. Our car would disappear over the horizon in a trail of dust, leaving me stumbling across the Gobi on foot. Alone.

So one day months ago, when we weren't battling a car fiasco, I raised the matter.

"You know, Bernard," I started out calmly, using my mild, nothing serious tone of voice. "I can't do this Rally if I'm worried that every time I make an error you'll snap at me, or worse, that you'll get all huffy, grab the GPS, and tell me you'll just do it yourself." Bernard wiggled his eyebrows, as he does when he's trying to project patience but can barely contain himself. "And then do that crazy eyebrow wiggling thing you do when you're annoyed." I heard myself getting strident, as I do when I think I'm being helpful and Bernard can't see it.

Then I offered my bargain: "And I don't expect you to drive 7,800 miles with me flinching and gasping every time you get closer to the car next to us than I'm comfortable with. So let's make a deal." The eyebrows were still.

We made a pact. Bernard vowed not to sigh with exasperation, nor to wrench the route book, map, and GPS from my hands to figure out for himself where we should go. I swore to assume that the way he was driving was, in his best judgment, the absolute right way to handle the car at that moment. And I pledged to stifle any vocal accompaniment I might ordinarily have contributed. Which is why it simply would not do to let out a startled shriek only one hour into the race.

We're both on our best behavior on the way to the hotel. I focus on the mileage displayed on our Tripmeter and the route book directions, trying to find the buildings, overpasses, parks, railroad crossings, and exits it mentions before we've zoomed past them. Bernard repeats each direction I say, to confirm he's heard it correctly. It's a dialogue of lefts, rights, and straight aheads that we'll repeat daily for the next five weeks, sufficient distraction that soon the cars around us fade into a blur. The route book turns out to be a practical affair, and despite my misgivings I rattle off one instruction after another without error. That we're right behind another Rally car has no effect on my pride. Bernard can follow the car if he wants, but I know I'm giving the correct directions.

When we reach the hotel I flash my P2P badge at the guard, though it's obvious by our car alone that we're to park in the heavily guarded Rally lot. As he lifts the security bar I think, "We've won. Right here and now we've won. Because arriving in Paris isn't going to feel any better than this." Roxanne runs, we're back at the hotel, we're still married.

What more could I want?

Three, Two, One

It is a humid, pearl gray early morning late in May, when 127 magnificent old cars roll silently out of the hotel lot and begin their 7,800-mile journey, Roxanne among them. It turns out I needn't have worried about the scrutineering. The organizers want everyone to pass. They've accepted several Chevy Fangio Coupes with bodies that look like they belong to a dune buggy and have allowed in a car with sections of cardboard fastened to the wheel wells, a crude approximation of the obligatory mud flaps the regulations specify.

All is peaceful in predawn Beijing, the incessant traffic absent, the roads empty and beckoning. An hour later we're at Badaling, one of the most visited sections of the Great Wall. From miles away we can see it snaking along a convoluted ridge line above intricately folded slopes clad in low green shrubbery. Sections of the Great Wall, which at one time spanned 9,000 miles, were first built as early as 200 BC. Though now much of it has crumbled away, Badaling has benefited from its proximity to Beijing, securing funds for major reconstruction. Built of huge beige stones, this is no mere antisocial fence. At twenty feet wide, it's broad enough to allow horses to gallop five abreast. There are no horses here now, only thousands of tourists clambering from archery perches to signal towers, taking snapshots and buying cheap souvenirs.

As instructed by the route book, we park in a cobblestoned square in front of an ornately carved and painted gateway. It's so high I could stack my house under it twice and still not reach the top. At one time, the massive wood doors, carbuncled with huge iron studs, would swing open to allow passage of imperial coaches. Now, access to those doors is cordoned off, since they're the backdrop to the P2P starting line. The sheer size of the gate dwarfs the hundred or so classic cars below, a fitting tribute to the immensity of our undertaking. When we arrive, there's already a ragged, green satin dragon, with bulging plastic eyes the size of beach balls, writhing around the square. He snakes his way through the crowd, ogling small children and rubbing lasciviously against women's thighs. Stilt walkers in yolk yellow silk pajamas and red masks dip and prance, hopping stiffly as cymbals crash, drums boom, violins wail. My heart picks up the drummers' rhythm and feels ready to exit my chest as I realize it's my imagined movie trailer come to life. Normally I'd be congratulating myself for successfully foreseeing the future. Not now. If this part of the fantasy is true, then the rest of it, the part with the Gobi and me alone in it, also may be true. And that would be bad.

With force of will alone I put my hand on the door handle and open it. A few tepid rays of sun have conquered the dense layers of air pollution, enough to warm the day. I wander near the dragon, daring him to do his worst. I take photos, standing next to some smiling and laughing competitors in hopes their insouciance will rub off on me. I'm stiff with anxiety, which dissipates only a little when the dragon dancers and stilt walkers take a break, remove their masks, and I see that they're just school children. Either that or the Chinese are a remarkably well-preserved people.

The organizer calls through a bullhorn for cars to enter the starting area in groups of ten. When Car 83 is at the starting line I start to hyperventilate. Even if movement were possible at this moment, there's no turning back. Car 85 is tight on our rear bumper and Roxanne never was very good at U-turns. Then I hear "Car 84, take your place at the starting line, please." Television cameras are rolling, the checkered flag is lifted. In slow motion, so slow I can see every ripple and wave, the flag descends, Bernard gently presses the accelerator, and Roxanne rolls under the starting gate. It's too much for me. I tear up, from sheer disbelief that we are on our way. I have my doubts that we'll make it to Paris, but at least we'll have gone part of the way, even if that part is short. I give Bernard a weak smile and wipe my eyes. Then I tell him to turn right.

By the time we reach the first time control of the Rally 185 miles later, Roxanne is in serious trouble. Chugging up a hill behind a slow-moving truck her temperature gauge hovers on the red line. This is a bad sign. We're moving so slowly no air is going through the radiator to cool her engine, which is now apparently minutes away from blowing up. We barely make it to the parking area, but barely is still enough for the course marshals to stamp an acceptable arrival time on my time card. Popping the hood, Bernard reports that the fan, which is supposed to force extra air into the radiator, has fallen off its perch and has been blocking air from the radiator instead. Why did it fall off so soon? Because it was installed backwards.

Out come the tool bags, the towels, the bolts and screws I so carefully labeled and packed months ago. I'm happy to have them along, but honestly, did we have to need them so soon? Other teams saunter by, casting pitying glances. Most make an unnecessarily wide circuit, as if afraid by coming too close they'll catch whatever we have. Those whose cars are going fine can use this rest stop to visit the nearby Hanging Monastery of Hunyuan, an exquisite complex of buildings poised precariously on sheer cliff walls, complete with current monks and 1400-year-old Buddhas. Robert and Maddy are already up there, or so I imagine seeing their empty car near ours. Only Sybil and Nick stop by to commiserate. Nick spends a few minutes with Bernard, who's opened the hood to investigate what's gone wrong. The two men peer inside intently, pointing, pinching parts to see if they might be loose, talking quietly. Sybil gives me a hug. "We're off, dear," she says. "Such excitement!" Just having Sybil standing next to me makes me feel better.

"This isn't a very good start, though," I say. "We already have car trouble . . ."

"Ah, don't worry about that. We'll all be in that position soon. Anyway, the boys will get it sorted," nodding her head toward Nick and Bernard, who by now are carefully lifting the loose fan from in front of Roxanne's radiator.

An hour's been designated for the monastery visit, and that's all the time we have to make our repair before we're expected to clock out again and return to the road. To get a Gold medal, we will have to match our prescribed time slot for every time control during the day. Bernard's bid for Gold at present trumps my desire for Bronze, so it's important we depart and arrive on the minute. It'd be too depressing to already get a penalty on Day One.

Bernard sets to with determination. He grimaces, he extracts, he refits. There's not much I can do except search for a particular size of bolt or wipe off a socket wrench for him. I'm purely a set of hands with no brain. Now and then I glance at the monastery above us. The dark gray cliff face looks like it's been polished by hand over the centuries, and I wonder why religious buildings are so often placed in spots that are so difficult to reach. From my vantage point it looks like a toy, peopled with tiny Rally crews making their way along narrow wood walkways that connect the buildings. A request for a screwdriver brings me back to the hot tarmac. Bernard sweats while I loll about trying to look engaged in the serious work going on next to me.

Having time on my hands allows a new concern to surface: that Bernard may be doing much more work on this trip than I. The experience of Roxanne's rebuild has me hypersensitized to things getting out of balance. Keeping the car running is so obvious and essential that I can't think of anything I can do to compare. How important can it be to dispense bolts and wrenches? I swat away that niggling sense of inadequacy that recently colors so much of what I do, but it's too late. A score card's been posted in my brain, comparing me to Bernard, how much he's doing, how little I'm doing. Right now, I give him a one to my zero. Already I owe him.

After forty-five minutes, it's clear the fan won't go back on. Bernard stomps once around the car, to settle his aggravation. "It's missing a pin," he tells me. "It must have been put in loose and fell off somewhere between the hotel and here."

"No biggie," I say, reassuring myself. "We have over a hundred pounds of spares. Surely we have a pin."

In the hundred pounds of spares and extras I sorted, labeled, placed in Ziploc bags, and packed, there are no spare little pins. Without the fan, there's only one way to keep the engine cool enough. Tossing the fan in the trunk, Bernard disengages the side panels from Roxanne's hood, stowing them behind the front seats. Now most of the engine is exposed to the breeze. Bernard's panel-removal solution is effective, but without them, Roxanne's sleek lines turn lumpen and un-sexy.

Surveying the hundred-plus cars of the Rally in the past few days, I've become conscious that Roxanne, a car that had seemed quite special to me, does not have the coolness factor that many of the older, more glamorous cars have. The organizer also seems drawn to those old convertibles, the cars with spoke wheels and spare tires strapped to running boards. He's all over those owners, chatting them up, with barely a stray hello for us.

None of this bothers Bernard, because he has important work to do. He doesn't have time to spend wondering who isn't speaking to whom and why. Which is good, because there are only minutes to spare when he presses the hood closed and we take our seats. "Right on time," the Clerk of the Course says as we clock out of the time control. I give Bernard the instruction to turn right onto the highway. Since we're on a one-way access ramp entering three busy lanes going in that direction, this is so obvious as to beggar the need for a navigator to transmit the information. Bernard's game and repeats after me: "Take the entry ramp right and merge onto the highway."

Finally, we're into the countryside, making our way through a patchwork of small towns strewn across stony hill country. Trees are few, coal mines plentiful. While I can't see the mines, I can tell they are there by two things: the crushed coal roadways that intersect the paved road we're on at frequent intervals, and the trucks piled high with coal, their sides dusted black with coal residue, that turn onto the pavement from the hidden mines. The sky is murky, a lethal mix of coal dust and Gobi sand, which I inhale in gasps, trying to get by with as little air in my lungs as possible. Coming down a hill in one town I see what look to be three nuclear towers, their concrete not quite as pristine as I suspect it should be. Each tower is blackened with a sooty substance, and as we descend I can see chunks of concrete scattered around the base. It's easy to pick out the ragged spaces left in the towers. Then I read in the route book that the towers are a landmark, where we take a right fork. We'll be going right past them. In a moment of brilliance I intuit that to save myself I must hold my breath as we drive by. How that would stop radiation from entering my body I couldn't tell you.

Soon after, we come across a broken-down local truck. It's a big one, with a bulbous cab painted robin's-egg blue and a bed with wood slat sides, long enough to carry a small car. Its tires look stout enough to support the weight of a tank. The driver is going about his repair with a few measly tools, while his assistant tends a little pot of food heating on a gas burner. They've stretched a tarp from the truck frame for shelter. It's a sobering thought that they're camped here till the fix is done. To make sure their truck doesn't roll, they place cinderblock-sized rocks under each wheel. Good plan, I think. With one small deficiency. I begin to notice large rocks in the middle of the road, left there by a repaired truck that's driven away. Until we reach our hotel, I scan the road for rocky obstacles and ponder the unavailability of roadside assistance should Roxanne break down.

Thankfully, we are on a good facsimile of an expressway for much of the way from Hunyuan to Datong, where we will spend our first night. Even finding our hotel in this strange Chinese city turns out to be fairly simple, as it's located right off the main square. There's no time to celebrate what is one of the most momentous achievements of my life. "Well, Bernard, we made it!" is all I can think of to say, almost too tired to feel exhilarated.

"Bravo, cherie," he tells me. "My little navigator!" He gives my hand a squeeze. In one way, it's anticlimactic. Then again, we both seem to feel we've now crossed an invisible line. Before Datong we aspired to do the Rally. Now we're doing it—*we're in the race*. All in one day, a number of things that have been gremlins on my shoulder for over a year have come to pass, and I've survived. We've had a breakdown, yet Bernard found a workaround that kept us moving. I've used the route book and all my navigator tools, if not with ease then at least correctly. I've relayed directions to

Bernard in a way he could follow. He has not snapped at me and I have not yelped. We are at the proper hotel, where there's a room, a shower, and dinner waiting. We are truly on our way.

After a day of general industrial ugliness, the hotel's manicured grounds, neatly planted with geraniums and petunias segmented by narrow gravel paths, are a refreshing sight. The scene that greets us when we pull in that evening is one I'll discover will be repeated many nights. Despite stern-faced, rifle-toting security guards at the gates, hundreds of local citizens have made their way into the hotel's courtyard and are wandering around admiring the cars.

Bernard immediately goes off to the mechanics' triage center to see if they have a proper pin to put the fan back on. I feel puffed up with immense satisfaction, as pleased with myself as if I'd swum the English Channel. Grabbing our time card, I head into the hotel lobby to sign in at the FTC, which is swarming with Rally teams, euphoric simply because they, like us, have completed the first day's drive. Maddy's at the reception desk, already checked in, waiting to get a key for her room. She and Robert have a car number much lower than ours, and I know they will always arrive before us, unless they have trouble on the road. It's thanks to Maddy's instruction that I know exactly what I'm supposed to do when we arrive. I give her a happy wave and she waves back. "Maddy," I have to yell to be heard over the clamor. "We got here. And get this: no mistakes!"

"Good for you!" she shouts back. "I told you it wasn't that hard."

After my time card is scanned to show we've completed the first day, I join Maddy in the room key queue. "Let's have dinner together tonight," I tell her. "You won't believe what happened to us. Is your car OK?"

"Robert's outside checking a few things, but you know, that's what he likes to do, even if there's nothing to check."

"Yeah, Bernard's like that, too. How about meeting at seven?"

After signing in, I return to Roxanne to get our bags. A young couple with a small boy approaches me. They walk around Roxanne, peer in her open windows, all the while nodding approvingly. They seem to admire me as much as they do the car. Shyly, the man displays his camera, points at me, then at his family. "Photograph?" I say, wiping my hands on my pants. "Sure thing." I move out of the way so he can shoot Roxanne's curvaceous lines unadulterated, but he motions me forward, to join his wife and child. Standing at Roxanne's side, the woman places herself next to me, hoisting her young boy onto her hip. She just about reaches my shoulder. We turn to the camera, me with my long braid coming undone, scraggles of hair catching in my mouth, and shirt already stained, she in her thin floral-print blouse and white capris, bobbed straight black hair neatly held with two red barrettes, toenails a nearly matching crimson. Her husband jogs backwards, then crouches. He shouts something to us in Chinese. We grin.

Into the Chinese Countryside

SIZIWANG QI

China is full of surprises. Pulling into a passage control, which is like a time control only without any time requirement associated with it, we confirm our existence and then step inside a cafe serving *huoguo* (Mongolian hotpot). I'm immediately enveloped by clouds of fragrant steam, redolent of meat and spices. The cafe is overflowing with a lunch-time crowd busy conveying interesting-looking tidbits of flesh and greenery with fast-moving chopsticks from bowls of broth into their mouths. Every plastic table is packed. We shuffle and sidle among the chairs until we find two empty ones, nodding to our Chinese tablemates who are already fully involved in their meals.

By waving both arms I manage to hail a sweating waitress. When I point at what's in front of our dining companions, she nods, sweeps her arm in a graceful arc, and departs. She'll have no trouble finding us again. We're two of the only whites in the place, the others being Rally crews who are already eating. When I turn around, I realize her arm sweep was not some local polite gesture. Behind me is a full wall of shelves and bins, stuffed with vegetables, fish, poultry, pork, lamb, and beef.

I count four sections, each easily five feet wide, divided by eight shelves reaching the ceiling. Every shelf is crammed with ingredient bins; there are another sixteen bins on the floor. I spy leafy greens, which I assume are bitter, plus orange and ivory chunks of various large gourds. There are, of course, the standard Chinese vegetables with which we're familiar, such as mung sprouts and bok choy, next to a greater variety of cabbages and sprouts than I knew existed. There are root vegetables, vine beans, all sorts of seaweed and things I don't have a clue about. There's an entire section with variations on a theme of tofu, cozying up to a section of nothing but noodles. Then there's the sea section, with basins of raw shelled mollusks; fish that's filleted, whole or powdered, fresh and also dried; and of course prawns, all sizes. Squiggly fried things nestle next to a prickle of chicken's feet. Coxcombs snuggle up to lamb kidneys.

While our waitress is in the kitchen extracting fresh pots of broth for us, I have a chance to observe how eating hotpot is done. People flock to the ingredients wall with empty plates, returning with those plates mounded high with choice bits. I watch as they place a variety of food-stuffs in their empty bowl, pour a ladle of hot broth over them, and wait a minute or two for the items to cook. Then they start slurping. When their plate has no more ingredients left to cook in the broth, they get up for more. It's the Chinese equivalent of a salad bar, only, to my mind, infi-nitely more appetizing.

Our waitress returns bearing our personal steaming pots of clear soup, along with heavy white ceramic plates. This is our signal to get up, plates in hand. Like supplicants, we approach the wall. Bernard looks for things he's familiar with, returning with a modestly filled plate of sprouts, greens, cabbages, and shrimp. I start out with an unsightly pile of everything I saw everyone else taking. I'm in a delirium of native cookery and I want to try it all, but I barely have time to refill my bowl with a new mound of ingre-dients and broth to cook it in, when Bernard's looking at his watch. This being purely a Passage Control, we don't have to clock out at a set time, but we do have to reach the day's destination at the prescribed time. Yesterday we already had our first car problem; who knows what problem could confront Roxanne next. My brain agrees it's sensible to get back on the road, but my stomach begs to stay. My stomach is outvoted.

Soon enough, mining towns fall away and we're bumping along a narrow road through farming country. Light filters through a green curtain of weeping willow branches, which softly sweep our windshield. We progress slowly, stalled by endless short detours around the local water project. The chirping of crickets and occasional trilling of songbirds waft through my open window. We're going slowly enough I can smell the warm air, redolent of old manure, pungent smoke, and drying grass. I love farmland. Getting to see how other people work the land in such a far-away place is a real pleasure for me. We pass close to houses, huts really, with walls made from unmilled branches and roofs of thatch. Pigs stop rooting in the yard, ears perked forward in curiosity, snouts following us as we drift by.

The culvert project has resulted in numerous cuts in the road. Every few minutes, we bounce off the pavement onto badly rutted dirt tracks that take us down and around the slice in the road where a new culvert will be inserted. Yellow dust blows into the car, Roxanne bucks about and then we're back on the pavement. It's tedious going. A dry riverbed on our left seems to have been used by other vehicles who also tired of the continuous jolting detours. "Let's try that," I suggest to Bernard. I'm the navigator and it's up to me to dictate whether we can abandon the designated route or not. "It looks like it parallels our route for quite a while. I think we should be OK."

This is planting season, and by all rights the riverbed should be flowing with water. Instead, the rocky ground looks parched and poor. A man plowing with a team of oxen looks up, startled. He rubs his eyes, perhaps wondering whether he's hallucinating from the hot sun. (Or maybe he's just clearing grit from his lids as we drive by). Other Rally cars see us taking off on this new route and elect to follow us. This is one of those aspects of group behavior that I find fascinating. The people behind have no idea whether the car in front is going the right way or not. They're all just looking for relief from the responsibility of having to understand the route book correctly on their own. Merely by the fact that we've made a choice, any choice, they're willing to go the way we go. Though I'm about to yell back at them, "We don't know where we're going," I decide instead to let them come. Roxanne's earned her chance to lead.

"You know, Bernard," I say. "This sort of thing, this riverbed drive, is exactly what I had in mind when we signed up for this rally."

"I know. It's way more interesting than those main roads we've been on. I don't even understand why they've put us on those boring roads."

"Why don't we do more of this? You know, pulling off on side roads, checking out what's around the bend. Maybe we'd meet the local people. We could just stop in front of someone's house, and when they see Roxanne, they'd come talk to us." I'm a little wary of pushing this idea. As far as I know, Bernard's still bent on Gold. Going rogue could put the kibosh on that forever.

"With all these other cars, too?"

"No. We'll let them pass us. I'd rather go on our own." We're only one day into the Rally, and already I'm abandoning my mission of becoming at ease with crowds of people. Bernard's not quite ready to buy it.

"But we still have to check in at each time control," he says, as if I could have forgotten.

He has a point. We are in this to do the Rally thing, whatever that might be. I bid good-bye to my momentary hope that we were done with competition. "Of course. Sure. We'll only take detours if we think we have enough time." I finished with, "And I'll make sure we can get back on the main route before a Control," though I have no idea how I'll be able to do this.

Our plan in place, we stop, thinking the other cars will pass us. They stop, too, apparently thinking we are discussing a strategy which they can again follow. After a few minutes of no one budging, I wave my arm out the window in that classic signal that says, "Go on around us." Once they're all safely ahead, I start looking for an opportunity for us to sneak away and explore.

Approaching a town, I spy a side road on the left, a small lane really, that looks perfect. It's so tightly bounded by tall bulrushes and reeds that I can only see a short distance. That alone is seductive. We have plenty of time to wander, because the route book says there's only 60 miles more to our hotel and that's on a highway. "This looks like a good one, Bernard. Let's turn here and see what we find."

Bernard's about to follow my instruction when we notice a policeman standing in the middle of the lane. He's in a white uniform with gold braid and wears a white peaked cap with a red ribbon. Despite the odd picture our Roxanne must make, he stares straight ahead, his face impassive. "That's odd," Bernard says. "He seems to be blocking the road. Maybe there's an official convoy coming this way and they want to keep all traffic moving." We continue on, looking for another opportunity. The next side road, too, is blocked by a policeman, his white-gloved hands rigid at his side. At a roundabout, there's another one. Policemen everywhere, shoulders back, feet planted, blocking any possibility of leaving the main route; at traffic circles there's a policeman at each possible exit, plus one in the middle, one arm out, white-gloved finger pointing at the exit we're permitted to take. It seems that Chinese bureaucracy has withdrawn its earlier commitment to let us be. Perhaps bribes were expected and not forthcoming. Whatever the reason, every few miles there's a guard, arm extended at right angles, pointing the way, the only way, we're allowed to go.

There's an upside to their assistance. For the past two days, I've queued up with the rest of the navigators each morning, eager to grab a copy of the change notes that amend our route for the day. Just knowing where I need to be at the start of the morning has given me a sense of achievement. Each time I tick off a waypoint or instruction, it's one more direction finished, one more instruction that I didn't botch, one more page of the four-inch-thick route book I can turn. I can't say that I've gotten cocky about being a navigatrix, but I am a step above totally unsure. Still, thanks to those white gloves pointing us in the right direction, I now have absolutely no worries. Any time I'm remotely hesitant I need only look for the finger and I'm back on track.

The presence of the guards announces our coming to every town. It seems we're celebrities, the cause for festivities. As we drive down these main streets, welcoming crowds line the roadside and laborers lift hands blackened with dirt. Mothers gaze proudly at the toddlers they hold aloft, as if to say, "You have the fancy car. But look at this baby I made." Their smiles and waves remind me of exactly how I felt when the Colorado Grand Car Tour came through my village: proud to live in a place such cars would drive through. Here, though, we're not allowed to stop, so all I can do is wave back.

The Chinese countryside, with its small farms, primitive houses, and ancient trees, is much like what I'd imagined. The towns and villages are not. From the little I can see as we drive along, there's nothing either prosperous or individual about them. In one town after another, the highway simply expires into litter on either edge. Soot from the surrounding coal mines covers everything, leaving doors and windows streaked with gluey grime and turning even the litter underfoot to black. This blackened layer, made up of food peels, strips from plastic bags, glass bottle shards, newspaper pages, and whatever someone didn't need or couldn't reuse, is the defacto safe zone for those not moving at high speed. It's crammed with pedestrians, motorcycles, men wheeling carts, and women pedaling bicycles. They bustle in and out of the single row of shops that parallels the highway on either side. All the shops are identical in size, about twelve feet square, no matter whether a hairdresser, grocer, restaurant, or furniture emporium. Perhaps this egalitarian assignment of space is a vestige of Mao. It seems stifling to me. After all, what would spur someone to build their business if it's impossible to get a larger space once it started to grow? The riot of prosperity and relentless march forward I saw in Beijing hasn't reached here. Though everyone has a cell phone, everything else about their lives seems stuck in a time warp.

We figure the Beijing officials who sanctioned the Rally were caught by a fit of remorse at letting so many foreigners see just how backward the countryside was. To placate any grumblers, perhaps to save entire careers, they posted police to keep us moving. I can't tell whether it's the coal smoke or this squeezing out of any individuality that makes me feel like I'm choking.

Frozen

SIZIWANG QI

As we get close to our stop for the night, we enter Inner Mongolia. Though I thought from the name it'd be in Mongolia, it isn't. It's in the northeast of China, nearly straight north of Beijing. We have one more day in China before entering Outer Mongolia, which also sounds like it's in Mongolia. And it is. The hills, farms, and coal mines of yesterday are all gone. In their place are windswept, featureless plains, which in summer must be green waves of grassland. Now, what grass there might be is just a brown stubble coming off a long cold winter. I'm not enthralled that the landscape has changed to brown stubble, but then I'm not yet aware that this is going to look like a tropical jungle compared to what's ahead. Here, sand dunes rim the road. Objectively, this is evidence of desertification from the Gobi. Subjectively, I call it Mongolia's revenge on China for taking so much of their territory. Perched on the dunes are bronze dinosaurs. Life size.

"Bernard, it's *Brontosaurus*," I shout, taking a break from my monotonous rights and lefts. "Hey, and that's *Triceratops*." I do know my dinosaurs. Soon we're passing *T. rex* and *Stegosaurus*, both lying on their side. At first I think they may be posed as sleeping dinosaurs. Then I realize they have suffered an ignominious defeat against the wind, which appears to have knocked them off their twenty-four-inch diameter feet. Just ahead is an enormous rainbow-like arch, painted in five colors. It spans the entire empty six-lane highway and is bristling with national flags. We've reached the heart of China's dinosaur region, where there have been and continue

85

to be fossil discoveries that rewrite the history of dinosaurs every year. In truth, the dinosaurs discovered here are such small creatures that only a paleontologist would find them sexy and exciting. None of those little ones have had bronze statues made of them. A statue of a two-foot tall flying lizard not only wouldn't be as eye-catching as *Brontosaurus*, it would soon be buried in the growing dunes.

Bernard eases Roxanne onto the soft shoulder so I can take a picture. While still trying to organize myself, the wind pulls a power move, nearly yanking the car door out of my hand. It takes my full body against the door to shut it. I scuttle around at crab level to photograph a supine velociraptor and then duck-waddle back to Roxanne. Any wind that can body slam a dinosaur on its side deserves, and gets, my respect.

The closer we get to the border, the less Chinese the people look. To me, they look Mongolian, with ruddy cheeks and broad faces. Which of course, they are. So it's fitting that on this, our last night in China, we sleep in a tourist yurt camp, where I learn that the local name for a yurt is *ger*. China's a big country with the world's largest population. This particular *ger* camp can sleep a modest 3,500 holiday revelers. It's as if all of Chicago booked into the same motel. At first I'm baffled by what would draw so many to this place. Why come out to the windy grasslands to sleep on lumpy mattresses on the ground and to plow against gale force winds to reach a shower hut where you bathe with cold water in buckets? Clearly, Chinese holiday revelers enjoy playing rustic Mongolian herders, because the camp hosts tell us that during high season, the place is full. Then it strikes me this isn't all that different from home, where playing at being a rustic cowboy has created a whole branch of the vacation industry. It's not just in movies that Americans go to dude ranches to sleep under scratchy blankets, get saddle sores, sneeze from horse allergies, and eat too many beans for a week. Chinese and Americans have more in common than I thought.

To the envy of many of the other crews, we're assigned one of the "modern" *gers*, with a bed and a private bathroom. I'm shown a real *ger* by Ralph, who's assigned to one for the night. It's a one-room round felt tent, with bed rolls on a dirt floor, a wood burning stove, and showers in a shared bath house. "Would you perhaps like to trade?" he ventures. "Go for the authentic experience?

"Thank you. Absolutely not," is my unhesitating reply, before I discover that our concrete yurt facsimile, for all its sturdy walls and tiled floor, has no heating at all.

In the parking lot before dinner we see our new friends Eduardo and Franklin. They stand next to their car, hands on hips, heads bowed in glum silence. The two are an odd-couple of a team, Eduardo a flamboyant irrepressible Argentine and Franklin his fastidious, playfully grumpy, American counterpart. Now Franklin's ruing his decision to leave the car arrangements to Eduardo, because the rusty old 1937 Ford that Eduardo procured is in terrible shape. No doubt at time of purchase Eduardo was distracted from the corroded underbody and the decaying engine by the car's newly reupholstered butter yellow leather seats and ivory soft top. It's dashingly elegant unless you look close. What they tell us is that, earlier that afternoon, desperate to stem the tidal wave of oil leaking from their car, they had high hopes of making a repair in the back alleys of the dingy towns through which we've just driven. Somehow they persuaded a road guard that they needed help. Once he let them pass, an eager flock of pedestrians and pushcart peddlers escorted them to a backstreet repair stall.

Franklin recounts how the mechanic spent hours deconstructing the Ford, welding bits and pieces here and there. Miracle of miracles, he somehow fixes it, and they go on their way splattering only droplets in their wake. The fix lasts for one hour, just long enough for them to reach the evening's hotel. There, as if on cue, five quarts of oil scrounged from neighboring mechanic stalls splash unceremoniously onto the parking lot. As they tell us this, Franklin gives me a glum smile.

"It'd cheer me up greatly if you two would join us for dinner," he says. I'm beginning to realize that making dinner plans is part of the Rally ritual. The navigators want a chance to find out whether turning left at that railroad crossing after the third roundabout next to the small gas station was a personal error or a route book mistake. We also want the chance to say words other than "right" or "straight on," not to mention simply speaking to someone other than the person we've been in a car with for hours. The drivers need to delve into mechanical problems with others who might be able to help, to share accumulated wisdom or, if nothing else, commiserate. Everyone wants to sit with someone else and get the benefit of their expertise and their sense of humor.

Even though the organizers have ordered dinner for us each night, the thing to do seems to be to arrange ahead of time with whom you'll be sitting. It's another throwback to my teen years, this time to the Saturday night dating game, and as such it's a distressing reminder of something at which I failed miserably. My keen pleasure at Franklin's invitation is sad proof that I haven't matured as much as I'd hoped since high school.

I'm flattered that Franklin wants to dine with us. "We'd love to," I tell him. "Maybe Bernard can come up with some ideas about your oil leak."

"No, no!" Eduardo interjects. "Too depressing. We will drink wine and talk about women!"

That night Bernard and I discover that the legacy of a people accustomed to sleeping on mats on the floor is a mattress that is more a concrete slab wrapped in a bedsheet. I'm a side sleeper and soon my hip bones are burning from jutting into that unyielding pallet. I flail and flop around, trying to get comfortable. The temperature drops precipitously. Our only cover is a thin white sheet, which Bernard tugs to his side and I to mine, as we each try to enclose a small space warm enough to sleep. At 2 AM Bernard mumbles, "We have sleeping bags in the car."

"It's good to know they're safe," is all I can offer, too tired from the day and too cold to go out to the car to get them.

"These Chinese really are tough. Or crazy. Because being this cold is ridiculous."

"Are you sure there are no blankets in this?"

"Positive. I checked before we went to dinner." Bernard hugs me to him, and some time before dawn, we both doze off.

The next morning, as I pull open drawers to make sure we've repacked everything, I discover two lovely fluffy blankets safely folded in the bedside dresser. My mental scorecard lights up again.

Borders: Take One

The official start of the P2P's first day in Mongolia is delayed. Bleary-eyed from our shivering sleepless night, we couldn't be more thankful for the nit-picking of Chinese officialdom. There are three hundred people and their associated classic cars to clear through the Erenhot border, and these guys are taking their sweet time. They've never been asked to handle so many cars at once, let alone foreign makes they've never heard of, like Sunbeam, Itala, Brassier, La France, Alvis. All the drivers are ordered to stay with their cars while navigators crowd into the large immigration hall, car documents in hand. Ever so slowly, three small, officious men in over-sized military peak caps scrutinize papers. They look very smart in their white shirts, creased khaki pants cinched overly tight at their slender waists. They squint at passports stamped with car authorizations, trot between their respective booths to get a second opinion, occasionally make eye contact to check that the person before them matches the image on the passport.

I edge along, muttering pardon me's and sorry's till I find a place next to Sybil. "God am I glad to see you," I tell her. "I hate these crowds, this shuffling along."

"I do, too," she laughs, another thing we find we have in common. Since our introduction that night back in Beijing, we seek each other out most evenings to trade stories, opinions on the day's events, and whatever gossip we've managed to pick up about other competitors, which isn't much. As the queue inches forward, I tell her tidbits of my New York childhood, and we trade our hopes and worries about Mongolia. Already, in three short days, her olive skin is attractively tanned from open-air driving.

She tells me about other rallies she's done with Nick, and I reveal my worries about this one. Now that the easy stuff in China is over, I can feel my shoulder muscles contracting like rawhide on a rain-drenched saddle. We're about to leave the comfort of easily identifiable landmarks like buildings, monuments, paved roads, and streets signs. All those white-gloved hands pointing directions will be staying behind, too. According to the route book, for the next eight days we'll be using GPS waypoints, a set of numbers created by satellites, to find our way. Landmarks will be few and undistinguished, an occasional telegraph pole or a railroad track the only manmade objects to help us identify whether we're going the right way. Wood poles and iron bars aren't the most distinctive of features, especially when there are miles of them. All I can think is how in the world to differentiate the right pole or track from the wrong one, while trying to find my way through a wasteland of desert. That's not all. We'll be doing time trials in the Gobi, and while I understand the concept of them clearly by now, I still feel wet behind the ears as a navigator, not at all sure I want to test my skills and nascent confidence against the clock.

When the hubbub in the waiting line gets too loud, officials shout at us to be quiet. At least we infer so from their harsh tone of voice and the frowns on their faces. When it comes to not speaking Mandarin, it turns out I've been in good company. The room grows still, but only briefly, and then the chatter and laughter build again, like an orchestra tuning for an overture. Normally I'm so impatient that if there's even one person ahead of me in line I dissolve into twitches. Impatience could be called one of my chief features. Or more accurately, my greatest flaw. My reaction to knowing that the people in front of me will move to the next thing before I will is physical, a combination of jaw clenching, muscle tensing, and shallow breathing. My brain becomes undisciplined, unwilling to focus on a conversation, conniving instead on how I can right this unfairness by sneaking to the front. Would that I could say I do these things unconsciously, but I don't. My intolerance shames me. With Sybil's company, and no route book demanding attention, for the first time in my life I feel relaxed in a crowd. This is such a novel experience that I smile at the ceiling, marveling at what it feels like to be too happy while waiting in line. These couple of hours of companionable banter are more welcome to me than a hot shower at the end of a long day's drive. Almost.

Once clear of customs and reunited with Bernard, we drive across a strip of no man's land and enter Zayman Uud, the Mongolian side of the border. This is a hallelujah moment, something I've been waiting for since we hosted those Mongolian scientists at our home the year before. I remember clearly how their delight matched mine when we realized how similar our home landscapes were. I look around, hoping for something familiar in the scenery. The best I can do is liken these surroundings to Sand Dunes National Park in southern Colorado. Even that is a stretch, as the terrain is hardscrabble and grave with no lovely rounded, fine dunes rising anywhere. The ground is parched, having received just that bit of moisture that tempts green things to grow into scraggly blades that wilt in a few days. For no reason at all, I held a hope that the landscape on the Mongolian side of the border would be different from what we'd just driven through in China. I wanted this to be true because already I longed for a landscape in which I could feel at home, a landscape that would welcome me, that would give me that same feeling of comfort that I get when I enter someone's home and smell coffee and chocolate and cinnamon. I brush aside my disappointment, focusing instead of how good it feels to be reunited with Bernard. There are thousands of Mongolian miles ahead of me, and there's no reason not to be confident that up ahead I'll see countryside that reminds me of home.

For the time being we bide our time in a sandy depression, a holding area where all teams have to wait until everyone has finished with the border formalities. Each Rally crew handles the mounting tension differently. I offer a "Bon appétit," to the cheery blonde Finns, who have flipped open the table and storage cupboard cleverly built into the side of their butter yellow Packard Coupe. As I walk by, I see they're snacking on tinned fish and sipping coffee. "Good luck," they reply, raising their plastic mugs. The lithe raven-haired driver of a black Citroen arranges his lanky, T-shirted frame on the balloon fender of his car, crosses his arms, and takes a nap. I hang out, waiting for him to fully relax and then roll off. Yes, I'm that desperate for amusement. A few diehards work on their cars, reaching into toolboxes the size of a child's lunchbox, roomy enough to hold two wrenches, a few screwdrivers, and a modest assortment of spare nuts and clips and still have room, if pressed, for a PB&J sandwich. Either they're woefully underprepared, or we could make a killing selling some of the hundred pounds of tools, spares, and every size of nut or bolt we packed, for that special moment of need.

Bernard and I are neither tired nor hungry nor inclined to inspect Roxanne's engine parts one more time. All that's left for us to do is pace. For once Bernard joins me in worrying. Through China we've been on paved road, a kindness on the organizer's part that allowed everyone to test their car and make sure everything was working, or tight, or dust proof. Except for the unfortunate incident of the fan falling off, Roxanne has held up superbly, and after Bernard's extemporaneous removal of her side panels, she's stayed calm, cool, and collected.

Mongolia's dirt tracks promise a whole new story. Given that her fan was jostled loose on a smooth road, all manner of things could fall apart once we get onto truly rough track. I picture the steadfast, hardworking Roxanne with her doors, fenders, and hood flying off left and right, leaving Bernard and me exposed in our seats, riding along on the bare chassis. I have other worries now, too. As we're moving into wilder territory, open country with no villages to provide civilized landmarks like streets and bridges, I realize that my earlier navigational anxiety was mere self-indulgence. In a city there's always someone you can ask for directions, even if your question is conveyed in sign language. If you're completely lost, you can even pay a taxi to guide you. Who's going to be around to help if I get us lost in a featureless expanse of sand?

After several hours, all the cars have arrived. We notice some drivers revving their engines. Car 1, a 1907 Itala, splutters and burps to the start table. This titan of an ancient car is my standard bearer. It has an engine bigger than a Formula 1 Ferrari except that, at its maximum of 45hp, it puts out about as much power as a snowblower. It's a carapace on wheels, fenders and running boards bristling with chains, levers, and other mechanical bits that newer cars hide beneath the hood or under the body. It is so heavy and complex to drive I have to believe that, if they can do it in that car, we can handle Roxanne. The driver and his wife, a quiet pair, have dressed the part. Each wears a skull-fitting leather helmet, goggles, knee-high lace-up leather boots, a long duster for chilly mornings, and a scarf wrapped around their necks, ready to pull over their noses if the dust gets bad. They're signed off, and, with a faster series of pops and bangs, they head toward the desert. From there, the starter's white flag drops once a minute, releasing one car after another into the wilds beyond.

The eighty-four minutes we have to wait feel like an endless age as we're each gnawed at by the sharp teeth of uncertainty. So deep are we in our respective reveries that we're startled to see Car 70 at the starting desk. "Quick Bernard, we have to get in line," I shout. We jump from daydream to action, racing through a last-minute check to make sure nothing's left behind. I slide into the car, grab my time card, click the 4-point harness closed. "Do you have the route book ready?" Bernard yells, his voice rising with the strain and excitement of the moment.

"Of course I do. I'm the navigator. No worries," I lie.

Bernard turns on the ignition. Kathunk. He tries again. A third time. Roxanne won't start. For a moment I think she's refusing to go into the Gobi. But no. Roxanne wouldn't do that to us now. Something's surely wrong, but there's no time to find out. We have to take our place in line or lose it. That means we'd be relegated to the end of the line, starting only after every other car had left. That wouldn't be the end of the world, but with the many penalty minutes we'd be assessed, it'd probably be the end of Bernard's quest for Gold. Adrenalin sending sparks through my body, I jump out and lay a shoulder into a fender alongside Bernard, feet searching for purchase in the light sand as we struggle to get Roxanne up the incline to the starter's table. Other crews whose departure comes much later lend muscle to push us up the slope. Roxanne weighs as much as a small Panzer tank, and I put every ounce of effort I have into moving her, fueled by desperation and the knowledge that the calories I burn would be the equivalent of one full Nautilus circuit at the gym. There's the thought as well that it would be rather disturbing for all the people at home who have told me they'll be reading the daily Rally reports to wake up and see "Rally crew squashed when car rolls over them."

"Our engine's quit!" I shout to the marshals. "What do we do?" I am one unhappy navigator. Here I'd just begun to feel confident about the time control procedures and now I don't even have a car for them to time.

"Just roll 'er on through," is the nonchalant reply. "As long as she crosses the line, you'll be noted as taking your start on time." This seems a bit lackadaisical to me. Here I thought the Rally was about cars moving, not cars being moved. Never mind old assumptions. It's their rules, not mine, and right now I'm glad the rules bend in my favor.

A course monitor initials my time card, the white flag drops, and we push Roxanne across the starting line, keeping our crawling momentum going till she is under the concrete awning of an abandoned gas station next door. That's how we start our drive through Mongolia: on foot.

Minute after minute other cars are flagged off and lumber by us. I wave, projecting good cheer while inside I feel like I'm being twisted in two. I'm wondering how good Bernard really will be at fixing Roxanne on the fly. Maybe, without telling me, he's testing himself to see just how much he can do. What if he can't do it all? Each car that passes is one more car that will get to camp before us. Here I was just starting to feel like I had a comfortable space within this group, and now they're all bypassing us. All I want at this moment is to keep up with the Joneses, all three hundred of them. After ten cars have gone, Bernard calls out from under the hood, "Got it. It's minor, really. A linkage from the gearbox is out of adjustment. I can fix this in no time." I don't even realize I've been holding my breath till I exhale. "You are one swell guy!" I holler back. The problem he's described means nothing to me. That he can fix it means everything. Another five cars and we, too, are back in business.

Sagging into my seat, I'm lavishly happy that we won't have to spend the rest of the day trying to repair Roxanne at a bleak border station with no services. We're in Mongolia for sure now, a place with a population the size of Brooklyn, in an area the size of Texas, California, and Montana combined, with West Virginia thrown in as a bonus. There's literally no turning back, regardless of whether we want or need to. The organizers have told us that China will not let any of our cars reenter once we've exited. Seems like three days of foreigners driving helter skelter over their roads is as much as the Chinese could bear.

The first mile of Mongolian road is a concrete slab, built to imbue the border with a sense of modernity and permanence. Like many third world projects, this one never was finished. Either money ran out or drained straight into the contractor's pocket, leaving the fine concrete with an eight-inch drop to the sand. Given that cars are vastly outnumbered by people in these parts, the road has become a sidewalk. It looks like half the population of Mongolia is streaming toward the border, most likely having arrived here by cadged rides from Ulaanbaatar. In simple T-shirts, slacks, and loose flip-flops, carrying cloth bundles or plastic shopping sacks, people weave and wander around us like a school of tropical fish through a coral reef.

We're off into Mongolia, and this strikes me as a major event worth acknowledging. I'm already accustomed to the eager, excited crowds that mobbed our car at each fuel stop in China. I wave my arm out the window and some return the gesture, but most just walk by. Suddenly there's a loud crash, followed instantly by a sharp bang. I hunch reflexively. As a child of the sixties, I'm a veteran of school air raid drills. I now execute a perfect duck, knees cradling my head, arms covering all. "What the hell was that?!" I shout from between my elbows, as Bernard shouts, "A rock. Someone threw a rock at us!" I peer up and see the windshield on Bernard's side is a crazy blossom of cracks. Bernard keeps driving, giving me only a second to spot the culprits: a small group of cute tousle-haired young boys, who mockingly wave rock-filled hands. They're laughing.

"Slow down, Bernard. I have to get out." Bernard knows that I'm irrational and that rock-wielding kids are nothing to trifle with, so he does the smart thing. He speeds up. I yell at him to stop. He ignores me. Before I can even start fumbling at my seatbelt latch, the boys have faded into the flowing crowd of pedestrians.

As Roxanne thunks off the concrete pavement onto the sandy track that heads to the desert, I realize I must be ridiculously fragile. Something as modest as a rock thrown as a prank, as unimportant in the grand scheme of possible car problems as a damaged windshield, has thrown me completely out of kilter. Bernard, as I expected, stays calm. "Just drop it," he says. "It's done. Maybe we can get a replacement in Ulaanbaatar." I could use some commiseration, but all he gives me is practical advice. I lower my head, nursing my wounded pride, and pick at the sparkling splinters of glass that glitter in my lap, souvenirs from where the sharp tip of the rock poked a hole in the windshield.

Three days in and I want to scream with vexation. Because it's not about the windshield. It's about that year and a half, and all our efforts to make Roxanne beautiful and worthy. If I cared to admit it, it's also about my own efforts to see myself as worthy, to be the half that makes the two of us a whole.

Time Trial

ZAMYN UUD-SAYNSHAND

I count telegraph poles and keep track of GPS waypoints for several hours before we reach a flag stuck in the ground, beside which are standing two course marshals. It's the start of our first time trial, which sends an entire migration of butterflies coursing through my stomach. Here's what's coming over the next three minutes: The route book distances will be in yards, not miles, which I am to holler in a high volume litany to Bernard. Our car hurtling over rough ground at 50 mph will cover two hundred yards in eight seconds. Bernard either gets it and does it, or we crash.

My monologue should go like this: "Two hundred yards left turn, 150 yards left turn, 75 yards left turn, LEFT TURN NOW!" Getting the distances right will require a level of concentration I've displayed once in my life . . . when I fought to stifle nervous laughter welling up from the pit of my stomach as I waited to say "I do" at our wedding. There'll be no time for fact-checking. That's bad. But what's good is that there'll also be no time for back talk, none of the "Are you sure" and "What did you say" of earlier days. The time trial gives me permission to shout at Bernard all I want.

I can tell Bernard's thrilled to put Roxanne to the test; a smile has been playing across his lips for the past half hour. "Don't worry, cherie," he said a while back. "Just read me the directions, one by one. But fast. And clear. And loud. We'll do fine."

"What if I lose my place in the book?"

"You won't. Mark it with your finger, and just slide that finger down the page." His confidence does not reassure me.

"I have to look at the Tripmeter at the same time. And some of the directions are just symbols. I need time to remember what they mean," I tell him, looking ahead in the book at what's to come. I swallow hard. This may be the last time I have a chance.

"You've been perfect these past few days. This isn't any different. It's just faster. I'll still repeat everything you tell me."

"Hello, luv," says one of the marshals, sticking his head in my window. "Ready to have a go?"

"Oh god. Yes. No! I don't know. What do we do?" I'm breathing in short gulps.

"I'll scan your time card, and Bernard, when this car ahead of you leaves, you pull up level with the flag." My heart feels about to leap out of my chest and stay behind as I listen to my first ever "Three, two, one, GO!" Bernard mashes the gas pedal. Like a cannonball we shoot across the starting line and into the desert. Charging along, Roxanne stirs up a dense powdery cloud. She careens off boulders, brutalizes small shrubs, dodges telegraph poles and any other inanimate object too stubborn to get out of her way. We swoop up small hills and are momentarily airborne. I let out a whoop before Roxanne slams back to the ground and the breath leaves my belly with a strangled "Aaaargh." We are going so fast we overtake other cars. "Gee," we mutter. "Don't want to cover them in dust." Then we blaze past them cheering mightily. Bernard eyes me carefully after the finish line, to see if I am frowning. "Bernard! I loved that!" I exclaim and bestow on him the broadest smile he's seen in days. He smiles back, proud of how he's driven and delighted at my delight.

We head back onto the normal route, feeling all shiny and bright with the thrill. It takes us some moments to notice that Roxanne, instead of gliding along serenely as she normally does, is now unnaturally bouncy, moving like a drunken sailor rising on tiptoes and then collapsing at the knees. Each washboard sends her trunk soaring and then jouncing back to within inches of the ground. This seems a bad sign. Pulling to a stop in the scrub, Bernard slides under Roxanne on his back. Emerging a minute later, he slaps the dust off his hands, then turns his back to me so I can brush away any Gobi detritus clinging there. He shakes his head, then lifts furious eyes and confirms my fears. Roxanne is injured. The thick steel mounts that attach the rear shock absorbers to her frame have sheared off. Both are broken. Without them, every ripple in the road is magnified, transferring stress to her leaf springs that they were not designed to handle. One of them appears to have sustained a hairline fracture. It isn't a mortal wound, but it will take doctoring, the sort that can only be done from under the car, standing in a service pit. We drive on.

"This should never have happened," Bernard says, thankfully keeping both feet on the clutch and the gas pedal instead of kicking himself in disgust. "I made those shock mount measurements myself. They should be perfect." The butterflies in my stomach have metamorphosed to gargoyles whose sharp claws now dig into my gut. Neither of us wants to state the obvious, but we're both thinking it: if we'd been able to test drive Roxanne, we'd have found this design flaw while there was still time to fix it. As it is, we creep the rest of the way toward that night's camp at Saynshand, our speed reduced from modestly ground-covering to slow enough for me to count the blades of dead brown grass as we drive by.

Sandstorm

SAYNSHAND

Eight hours after leaving the China-Mongolia border, we arrive at dusk at our new digs, a broad shallow bowl in the desert, surrounded by dunes. It must have seemed like a lovely protected spot in which to pitch camp when the organizers were there a year ago, in calm weather. Now though, the bland, featureless bowl hosts only a few scattered Rally cars; it's more discouraging than rewarding to arrive there, especially with a hot wind blowing grit over everything. Over the course of the day, Bernard's right eye has been swelling shut. I think the hacking cough he was plagued with in Beijing, the one we attributed to the dense pollution, is an infection that's left his lungs and taken up residence in his eye. By the time we pull in to camp, it's gummed nearly shut with goo.

"I've got antibiotic drops for that, Bernard," I say, thinking I'll reassure him. Before I can even dig out the medicine kit, he dismisses my help. I'm his wife, and one of his unwritten rules is that he cannot accept medical advice from me. "No, no, leave it," he says. "It'll get better." The euphoria of our first time trial is long past, and we're both trying to stifle bad moods, so I let it go. Besides, already the breeze has stiffened. Wisps of sand skiff along the ground. Like prying fingers they find poorly sealed car doors and sneak into carelessly closed car windows. It seems barely moments before a wild wind arrives and the depression in which we are camped turns into a sink in which all the sands of the Gobi appear to be collecting. Radios crackle between organizers, camp staff, and course marshals. The advice for those still in the desert is to stop where they are and retreat into their cars to escape the swirling airborne sand.

We're both distracted with concern about Roxanne's broken suspension, whether we'll find a workshop to get her repaired, or if she even can be repaired around here. The abrasive sand blowing about insists on our attention, though, making clear there'll be no working on the car. More pressing is our need for shelter for the night. "Let's get the tent put up," Bernard urges. "This storm doesn't seem like it's going to die down any time soon." I visualize our pop-up tent airborne on the rampaging wind, me hanging on to one corner as it whisks me into the next country.

"OK, here's the plan. When the tent springs open I'll unzip the flap and launch myself inside to hold it down. You do the attaching." I feel sneaky but pleased about this division of labor. I'll be protected while Bernard's braving the elements. We open the tent and I immediately spread-eagle myself inside, arms and legs stretching to the four corners while Bernard lashes the tent to Roxanne's side mirror. I only hope that mirror is bolted on more securely than the radiator fan. He grabs our water bottles from the car and joins me inside, where we hunker down to consider our options.

"Are you hungry?" Bernard asks, looking at his watch and noting it's definitely dinner time.

"Starving," I say. "By the way, when I was walking around waiting for the start this morning, I overheard the organizers say something about cold beers at the end of the day."

"Beer? Let's go see if it really is cold, and give the camp staff some moral support." That's my Bernard, always ready to think about others. The tent flap is nearly ripped from my hand when I unzip it, even though I open it just enough so we can wiggle out on our bellies into the furious hot blast of the storm. From there we scuttle the few hundred yards between Roxanne and the listing dining tent like a couple of sand crabs. The exfoliation special my face gets along the way is not only necessary, but free.

By clenching my eyes into slits, I can see on my left that every green canvas Port-a-Potty has been blown over. The green heaps next to them used to be the shower stalls. Glancing to my right, I make out forty-odd cars; the rest of the Rally must be stuck in the desert. The cars that have arrived are arrayed chaotically in the modest depression, as if they pulled into the camping area and abandoned any semblance of orderly parking. This is our first night under the stars, though now it's debatable whether we'll even see them. Everyone's been looking forward to the adventure of sleeping out in the desert, but the cars I see around me look pathetically small and helpless in the wasteland of blowing sand. Those crews who have succeeded in erecting a tent have tied it to their car, just as we have. A few crews seem to have abandoned the idea of pitching a tent altogether, opting to sleep in their front seats instead.

At the dining pavilion, several staffers struggle with the support poles as the tent gyrates in the shrieking sandstorm like a hip-hop dancer. Peering into the murky interior, we spy a table set with chunks of cheese, biscuits, a stew, and trays of sliced tomatoes, cucumbers, lettuce, and carrots. There appears to be a dusting of glittering bread crumbs over everything. "Oh my god, this looks delicious!" I say. "Bernard, look. Fresh tomatoes. Salad! Deviled eggs!" I lift a pot lid and feel my legs go weak. "Bernard, beef goulash." I inhale the savory steam rising from the pot, redolent of stewed tomatoes, paprika, and onions. All my worries vanish. No matter that our dinner will be gritty. We are out of the car and food is at hand.

Filling plates, we sit with our backs to the wind, alone in what appears to be a swiftly collapsing dining tent, and stuff the gritty food in our mouths as fast as we can, spitting out grains of sand as we find them. It's better than a three-star Michelin banquet, a meal Bernard and I can share quietly to help dispel the hours of grimness after the time trial. We can't let animosity build up between us already. If the rest of Mongolia is like today, there'll be too many tough aspects without adding a heaping helping of general gripes to the mix. Besides, we're not angry at each other, we're distressed at circumstances that prevented us from ferreting out Roxanne's shock absorber problems before she shipped.

The storm howls and thrashes, its violence testing the strength and stamina of the human pole supporters. They're locked in combat with the tent, which writhes and twists in their grasp. It is obvious that we have only minutes before this structure, too, will collapse. We diligently gulp our beer, made thirstier by the knowledge that it may be awhile before we get another. More staff scramble about to save the dinner offerings from further ruin.

Back outside the now swooning dining tent, it is pitch dark, a blizzard of swirling sand. The trip we made with ease half an hour earlier is now an impossibly obscured distance through which we must retrace our steps. My headlamp, normally bright enough to read by, can barely illuminate the hand in front of my face. The wind seems to shriek with pain. My instinct is to cover my ears, to protect them from the high-pitched keening, but I need my hands to shield my nose and eyes from the grains that are frantically, insistently trying to invade them. In the midst of this swirling chaos I feel as if I, too, am spinning out of control. I don't even know for sure which way is up, let alone which way is Roxanne. To hell with sand in my nose, I say to myself, and grab for Bernard's hand. Slowly we pick our way in what we hope is the direction of our car and tent; when we dare raise our heads for a second, we peer into a shapeless darkness. In the distorted frame of reference that is a Mongolian sandstorm, I have no idea how long or how far we've crept, when Bernard finally points out a humped shape in the otherwise featureless foreground. Roxanne, right where we left her.

Safely at the car, I still have to figure out how to relieve myself in a vicious wind with no Port-a-Potty available. This is minor compared to what I later learn is the unpleasantness suffered by the 140 people caught in the desert when the sandstorm arrived, Sybil and Nick among them. I squeeze myself next to the running boards, hope I'm squatting in the right direction, and spare a grateful thought that, given the weather, no one's likely to walk by. Done with that duty, I belly-crawl into the tent, Bernard grabbing my arm to guide me. We sit there for a bit, still holding hands, the escalating moan of the wind making us feel that much safer inside. A warm cloak of relief envelopes me as I crawl into my sleeping bag and shove earplugs into my ears. Drowsily I run my fingers through my hair, taking note of the thousands of grains of sand that now reside on my scalp, tiny fellow travelers on the road to Siberia. Then I search out

Bernard's hand again, reassured by the warmth of his skin that he's still there with me.

At dawn the next morning, Bernard awakes with his right eye sealed shut with yellow, crusty muck. Some time during the night the sandstorm blew itself out, so when we crawl out of our tent, it's eerily quiet. "I'll take another look under the car. I have to know what's happened so we can figure out how to fix it." I wander over to the re-erected dining tent, where I find Sybil nursing a steaming mug of tea. "My God, you're here! When did you get in?" I ask her.

"Just now," she says, explaining that they came upon their friends Richard and Jill whose 1929 Bentley had broken down, and decided to stay in the desert with them to ensure they were OK. "It was such fun," she tells me. "We took out our stoves, made tea and broth, had tinned fish and biscuits.

"Weren't you worried about the storm?" I ask, incredulous that someone could have met adversity with such a blithe spirit.

"Not at all. One of the marshals managed to find us and told us to stay put. So we knew someone other than us knew where we were. When the storm blew out, you should have seen the stars. It was marvelous."

"Sybil, what about your Gold?" I ask her, knowing that Nick, like Bernard, has his heart set on one. In my humble opinion and disregarding the affection I already feel for this couple, I've already decided theirs is the most beautiful car on the Rally. It's the color of a precious gem and has the long, slender, lightweight lines of a greyhound, as compared to Roxanne's more ponderous St. Bernard frame. It deserves to win a Gold medal.

"Well, I'm afraid that's gone. But, you know, that's OK. Now we can relax and enjoy the Rally." Then, our eyes catching, we both say, "Maybe!"

I'm about to fill her in on our experience when Bernard arrives. I can see clearly now that his eyelid is swollen and red. In as offhanded a manner as possible I say, "Perhaps the Rally doctor has some suggestion for you." Since the doctor's not married to Bernard, I'm hoping his opinion will carry more weight than mine. We wander through camp, looking for cars of people we know, noticing that barely half the Rally made it in before the storm. Some have tents next to them that look like squashed fruit, the owners having given up on inserting the support poles in the proper places. The storm clearly hit everyone with a knockout punch, and we seem to be the only ones stirring. Where the rest of the Rally is, who knows, and I silently bless Bernard for getting us through yesterday. Near the edge of camp we finally find the doctor's van. Its hood is smashed, the windshield shattered out, and the roof a crumpled mess. "My god, Cyclops, I hope they're OK," I say.

"Well, somebody put up their tent, so they must be," he grumps, in no mood for jokes.

It seems unkind to knock on their tent flap at this early hour. Back at our tent, Bernard dabs at his eye with a damp tissue. When we do finally find the doctor in the dining tent, all in one piece, but with hands shaking as he pours himself a mug of coffee, Bernard lifts his face with its red, swollen eye and asks his advice. "I can check it further this evening," he's curt, sounds frazzled, as I would if I'd survived a launch and flip in the Gobi. "Meantime, if you have some antibiotic drops, that's what I'd prescribe." The scorecard lights up. We're even.

Giving Up Gold

SAYNSHAND-ULAANBAATAR

We grab a few rolls off the breakfast table and head out. There's Roxanne to tend to and only one mechanic in Saynshand. "Having the number 84 is really a liability," I say to Bernard as we're packing the car. "I mean, if we're to toe the line and leave at our sanctioned time every day, we'll always be leaving an hour and a half later than we could. We're up at 6:30. We could even leave at 7:30, if they'd count that as legal. But no. We have to wait till they say we can go." My natural impatience, so successfully tamped down while the going was easy, is asserting itself with vigor. "How can we ever get to a repair shop, make our start time and still get in at a reasonable hour?"

"That's right," is Bernard's terse response, which doesn't answer my question. He's angry, at himself for the shock absorber calculation error he seems to have made, and at the Greeley mechanics who, by procrastinating on their tasks, made it impossible for us to stress test our car before departure. We passed the lone mechanic's shop on our way in last night, and so we know that it's as small as a horse stall and, if the shabby exterior is any indication, minimally equipped. If we're not the first ones there, it could be many hours before the sole mechanic is able to tend to our needs. "When would we be allowed to clock out if we stayed?" he asks me.

"Today it'd be about 10:30, because Car 1 is scheduled to leave at 9:00. If they're even here."

"That's impossible. We can't wait till 10:30. We'd never be able to get Roxanne repaired *and* finish the drive to Ulaanbaatar! Come on. Let's get going." Bernard's aggravation at objective rally rules is a good indication of how unhappy he is. The MTC isn't even open when we leave. If it had been, we could have clocked out early, simply receiving penalty minutes. As it is, we won't be recorded as having clocked out at all. This is a grave matter, since only those recorded as leaving every morning, and of course passing through every time control and running every time trial, can stay in the running for Gold. I feel profoundly sad for Bernard. At the same time, I know that the decision to focus on fixing Roxanne at the expense of the Gold is the right thing, the practical thing, to do. In this sense, it, too, is the Bernard thing to do. I keep to myself how relieved I also feel that the competitive edge required of me if we're going for a Gold is no longer expected.

Saynshand's mechanic chooses this particular morning to sleep in. Roxanne's problems are a pressing matter only to us, of course, and it's a long, frustrating hour before he shows up. When he does, he rubs his bleary eyes in disbelief. Watching him, I can't tell whether he's seeing his fondest dream or his worst nightmare come to life. During the time we've been waiting, six other Rally cars have pulled in behind us on the greasy concrete in front of his shop. This is more business than he sees in a month. Perhaps more than he sees in a year. Their presence is the main reason why we did not dare do the half hour drive back to the MTC to clock out properly. To do so would have meant giving up our spot. We thank goodness we're early risers and therefore can claim first dibs on the mechanic.

Bernard is at the man's side in an instant. After a brief palaver in sign language embellished by the limited number of English words they know in common, the mechanic disappears into the grimy recesses of his shop. I hear the scraping of a chair, a box fall, some clanking and then he's back. Allowing ourselves to puff up a bit with hope, we turn to the mechanic to see what he's found. Roxanne is a hefty girl, and it'll take some substantial metal to repair her. Like a child offering to share his favorite candy, the mechanic extends his hands toward Bernard. In his cupped palms are unburied treasure, a modest selection of small metal bits and pieces he's saved over the years. His eyes are hopeful and apologetic. Thus we learn that, in a country where horses still outnumber motorized transport, and where most of the latter are small motorcycles, there are few steel scraps to choose from.

Bernard sighs and smiles. We are good at reading each other's expressions, and his eyes convey that none of these really will do. He pokes through them anyway, turning the pieces over, hefting them to assess their mass, admiring them to give the mechanic encouragement, eventually picking out the stoutest of the flimsy options. The mechanic amazes us, doing more with a handmade welding torch jury-rigged with suspect threads of frayed cable than many American body shops do with all their fancy acetylene gadgets. He's so thorough it takes him four hours, during which time some of the six other Rally crews borrow his tools and get to work on their cars themselves; others give up and leave. By the time he's done, the rest of the Rally is long gone. That includes the Rally mechanics, the ones who check the road for cars in trouble and who stay out late to make sure everyone's made it to the day's destination. Ahead lay seven hours of rough track to Ulaanbaatar and the end of that day's trek. We are well and truly alone in the Gobi.

As we drive out of town, looking for the prescribed telegraph poles to guide us, we see a dead Rally car perched on a dune. It's a turquoise blue 1930 Delage D6L. Queued up behind it are two other vehicles, which I'm able to identify by their competition numbers. One's a canary yellow 1927 Rolls Royce 20 Tourer, the other a 1931 Ford Model A. The car teams loaf about in the sand, looking broadly pleased with themselves. The object of their ardor is a local transport truck backed up at roughly dune height. It has a wide cargo bay that's at least twenty-five feet long, with walls of wood slats painted sky blue. They've found a way to get to Ulaanbaatar without having to drive, and they're thrilled about it. The problem is that the truck driver does not have ramps to span the empty space between the bed and the car that needs to be loaded. Assembled townsfolk mill about, admiring the cars, hoping for some action. The men divide up, rolling up their sleeves, joshing in that masculine way that conveys they do not consider lack of ramps an obstacle. Four go to the back to push, two others hunch under each front fender, ready to heave upwards, and one leaps into the truck bed where he grabs the hauling end of a coarse rope. To a raised cry and chant, they push, shoulder, and pull that car into the bed. This strikes me as the way to go.

"Bernard, it's a long way to UB. Maybe we should let a truck take us?" I say, my voice quaking. As far as I'm concerned, if a truck could take us all the way to Paris I'd be happy. The Gobi is so big, so wide and empty—so endlessly burnt and brown—and I am so small and unimportant by comparison. It's too dismaying to say this aloud, but it seems the greater the vastness, the weaker my assurance. If only to humor me, Bernard stops next to the truck. We ask how long it would take to haul our car to UB. The driver draws a one and a two in the sand. Twelve hours. That's after a truck has been found to accommodate us, since the present long-bed truck is full. Even to me that seems too much.

"Dina, we can make it," Bernard says. "We'll be fine." I've seen the look in his eyes at the mechanic's, and I know this isn't strictly true. If Bernard can fake that everything's OK, I will rise to the occasion and fake it, too. "OK," I say. "So, let's go."

I hide my jagged nerves by forcing myself to speak directions in a calm voice, but I'm besieged by the notion that we are by ourselves in this wild, lonely place in a car that's not running well. I start to make navigation errors. The more I make, the more nervous I get. "Bernard, I think we've gone off track," I finally say. The amount of pride I have to swallow to say this is so large it nearly blocks my throat. After four days of getting us where we needed to go, a part of me was starting to think I might be able to manage the remaining 7,000 miles to Paris flawlessly. Now, though, we have come to a stop on a promontory with a great view over a whole lot of nothing, except that to get to it, we'd have to descend the slope below which is strewn with major boulders. I know I'm a Gobi novice, but even to me it doesn't seem probable that anyone would plan for us to slalom downhill through those obstacles. I cringe, waiting for recriminations to start, as they have in years past when Bernard and I have gotten lost on the road. I'm expecting to be given a stern lecture about how I should have spoken up sooner, looked around better, used my sense of direction. I would be unable to explain that I'd thought I'd been doing all those things.

"You're right," Bernard says. "This doesn't look right." He's enjoying himself, doesn't seem fussed at all. The Miracle of the Gobi doesn't stop there. Sensing how unhappy I am about my mistakes he now rises to the occasion. "Don't worry about it. You're doing so well, cherie," he continues. "I'm so proud of you." He leans across to give me a peck on the cheek and squeezes my hand reassuringly. I hand him the route book and the GPS. "Look here," he says. "We went off track just a little ways back." I have to gulp when I see what he's discovered. If we hadn't stopped, my modest navigation error would have led us far in the wrong direction. Bernard's unconcerned, though. He's looking into the distance, surveying the field. "I think I can just drive down this slope and we'll be back where we should be." Though I feel like a dope, at the same time I'm hugely relieved. In a few minutes I'm also justly proud. My mistakes have given Bernard a chance to drive where no one else on the Rally has gone before.

I know for certain we're back on the proper route when, half an hour later, we pass one of the few stable landmarks the organizers have been able to offer us: the hamlet of Lun Bag, which used to be the site of the largest Soviet air base in Mongolia. It's now empty of military personnel, the Soviets having skipped town in the 1990s. Mongolian families have moved into some of the abandoned flats; others have pitched their *gers* among the cracked concrete huts. It's a derelict and uninviting place, but even so, I search the landscape for highlights I can memorize, in case I need to make my way back there on foot if Roxanne collapses for good. All I see are sand, gravel, rocks, and shrubs, none of which is a likely candidate for landmark of the month. The route book instructs us to continue on the so-called road, which in my opinion barely qualifies to be called a track. To me it just looks like tire treads where someone else decided to drive. As fate has it, it's not long after passing Lun Bag that we feel Roxanne's rear end sink with a thud. Four hours of repair, gone.

With a sigh, Bernard pulls over and climbs out of the car. Around us the barren, parched hills of the Gobi stretch to infinity, as they have since we entered Mongolia. I've been searching in vain for those verdant slopes and lush valleys I saw photos of last year. All I see, for hours on end, are brown plains, rocky outcroppings, and tufts of dead plant life. Mongolia is so far inland that no sea moderates its climates. No island of clouds breaks the gauzy blue of the sky. No afternoon shower drops its curtain in the distance. In this unrelieved arid solitude, baked by a merciless sun and chapped by the wind, I stand by the car, as insignificant a speck on the landscape as a flea on an elephant.

Looking down at the dirt with distaste, Bernard kneels to peer under Roxanne. "Shock absorbers are broken," he says, and lets out a breath of exasperation. He bounds up and trots back to Roxanne's trunk, where he grabs his flashlight, a large wrench and other tools, along with some paper towels. Years of fastidiousness with his tools are not going to be ignored just because we're in the desert. Meanwhile I've brushed the sharp pebbles and stones away from where I know he'll have to lie down. Then he's on his back, wriggling under Roxanne, inspecting the rear shock absorber mounts and muttering curses to himself, and, perhaps not coincidentally, taking advantage of the only spot of shade for hundreds of miles.

Fifteen minutes go by before a ruined shock is flung aside, followed fifteen minutes later by the second one. "That's all I can do now," he says, his voice muffled by Roxanne's body. He inches his way out from under Roxanne using elbows and knees to move forward without shredding his shirt, then gathers the set of broken shocks and turns them around a few times. "Same problem as last time," he says. Tossing them behind his seat, he puts his hands on the small of his back and stretches, then lowers his head and shakes it. "Well, nothing more to do here. Let's go," he says, climbing back into the car.

Eying each other is the only communication we're up for. We motor slowly onward, as Bernard babies Roxanne's fragile suspension. Our beloved Roxanne lists forlornly to port, unable to handle the load of spares and tools we've crammed in her trunk alongside her extra-large retrofitted fuel tank.

My outlook turns to benign irritation as the sun drills a hole through the metal roof. The first air-conditioned car was a 1939 Packard, but

Cadillac, the LaSalle's fancy cousin, didn't get air-conditioning until 1941. Roxanne was made in 1940, and the only air conditioning she has is the natural sort, supplied by an open window. My window's down, offering as much cooling effect as if I were fanning myself inside a 400-degree oven. We crawl along at a pace that would make a beetle swimming in molasses look like Michael Phelps. I can attest that nothing seems to get closer when you're going 9 miles per hour. The one benefit of our pace is that we don't even raise a dust cloud. That's left to the few other late Rally cars that every once in a long while whiz by, covering us in yet another layer of Gobi powder. One by one they disappear around a tufted hillock, reappearing soon thereafter as a plume of dust on the far horizon, already depressingly closer to Ulaanbaatar than we are, or may ever be.

By mid-afternoon, our tempers frayed, we have sunk into glum silence. Our mouths are gummed shut with the dust, our food and water covered by the fine powder carried on an otherwise welcome breeze. We avoid the fuel gauge, knowing there are no gas stations to tank up anywhere before UB.

I invent a pastime to cope with my mounting aggravation. It's called Endurance Rally Solitaire. In this game, I prohibit myself from looking at my watch or the speedometer for a set period. I do this for five minutes, fifteen minutes, whatever I can endure. During that time, I force myself to think positive thoughts, such as how we'll soon hit a smoother stretch of road and be able to let 'er rip at 15 miles per hour. I think about how quickly we'll reach UB and be able to get out of the car once we achieve that brave new speed. I whistle happy tunes, picking sand out of my hair, drawing figures in the dust that now swaths the dashboard, anything to distract myself. Finally I peek at the odometer, confident that we've covered a heartening distance, only to find that we've advanced barely six miles. Soon my game is aggravating me as much as knowing how much distance we haven't yet covered and how much time we've spent not covering it.

Moving in slow motion magnifies everything. Each breath I inhale is a long inward sigh. The sun can't seem to move along its normal arc to the horizon. The cracks on my fingertips, desiccated from constant use of anti-bacterial baby wipes these past few days, are splitting into deep crevasses.

Worst of all, as my spirit flags, my own voice starts haranguing me. "You're not going to make it. Give up. Go home." This is not the voice I want to hear. I believe I've set reasonable expectations for myself on this trip, beyond just not vomiting in the car. And OK, I haven't quite met all of those. Yet. That doesn't mean I should be giving up. It's demoralizing to me to have made mistakes, despite knowing that Bernard, too, has made mistakes. Big ones. After all, the onus of Roxanne's Gobi-worthiness rests on his shoulders. What could be a more visible sign of a major flaw in his design than that Roxanne's shock absorbers have broken twice in two days? If he's demoralized, though, he doesn't show it. I try to do likewise, putting a patch on my damaged ego, offering myself a little forgiveness for my earlier navigational errors. We're careful now, each recognizing in the other bruised fruit that needs to be handled tenderly.

Ulaanbaatar Pizza

ULAANBAATAR

It's deepening dusk when we exit the desert. Even before we reach the shack-lined outskirts of UB, I know we're near because of one clue: asphalt. After hours of potholed tracks and sand, I find the existence of pavement and road signs not only deeply meaningful, but cause for pure joy. Even the traffic jam we get stuck in not far from our hotel is a relief: if we break down now there'll be plenty of people to help us. The image of Roxanne's dragging trunk can't stifle my ecstasy when I step under a stream of hot water in our hotel bathroom. It swirls the sand and dust out of my hair, turning gritty and brown before it's sucked down the drain, taking my bad mood of that long day with it. I chant, "Rest day, rest day. Rest! Day!" as the water pounds down. Right now I'm all for reveling in my deep pleasure that we will stay in one place for two nights, and ignoring the big stinking bull in my china shop: that when we drive out of UB, we'll still need six more days to cross Mongolia.

Feeling bright, polished, and ridiculously optimistic, we go down to the hotel lobby. In a routine already firmly established in China, the lobby is where everyone in the Rally mills about, chatting with the organizers who staff the information desk, looking at the day's results and the next day's start times posted on a red velvet bulletin board, glancing out the glass lobby doors to see who is repairing a car in the parking lot. In a departure from that past few days, though, the Rally is now split in two, with many of the participants lodged in a different hotel from ours. UB doesn't have a hotel big enough to house all of us.

I look around for Maddy, Sybil, and the rest of our small group of friends. My need to share stories with them has become like an addiction, so intensely do I look forward to it. It seems whatever I've suffered during the day will be put to rights simply by telling them about it. My hopes for a fun evening are dashed when a staff member tells me they are in the other hotel. Of course we do all have cars, and there are taxis on the street. But the notion of getting into a car again, even one driven by someone else, is too off-putting. We look around for anyone we know and notice Matthieu by himself.

"Bernard," he says when we circle into view. "How is your car?" and he gives Bernard a hearty slap on the back and me a warm hug. I'm learning that in Rallyworld, if you want to show you're glad to see someone, you inquire about their car, not about them. The answer to the former is crucial; the answer to the latter, immaterial. We're only a few days into the Rally, but already I have the impression that many, Bernard included, would keep driving their car even if blind and with a broken leg, viewing physical issues merely as a minor inconvenience. So although I would have preferred a greeting from Matthieu along the lines of "So glad to see you" or "How are you both?" I'll take what I can get.

Bernard fills Matthieu in on Roxanne's suspension issues while I stand by, half-distracted as I look around to see if others I know who were stuck in the desert have by now arrived. Matthieu listens with his head bent, in serious contemplation of what Bernard is describing. He smiles that smile that I was so charmed by two years ago, but then rubs his hand over his face as if trying to rid it of clingy cobwebs. The expression that emerges is haunted with concern. "I have some terrible problems with my radiator," he tells us, then rubs his face some more. "I'm afraid it's cracked. Aaachh! I will have to work on it tomorrow. I think I know what to do, but I need special equipment. We'll be at UB's Mercedes dealership. They're expecting us."

"You mean it's allowed to take your car to a dealership?" I ask, jarred back to the conversation by this unexpected announcement. Bernard, too, looks puzzled, but then smiles as he divines what they've done.

"You arranged this all from home," he says to a nodding Matthieu.

"Right!" Matthieu says. 'Every place where there's a rest day we called the Mercedes dealership and had them reserve three service bays, one for each of our cars." I'm seriously fussed about this. It strikes me as akin to getting a bootleg copy of the route book and driving it ahead of time. I gather words to scold Matthieu with my recently discovered notions of fair play, such as not sequestering the best services for yourself before you know whether you'll even need them. Then he looks at both of us with those piercing blue eyes, and I'm under his spell before he even says, "Bernard, we'll be there at 7:00 tomorrow morning. Meet us there so you can use their hoist to get under your car. If you get there ahead of us, just use my name." The route book urges "Enjoy your day off!" Thanks to Matthieu, we have something that, given our circumstances, promises more potent miracles than a visit to the local holy sites. Dealerships. What a fine idea.

It's like homecoming to walk into the oily bowels of the dark repair bays, shake hands with an overall'd mechanic, set about cleaning out the car while Bernard delves into repairs. Naturally, we expect to find replacement shocks here, so why not believe as well that somewhere in UB there is a windshield the exact size and shape to replace our cracked one?

Keeping us company are three cars from the 1920s belonging to Matthieu and his teammate James. Rumors began swirling about James even in Beijing. From what I've been told, he's probably the wealthiest man on the Rally, and even I can tell he's driving an extraordinary car. Everyone seems to want to claim at least a moment's camaraderie with him, but few have managed. It seems to me he keeps himself to himself, hence the rumors. Sybil pointed him out to me a few days back, which is how I discovered that this famous guy, whom I'd never heard of, was part of Matthieu's coterie of friends. At the time, Sybil and I stood there trying not to stare, much like two teenagers in awe of the football team's quarterback, both too star-struck to approach him, let alone say anything. Word has it that James's copilot is, in truth, his mechanic, and in fact is chief of mechanics for his entire car collection.

Searching the dealership for a reasonably clean rag, I wander near their car and learn something I shouldn't have. Bernard has always chastised me for eavesdropping on people's conversations, but I'm helpless to control the acuity of my hearing. Besides, I love hearing other people's stories. Now my finely tuned ears come in handy. I overhear James talking about organizing his plane to fly in more spare parts to Novosibirsk, to have on hand for the next rest day, seven days away.

Part of me is outraged. The Rally rules say you have to carry your spares with you or fix your car with what you can find on the road. That's why Roxanne is so heavily laden. Anything other than that is cheating and grounds for disqualification. Another part of me feels sick with envy at how lucky James is to employ someone to keep his car running and to have such wealth that he can get the parts he needs flown in for him. A not insubstantial segment of me wants to make friends with him immediately, hoping that if it comes to it, he can bring some spare parts in for us. Discussions about private planes and Bentleys are not what I'm accustomed to. We have one, modest, but beloved old car and just getting that one was a stretch. I feel so out of my league that, even though I want to use this day to at least say something to James so I can consider us acquainted, even if not plane-mates, I can't think of a topic of conversation.

"Bernard, guess what I heard," I whisper as I'm wiping the dashboard for the third time and he's sorting through bolts. I recount to him the bit about the plane. "What do you think we should do? Should we tell the organizers? Ignore it? But that wouldn't be fair would it?" Bernard only smiles, acknowledging what to him is another competitor's chutzpah, doing whatever he needs to do to keep his car moving.

The fact that I'm tongue tied in front of James is irrelevant. There's not much chatting going on, as each crew is deep in the guts of their vehicle, repairing much worse problems than ours. There's a standoffish feeling for the first couple of hours, as if each team doesn't want anyone else to know just how badly damaged their car is. Then we all realize we have to make the most of this opportunity. Tools are shared, a spare part offered to someone who needs it, the shop vac trundled from one bay to the next.

Bernard has been passionate about race cars and rallying since he could drive.

At age four, I mounted my first alternate mode of conveyance...and fell off.

Roxanne was a grand lady when she first arrived. *(Courtesy of Bernard Gateau)*

Roxanne was stripped down to her chassis and rebuilt with every single bolt, nut, and wire new. *(Courtesy of Bernard Gateau)*

The parking lot of our Datong hotel in China was packed with classic cars.

When a construction project made driving the route too torturous, we went off-road instead. *(Courtesy of Bernard Gateau)*

Sometimes we had a rare glimpse of the local wildlife, like these Bactrian camels. This small herd was moving toward summer pasture.

Directions outside of Saynshand, Mongolia, were not reassuring.
(Courtesy of Bernard Gateau)

A Siziwang Qi (Inner Mongolia) ger motel that can house 3,500 guests.

On lucky days, I had time to make sandwiches for the road from the offerings at breakfast.

Our campsites in Mongolia would have been lovely, if we'd had time to enjoy them. We arrived each night between 8pm and 10:30pm.

Only 65% of the Rally made it to the Mongolian border under their own steam.

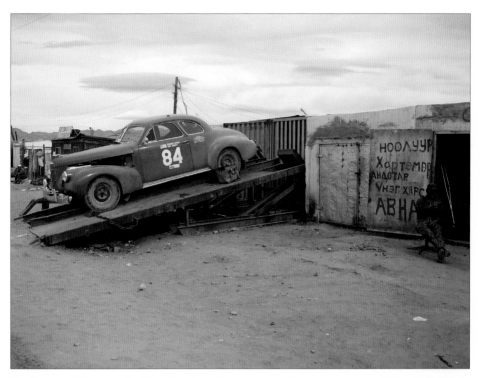

Finding a public ramp in Khovd, Mongolia, was cause for great joy, even if Bernard did have to stand in garbage to inspect Roxanne's undercarriage.

In Novosibirsk and Yekaterinburg, Russia, the luxury of the Ford and Volvo dealerships, which invited us to their service bays for a day of repairs, was unbeatable.

After a day on a long-haul truck heading to Moscow, we were thrilled with our room at this Trans-Siberian Highway truck stop.

Bernard and I pose at the Paris finish line. *(Courtesy of Elisabeth Stift)*

Hours of concentrated work are broken by the arrival of eight boxes of UB's finest pizza. As the only woman there, it seems to fall to me to distribute the food. "James, do you want some pizza?" I ask, and I'm so nervous that I'm speaking to this august personage that just this simple sentence makes me quail. "Oh sure, thanks Dina," he says. He knows my name? That means we've been introduced in absentia by Matthieu. Which means Matthieu hasn't truly been ignoring us after all.

Feeling a happy esprit de corps, I open our box of pizza and find a dreary facsimile of the real thing: damp cardboard crust smeared with sludgy tomato paste, oozing orange globules from rubbery cheese melted on top of a Mongolian's idea of Italian pepperoni. Everyone else, too, is looking in their pizza boxes in horrified silence, as if they'd found cockroaches in the box instead of just bad pizza. Then, as if choreographed, we delve in. Frowning faces relax as hands stained with hydraulic oil and axle grease lift soggy slices for another bite. Those pizzas disappear in minutes. We all agree they're delicious.

A Good Day

ULAANBAATAR-KHARKORIN

The next morning starts poorly. I'm in the lobby of our hotel extracting millions of Mongolian tugrugs from a willing ATM machine, when Franklin shambles over. He puts his arms around me in a droopy hug. "This is goodbye," he says. He and Eduardo have retired from the Rally, their middle-aged Ford too rusty and leaky to continue. A Dutch couple, too, have retired, the entire chassis of their Bentley having cracked in half. All I have time for is a promise to keep in touch. We've fixed Roxanne, though not her windshield, and Bernard's already waiting for me outside. As I carry our bags out I feel morose. I can't help but think it should have been me leaving, not two crews who are more experienced than us. Yet here we are, ready to head back to the desert and six more nights of hard driving and camping.

As has happened on previous mornings, my services as navigator are not particularly necessary. That's because the MTC is in UB's Sukhbaatar Square, an immense gray quadrangle rimmed by austere, colonnaded Soviet-era buildings. The city elders have organized a major welcoming and bon voyage ceremony for us. It seems half of UB is streaming in that direction, so I close the route book and instruct Bernard to follow them. The morning is warm, and with the window open I can hear the ceremonial band playing syncopated versions of Beatles classics and an occasional Souza march from many blocks away. When we round the corner to the square, we see a parade ground so vast that the triple row of Rally cars parked on one side look like tinker toys. Across from them is a jury-rigged bandstand draped with red polyester skirting. It's replete with a full swing band of horns and percussion, and a mike at which stands a significant person declaiming good wishes to the assembled multitudes. At least, that's what I assume he's saying, since not only is the mike weak and the sound system crackling with static, but the official is speaking Mongolian. Townsfolk mill about, some in city clothes, others in embroidered silk tunics and brocaded caps. I open Roxanne's door so a child can be placed on her seat and a photo taken. This time, though, I'm not invited to participate.

We're only two days into Mongolia, and the struggle to get just to here has taken its toll. By now more than half of the cars that started the race have suffered one or more calamities. Many sank over their hubs in deep sand, where they wallowed like floundering mastodons till a faster, sturdier car arrived to pull them out. Some disintegrated, fenders and bolts launching themselves suicidally onto the dirt road, doors hanging crookedly off hinges, springs wheezing as the cars groaned over miles of washed-out track. It's not just vehicles that are in dire straits. Three crews broke up as well, driver and navigator brandishing one-way tickets home, fuming about how miserable the Rally turned out to be. One navigator simply abandoned his driver, leaving him to complete the remaining 7,000 or so miles alone. Everyone grumbles about how Mongolia is not what they expected. No one seems able to fathom how we're going to make it to Russia, much less Paris.

If not totally cheery, I am basking in a pleasant sense of relief. Roxanne's shock problems are fixed, and she again handles like a champ. When we leave UB, though, the initially alluring asphalt turns into a patchwork of potholes connected by fragments of tarmac, the damage done by a continuous flow of cargo trucks going to and from Russia. We try the dirt tracks next to it and find them smooth enough. Roxanne's rugged off-road tires grip the loose gravel like suction cups, and as we surmount a low hill and plunge back down to the short-grass prairie, it feels like I'm on a sailing ship. Even the unremitting brownness can't dampen my spirits. Though there's still no place to stop for lunch, there are things to see besides rocks and dead grass. Herds of shaggy, brown and black cashmere goats browse by the roadside, shepherds on motorcycles moving them along toward the hills. Whirling dervishes of local sandstorms, which seem to twist up out of nowhere, whip across the road and hightail it for the horizon. I haven't yet seen a Mongolian pony, but I'm hopeful. After all, if it's true they outnumber people here thirteen to one, they must be somewhere.

We make quick work of a short time trial. Directions spew from my mouth like bullets from a machine gun. Bernard manhandles Roxanne's bulk, swinging her left, right, charging forward, braking a split second before we have to make a hairpin turn, using centrifugal force to pull us around the badly banked, gravelly curve.

At camp that night, after dutifully signing in, I check the time trial rankings, set up on that red velvet bulletin board, which now stands in the organizer's headquarters tent. What I see astonishes me. "Bernard," I call as I run back to where Roxanne's parked. "Guess how we did in the time trial."

"We did well?"

"Better than well. We got in the top ten!"

He stands up and brushes his pants off. A big smile, the biggest I've seen in days, spreads across his tired face. "Ha!" he says. He's never one to gloat, but the good news makes me feel talkative. I'm eager to find Robert and Maddy and Nick and Sybil, to see how they did and, yes, if the occasion arises, to share this tidbit of information about our accomplishment. A little gloating would do me good. After Bernard has finished with Roxanne and I've popped open our tent, we head for the dining pavilion, weaving through the colony of small tents that has sprouted, each one like a colorful mushroom growing next to a dusty car. People look up as we walk by, some wave, others nod hello. The camp has an aura to it. I think it's shared pride, partly an unspoken acknowledgement that we are a select group doing a difficult thing, and partly silent relief that we are not among those crippled or broken down beyond repair. I still don't know most of the competitors by name, which would have bothered me to no end before the race. Now, though, I feel I have my own small family. We gravitate to each other each evening, sharing stories and going over the next day's route. We find each other in the dining tent, or, if not, look for each other strolling around the camp after dinner. There's a double-helix binding all of us together, one strand joining people into groups, the other joining the groups into a whole. There's no doubt that I'm part of a great enterprise, and even though when we're driving during the day I feel as close to what I know of despair as I've ever gotten, in the evening the camaraderie in camp heals me.

The Nature of Things

Learning from experience and gleaning tips from Maddy when I need them, I am now an ardent convert to the route book. It has become my bible, and though I haven't donned robes, I am its slavish devotee. I ferry it lovingly to our tent each evening, pore over its pages with rapt interest, mark important landmarks with pink and blue highlighters, and then zip it into its very own red plastic P2P-embossed case when I go to sleep. I understand the book's directional symbols without having to think about it. My eyes instinctively swivel from the route book up to the Trip-meter and back to the page's mileage a hundred times a day, double and triple checking that we are where I think we are.

The route book can't always save me, though. It hasn't taken me long to learn that, when it comes to roads, nature is more capricious than any village council budget. Each morning we get pages of revisions to review. The further into Mongolia we go the more copious the changes. Sand covers a previously obvious road, floods wash out a bridge, someone's ruts create a new track in the wrong direction, a river is too high to ford, the deep winter snows have eradicated a track altogether. All of this needs to be explained, and an alternate route provided. With all the other naviga-tors, I line up early to get the change pages then annotate my route book so I'll know when the original instructions are no longer valid as well as when to resume following them.

None of this would matter if we didn't have so far to go. Somehow, in my in-depth reading of the pre-Rally advisories, I had failed to notice that the 35 mph average speed was the proverbial brass ring, something to aspire to but rarely achieve. After less than a week on the road, I have to throw my expectation of seven-hour days out the window, where it can bite the dust alongside my fantasy of eating tasty local cuisine at a charming cafe each day. We're doing ten plus hours of driving a day. That's without even stopping for anything other than fuel, as the only place to get gas is from fuel trucks parked near the outskirts of camp each evening. In a city as modest as Ulaanbaatar, the day ends with a further hour of bumper-to-bumper traffic. I'm already continuously tired. Having thousands of miles more to go is so daunting I can't begin to imagine how I'm going to make it.

Also in the category of mistaken assumptions is that I know absolutely there are areas of tremendous natural beauty in Mongolia. Somewhere. What I know haunts me. Those photos I looked at with the Mongolian naturalists are still branded in my mind's eye. I want to feel the cool shade of those deep forests, hear the babbling roll of rushing rivers, and feast my eyes on the rainbow colors of alpine wildflowers.

Our part of Mongolia is desert, plain and simple. True, it's desert in which things do survive, but whatever decides to grow here has its work cut out for it. The land we are traversing is too harsh to support even a modest hamlet. There's so little of anything but desert in this desert, that when we do see something other than low brown hills it's cause for great wonder.

Once, or if we're lucky, twice a day, we pass a solitary yurt, with a scrappy yard fenced with sticks. The herds are out and the house dog naps in the dirt. A bit of clothing flaps listlessly on a line in the scant breeze. We don't see people around the yurt, and I figure they're with their animals. Grazing must be very far away indeed as there's little edible growing on the packed coarse ground we're covering. All of this is as it has been for centuries, except for two novelties: a satellite dish fastened to a pole near the yurt door and two small solar panels rigged to provide electricity.

My favorite times are when we see Bactrian camels glide by in search of fresh grazing. The animals I've been calling camels all my life, those tall desert animals with the single hump that show up in Lawrence of Arabia? They're not camels. They're dromedaries. These double-humped animals outside my window are the real camels, and while there might be fewer of them now than a hundred years ago, they, at least, have no motorized equivalent. It's coming off of winter, and they're shedding. Great heavy patches of brown winter coat hang loose, revealing the smooth summer coat underneath, leaving them looking mangy and ill-kempt. They walk slowly and gracefully, lumpy philosophers deep in thought, covering vast distances to their summer grazing grounds, at home in these barren parts as I'll never be. Like a whisper they appear on the crest of a sand hill, and like a sigh they're gone.

Each morning, I parcel out our snack rations of beef jerky, gorp, and cookies, as if we were marooned on a desert island. Given our lack of inter-action with the local populace, we might as well be. The jerky was a last-minute inspiration when I was scrounging around for something snack-like to pack in Roxanne's trunk that wouldn't melt, wouldn't get stale, and yet would be appetizing to eat. I thank goodness for it every day, as it's often the only bit of protein that passes my lips. The gorp I made myself, picking out every ingredient that I imagined I'd like to taste in the middle of a desert. It abounds with hazel nuts, almonds, salted pepitas, dried sour cherries and cranberries, sweet golden raisins, and bittersweet chocolate chips. The chocolate chips both amaze and disturb me, as despite the heat, they never change shape. Whenever I offer some to Bernard I can't resist referencing other bizarre candy behavior, saying in a chirpy voice: "Melts in your mouth, *not* in your hands!"

A big part of what pulled me through the awful months of car rebuilding were my dreams of whom I'd meet and what I'd see in China and Mongolia. For now, I have to be satisfied with my limited interaction with the Mongo-lian camp staff and random village mechanics. Technically, of course, they are locals, but these aren't the random encounters that bring a trip alive. Aside from the crowds that surround Roxanne when we stop, I haven't talked to anyone who lives here. I turn to Maddy and Sybil for support, but they don't seem to mind as much as I do, and they don't understand why I do mind. We're here to drive, they say. It's a rally and that's the nature of the beast. When it comes to fighting reality, it appears I'm on my own.

As we're driving, I argue with myself instead. Doesn't driving by its very nature imply stopping? If so, how come we're not doing any of the latter? Already I'm starting to long for a more balanced approach to this drive, and with that comes the knowledge that, for the next thirty days, I'm not going to get it. My resilience never made it back to normal before we left for Beijing, and now it threatens to desert me, making small slights feel like major dramas and inflating minor problems into major fiascos.

Bernard's no help. From the get-go he's understood the idea of a rally. I assumed I understood it and neglected to ask him how he saw things unfolding. Now I see I was so far wrong that I can't even begin to explain to Bernard my disappointment. I have to find a way to come to grips with the Rally reality by myself. As for Bernard, he's focused on getting Roxanne, and by extension us, to Paris, and that takes all his time.

Trouble-Free Day, Troubling Evening

The repairs done in UB hold up for 230 miles. It's enough to get us to Kharkorin, Mongolia's first capital, while the sun is still high, despite an unexpected delay. While still deep in the desert, we pass another LaSalle, its driver puzzling over some problem with the engine. Seeing Rally cars stopped in the desert has become a common sight. When I saw them on our first day in Mongolia, I thought they were stopping to take pictures or have a snack, but I soon learned that nearly every one of them needed a repair. Sometimes a mechanic's van would be parked alongside, everyone working furiously to get the car back in the race. But with broken cars numbering in the high double-digits and only a handful of mechanic vans, most teams struggled on their own. Of the two signs the organizers gave us on Day 1, one saying *SOS* and the other saying *OK*, this man has put the *OK* sign on his windshield. As Bernard drives by I recognize the car. "Hey," I shout. "That's Gustav." Bernard slams on the brakes and backs up. "Oh come on, Bernard. Their sign says they're OK. This is the first time we're making good time. Let's keep going." We only know Gustav and his wife, Laure, through a handshake when we happened to park our similar cars near each other. From this I know they're French speakers, but I don't know anything else.

"Dina, they have a LaSalle. We have to see if they need help."

The two men put their heads together. I pick up smatterings of French, a language the two have in common, but if auto mechanics parlance in English was a stretch, figuring out what they're saying about the car in

French is an impossibility. Soon Bernard is dragging out our tool bags from the trunk. "Dina, would you see if we have any three-quarter inch bolts?" he asks me in French.

"Bien sur. On a beaucoup." I'm chagrined to have exposed the fact that I'm more concerned about myself than helping someone in trouble, so I dig through our tubs of spare nuts and bolts with unusual vigor, prepared to give Gustav handfuls of bolts to make up for my earlier selfishness.

As I walk over to the stuck car I can't help comparing it to ours. It's a few years older than Roxanne, a convertible painted matte black, and nowhere near as lovely as she is. When I give Gustav the bolts he nudges me toward his wife, telling me she doesn't speak any other language *but* French. She's sitting on a folding camp stool Gustav has set up for her, sunk in gloom, her fair skin an angry red from the heat, wind, and sun she's exposed to in their open-top car. Much as I love Bernard, not being able to talk to anyone but him for 35 days would lead to some extended moments of silence. I feel for the woman.

"Bonjour Madame," I say, addressing her formally because she appears older than I and I haven't really spoken to her before. I start babbling about the heat, the long days, the food in camp. She nods, but doesn't contribute much. Finally at a loss of what to say, I suggest that we all have dinner together one of these nights. At this she brightens, straightens from her slump, and gives me a forlorn smile. How happy this would make me, she tells me. I decide I'm willing to be this woman's go-to-girl every now and then if that'll make her feel better. At the time, I have no idea that Gustav has other plans in store for me.

Our lodging for the night is in a tourist camp of fixed *gers*, an exciting opportunity to leave our tent folded in the car. This is a proper Mongolian setup, not the faux Mongolia presented by China. As we near it we pass an aged monastery, Erdene Zuu Khiid, the first Buddhist monastery in Mongolia. It used to be home to a thousand monks. Like many ancient sites, it's suffered the ravages of time, not to mention the ravages of the Stalinist purges of the 1930s, during which all but three of the original hundred temples were destroyed. One of the ornately carved wood portals in the high white walls surrounding the monastery is open, giving a view of the stately ancient beauty of the remaining buildings. I get a first glimpse of two maroon-robed monks in Crocs striding purposefully across a derelict quadrangle as we drive by. We're sorely tempted to visit, but we have to clock in at the finish time control or face more time penalties, so we don't stop. Though we're out of the running for Gold or Silver medals, both of which require clocking out of the MTC every day at our appointed time, we still try to follow Rally rules if we can. This strikes us as more sporting, though from the way the organizers seem to dismiss us, I surmise we're the only ones who view it so.

We are higher in the mountains now, and there's a small river coursing through the fields around our camp. Though it's still not the flourishing landscape I'd imagined, the crisp, bracing air fills me with optimism. There's even green grass on which to park Roxanne in front of our assigned *ger*. As more cars arrive, a match is organized to display the skills of local Mongolian wrestlers. Inside the circle formed by Rally crews, two burly, olive-skinned men swagger in leather briefs in the afternoon chill. Suddenly, they whirl and lunge at each other, then grapple and twist until one tosses the other to the ground. The thrown one leaps back up, while the winner struts the perimeter of the circle, beating his chest and shaking his fists in the air in mock triumph. We roar our approval.

In a moment of insanity, a Rally driver unzips his trousers. He hops about tugging off his socks and pants, and enters the ring. I almost have to avert my eyes at the sight. His body is pallid and flabby in comparison with his opponent's swarthy skin and sleek, bulging muscles, and he's quickly covered with goose bumps. He looks ridiculous, but we all give him a loud hoorah of encouragement. The Mongolian wrestler, being a good host, allows him thirty seconds before tossing him on the grass. His pale shoulders now have green stains on them, but he's up and hopping about like a bantam cock, ready for another go. I hug Bernard with relief, both to be here on this night and because I'm so glad he's not the sort to jump in and tussle with a Mongolian wrestler. Though I do think he'd beat him if he did.

Another delight awaits me. It's the shower cabin I spied when we drove in, with a large hot water tank installed on its roof. I head there late, delayed both by the thought that I might make some friends if I let others go first and by a strange inability to find my hand towel in my duffel. By the time I walk in, it's clear no one else felt so constrained. The intoxicating steam billowing from completed showers is enough to make me tipsy. It is also proof that most of the fifty-six other females still on the Rally have already partaken of the joys of hot water. Rarely in my life have I disrobed faster. Clutching my modest travel towel to my even more modest chest, I abandon my dusty cargo pants on a bench and scamper down the slimy corridor, and I enter the first shower stall I come to.

By now I'm shivering, made colder still by the arctic draft blowing through the ill-fitting stall door. "Suck it up, Dina," I tell myself. "Hot water's comin'." I turn on the tap and wait. Some warm drops dribble from the shower head. The anticipation is killing me. I've seen the gravity-fed pipe leading to my side of the shower house, so I know hot water from that rooftop tank can reach me. Not to waste a drop, I crouch under the rusty shower head and hold my breath. There's a loud gurgle accompanied by the whining of pipes. A good sign. I swivel the wobbly faucet to what I hope is the fully open position and am deluged by water so cold it should be solid.

Gasping and cursing, I splash the liquid ice over my body to dispel the accumulated dust. All I manage to do is water a bumper crop of goose flesh. "Who even would notice that you've sacrificed yourself for their showering pleasure," I censure myself. "You idiot!" I add for good measure, to impress on myself that a lesson needs to be learned. In under a minute I'm out of the shower, dashing on tiptoes down the icy, dank hallway to the women's room, and have pulled my dusty clothes back onto my still damp body. As luck would have it, Bernard emerges from the men's shower cabin at the same time I step out of the women's side. Only he's pink and warm, where I'm chapped red and cold. We look at each other. "Don't even ask," I say. He puts his arm around my shoulder and I shrug it off, determined to have a good sulk.

Near dusk, a local herder brings ten Mongolian horses to the camp, the first herd I've seen. They're small beasts, with big heads and coarse manes, saddled and ready to be ridden. At best they're scrappy ponies, compared to the stout American quarter horses I have back home. Yet I am so enchanted to finally have horses around that I can barely contain myself. First, though, I turn to Bernard. "Will you come, too?" I ask, hoping to experience something with him on this trip that doesn't involve cars.

"No, I don't think so. Horses are your thing. I'll watch. Maybe take some photos." If he's trying to make up for the fact that he got the hot water, I accept.

There is a traditional saying in Mongolian: "A Mongol without a horse is like a bird without wings." Venus is bright and a few early evening stars are already winking when I mount a small, sinewy bay and trot off down the green. His gait is choppy, and it's hard to direct him. Perhaps Colorado horse language is different from what a Mongolian horse would under-stand. The dusty warm pony sweat and the fresh air on my face make me long for home. Still, it feels so poetic to be in Mongolia on horseback that I momentarily consider just trotting on, to be done with brutal roads and confusing waypoints. Bernard's figure recedes, becoming a small spot on the dark field. I thrill to be just me and the bay. Until I don't. The further Bernard fades in the dusk, the more bereft I feel, as if I've torn half of me off and left it behind. In the deepening blue dusk I canter a ragged circle and head back. Bernard raises his arms high in a victory sign as he sees me, and I sink into his enveloping hug as my pony is led away.

Like much Rally news, word has spread informally that a special dinner plus entertainment are arranged for that evening. For everyone. Thanks to the largesse of one participant with the connections to import cases of Moët & Chandon, there's also champagne for the entire Rally. The very frivolity of this gesture boosts our spirits, and I'm especially looking forward to sharing a toast with Bernard and our friends. Hoping to surprise everyone, I ransack Roxanne for some extra treats, pulling out our precious stash of beef jerky and some sticky sweet lemon energy bars. Thus laden, I take the long way to the dining hall, enjoying the feel of the clean night air with its hint of moisture, and the spring of grass under my feet. I relish this rare chance to be alone. On my detour, there's a small, fancy yurt I hadn't noticed earlier. Like in a fairy tale, it's small and squat, with a carved wood door and canvas walls covered in curlicues of blue and red embroidery. Light flickers in a window, and I hear low voices punctuated by sharp laughs. "Ah, a secret discovery," I think, already planning the memorable end to the evening that Bernard and I can have here. I pull open the door and peer in, expecting to see a few locals clustered round a bartender. Mongolians are hospitable and I have no doubt I'll be greeted by gestures to step inside. Instead I glimpse Matthieu, sitting in a sumptuously decorated yurt with his mates, bottles of wine open on the table, a Mongolian singer performing for their private pleasure. He looks up, sees me, just as James does. After our shared work day in UB, I feel I know James, or if not "know" then at least am acquainted insofar as he sometimes nods when he sees me. Though I've also noticed that sometimes he sees me and does not nod. I've forgiven the latter episodes, attributing it not to snobbery, but to him being distracted by his own car problems. Though since he has his own mechanic, I can't imagine he'd have any.

"Now's my opportunity," I think. "James is clearly a generous, thoughtful person, since he's the one who made the gift of champagne to the whole Rally." I expect him to wave me in. In that same second, James flicks the back of his hand at me. There's no mistaking the gesture. He's shooing me away. Matthieu doesn't move. I have been summarily dismissed.

I find myself yearning not to care, to relish instead the pleasure of horseback riding, of being on this endeavor with Bernard, of having made it this far. Yet there's no denying that people I hoped to befriend have signaled they do not want me in their clique. It hurt when I was thirteen, and it hurts now. Walking toward the dining yurt, I no longer am able to review my day with the same pleasure of a few minutes back. This slap to my sense of belonging stings as smartly as the ice cold shower that afternoon, though at least the shower left me feeling a little bit cleaner.

When I open the heavy door to the dining hall I'm hit by rollicking shouts. It's a wall of noise and bodies inside, as hot and dimly lit as a sauna.

Everyone's pressed together, open bottles of champagne passing from hand to hand, people drinking straight from the bottles. It's a veritable bacchanal. I grab a bottle by the neck, spy my own clique at an already fully occupied table, see Gustav and Laure talking standing with another couple, though Laure still doesn't seem to be participating. I weave my way through the crowd to Bernard. "Look," I tell him, handing him the bottle. "I got us some of our beef jerky for dinner." We each take a swig of Moet. "Robert and Maddy are over there," I shout, pointing into the teaming crowd. "Their table's already crammed. Let's find our own place to sit." Grabbing some empty chairs before someone else takes them, I pull the jerky bag out and fling it onto the table. "Help yourselves," I shout to the others at our table. No one moves. The jerky is one of the best decisions I made before the Rally. Not only is it organic beef, I've chosen a peppery, soy, sugary version that satisfies every one of my food cravings. To the uninitiated, jerky looks as appetizing as boot leather. "It may not look good, but it's delicious." They each take a tiny piece to be polite and soon all our hands are delving into the sack, tangy jerky washed down by mouthfuls of drily refreshing champagne.

Out of the corner of my eye I notice three tall Mongolian women striding through the crowd. They're dressed in claret silk *dels*, the traditional, loose-fitting Mongolian tunic buttoned on the right shoulder, the neck a high-fitted collar, the fabric falling in folds to the calf. Each wears a red silk and velvet ceremonial skull cap, perched low over her glossy long black hair. On their feet are leather boots with pointed upturned toes, richly decorated with bold-colored appliqués and embroidery. They're heading for a small raised platform and to make it through they hold their instruments above the crowd. The evening's entertainment has arrived.

What Women Do

Next morning, when I see James sitting in his convertible, a hot flush of shame rises at the memory of his dismissal. It's a beautiful morning, sun smiling, air bright, and I don't want to begin this day in a bad mood. I could walk right by him, but instead persuade myself to do something I'm normally disinclined to do when my feelings have been hurt: forgive. I smile and say, "James! That champagne last night was so wonderful. You really were generous with that, you know. You made a lot of people happy." Which is the truth, and it makes me feel good to say it. James looks at me. He doesn't exactly return my smile, but I detect a slight crinkle around his eyes that suggests he just may be pleased.

With a seemingly easy day ahead, we decide to leave at our assigned time of 10:30. This gives us a chance to visit the monastery we passed yesterday. We enter through an open gate in the expanse of crenellated, whitewashed walls that guard the sacred interior. Inside, scattered as if by some immense divine hand, are small wood and stone temples, each on its own raised patio. Though faded, I can detect remnants of what once must have been vivid yellow and red paint adorning each building. Now, only faint strips of color remain, the rest having been blasted by centuries of wind. Apparently neither the Mongolian government nor any NGO feels this monastery is worth saving, and there are too few monks to keep the place up. Amidst the echoing silence, we wander along stone paths blackened with lichen. I step onto one of the temple patios, careful not to crush the few blades of grass and an occasional wilting flower that have managed to grow there. Splintery temple doors are locked, broken windows boarded over, so we walk the temple's perimeter, inspecting faint carvings on the weathered exterior. It's quiet, so quiet I can hear the faint whistle of a light breeze. Despite this, the empty grounds resonate with an ineffable spirituality, as if to say, "You can tear us down, but you can't destroy us."

It's a glorious day to drive, sunny and bright with that crisp clarity you get at higher altitudes. We're back on the road when, with the monastery walls still in view, we make a left turn, cruise up into third gear, and the shock absorber mount gives way. Eight hours of work in UB have come to naught. We circle back to Kharkorin, the village we thought we'd said goodbye to five minutes earlier. "Car repair?" I shout out the window to a guy on an idling motorbike. He nods and makes a large circular wave with his arm, indicating "Follow me." We inch down narrowing lanes, passing tin shacks with babies sitting in the dirt out front, guarded by the family cur. Our guide points through a gate to a littered yard in which reside a few engines and motorcycle carcasses. Our repair shop. As Bernard backs Roxanne in, a thin, dark-skinned Mongolian in shorts and sandals stands up, a shock of black hair falling over his face. He drags on a cigarette dangling from his lips. Next to him sits his personal version of a welding torch, exactly what we're hoping for. Bernard sets about using hand gestures and sand drawings to explain what's needed. Soon there are several men leaning against their motorbikes, smoking hand-rolled cigarettes, contributing their advice.

I'm half inclined to vent some of my frustration by stomping around a bit. We're only a third of the way through Mongolia, with 1,120 miles to go before we even get to Siberia. There's been something so endless, so daunting about the landscape, so remorselessly punishing about the roads, that I feel undone. What I want is to do some serious emoting, but without offending any of the polite people here who have so willingly dropped what they were doing to help us. Bernard doesn't understand this sort of reaction. "What's the big deal," he'd say, fixing me with a steady gaze. "Why worry about what hasn't even happened? Who cares?"

Luckily, I'm cast a life line by a slim woman with a very bad haircut, her black hair sticking every which way from her head. She peers from the repair shack door and motions me in. Stepping across the greasy, littered threshold I enter her personal space, part office, part home, all in a narrow room six feet wide and twelve feet long. At the back, next to the small desk and twisted chair, both signs of prosperity, there's a two-burner hot plate. I love to make myself at home in people's kitchen, puttering about with the lady of the house, pulling out cookies and mugs to make a tasty hot beverage. Not knowing the formalities here, I spin around aimlessly, not sure whether to get to work at the desk or insert myself in the cramped space by the burner for some repair shop bonding. I feel a hand on my shoulder, see another gesturing to the ground, as my hostess politely but firmly insists I sit on a thin mattress piled with pink and floral quilts. Once I'm safely ensconced on the floor, we're both silent as she fills a tin kettle with water from a jug. I have all the time in the world to wait for that water to boil. She makes tea, tossing a few handfuls of leaves into a chipped tea pot. I watch. She hands me a small plastic cup. The brew is hot and strong, with a generous spoonful of sugar stirred in. Not speaking each other's language, we pass the time as women do the world over. She shows me dog-eared photographs of family. I ooh and aah. We laugh at our inept communication. I kick myself that I haven't brought photographs to share. Together we sip, compare wedding rings, analyze our shoes, smile, and so the minutes tick away until Roxanne is ready to carry us forward.

On the road again two hours later, we drive along in silence. I stare out the window. The landscape is still brown. Sometimes I have the impression that perhaps we haven't moved at all. It's hard to believe that the country-side could be even emptier than before, but it is. We're still far from the true peaks of the Altai mountains, but there's definitely snow melting somewhere. Occasionally, by which I mean once every few hours, we reach a small stream of clear running water, which we cross on yet another rickety plank bridge. Each one looks the same, a collection of splintered boards, board fragments, and gaps where boards used to be, these last perhaps the result of someone needing firewood more than they needed a safe bridge to cross. The bridges are musical, thunking like a drum as the loose boards seesaw under Roxanne's tires. I trust in their soundness for one simple reason: there are no toppled Rally cars in the stream below us. Near every bridge, and therefore near the water, there's inevitably a solitary *ger*. They're still simple affairs, but thanks to the increased water, they now have a tiny garden and a few stick-figure trees.

Bernard stops Roxanne every ninety minutes or so to check what's going on underneath. After one such inspection, he emerges with bad news. Roxanne's leaf spring has cracked further. I know what a leaf spring looks like because I saw one when we were rebuilding Roxanne. It's made of gently curved, heavy steel, with a little curlicue on each end, which is how it's held in place under the rear end of the car. It's a part I assumed had redundancy built into it, as it seemed to me there were always several leaves included in one spring. My assumption was, if one cracked there would be a couple of leaves remaining, to pick up the slack so to speak. I thought this was quite clever, a bit like our dual fuel pumps.

Seeing the furrows creased into Bernard's brow, I can tell we're in more than a bit of a pickle and that my assumptions about leaf springs were incorrect. I suspect that, if the leaf spring cracks through, then what I promised Roxanne would not happen, will. We'll be stuck in the Gobi, unable to drive out. I devolve to a response that I adopted when I was five years old and that even then didn't serve me well. I say nothing, believing that if I ignore the situation, it will go away. Just like then, by not speaking about my worry, my insides start to churn in turmoil.

Like me, Bernard now does what he does best. He relaxes in the face of looming disaster, one hand on the steering wheel, the other resting on the storage compartment between us. I follow suit. What's happened, happened. Wailing over it won't change it. I'm not resigned about this. It's more like I'm in the center of the hurricane, where it's preternaturally calm.

Bernard's eye is better now, but his face is starting to look drawn and etched with fatigue. I reach across to caress his rough, stubbly beard, remembering its brownness when we first met, noticing its distinct salt and pepper coloring now. With his free hand he covers mine and we drive on like that, his left hand on the steering wheel, my right hand on the route book, our two hands together in between.

Circus Elephant

BAYANKHONGOR-ALTAI-KHOVD

As we approach the towering Altai mountains, it becomes clear to me that the interaction we had with people in China, modest though it seemed at the time, is a thing of the past; that the P2P, which is taking us through such extraordinary country, is not going to yield the connection with the local populace of which I'd dreamed. On the positive side, this stokes a disproportionate delight when I finally see a Mongolian on horseback. There he is, a young man on a small but well-fed black pony. His blousy cotton shirt, cinched with a wide belt, billows in the ever-present wind. A long, willowy stick with a lash of string at its tip, with which he moves his goat herd, rests lightly on his shoulder. He's like a centaur, my own personal myth come true. After driving for hours through landscape that doesn't change, seeing anyone at all is cause for delirious joy. To see both a person *and* a horse at the same time? Well, I'd given up hope. He's a beautiful sight, a man and his horse in landscape that suits them both. We stare at each other. Out here in the true middle of nowhere, we're as astonishing to him as he is to us.

On the negative side, my tiredness each day is mounting, and the more spent I feel, the more of a struggle it is to maintain cheeriness. I've always been moody, the child described by puzzled adults as perpetually having a dark cloud over her head. One of the tasks I've set myself for the Rally is to put extra effort into being a good sport. Luckily, I have good people to learn from.

That evening in Bayankhongor, we join Robert and Maddy for dinner. "How was your day today?" I ask Robert, setting my dinner tray on the table. He ignores my question and says instead, "Let me get you a beer," and leaves. When he returns he plunks the chilled bottle on the table, gives my shoulders one of those squeezy little massage things, sits down, and bestows on me a devilish grin. "My day, you asked? Awful! Terrible! Right Maddy?" and he laughs so hard I'm not sure what to make of it.

She smiles broadly and elaborates, "We had six flats today." Robert is now wiping tears from his eyes, running his fingers through his dust-coated hair and mussing it into startled spikes.

"Six flats!" he echoes her. "I'm a lucky man."

"You are?" I ask, utterly lost.

"Yes. Because I brought seven spares." He howls with merriment.

Maddy bestows an affectionate, bemused glance on Robert. "Didn't that drive you crazy?" I ask her.

"What for? It gave me time to be out of the car and rest." Her hair, too, is sticking up in spikes, but on her it's fashionable, aided by the touch of lipstick and tight-fitting white T-shirt she's put on for dinner. I make a mental note to buy a sexy white shirt, ignoring that there are no shops to buy anything in, even if I did have time to do so.

I'm not the only one struggling. The web of anxiety in which I'm often entangled has snagged others as well. The atmosphere in the camp's dining tent at night is no longer as convivial as it used to be. Laughter is scarcer. People slump over their plates, eyes staring unseeingly at their carrots, too worried or tired or frustrated to talk. The whole tone of the Rally has changed. I hear that one of our early friends in Beijing, Ralph, is so lost that even GPS coordinates can't locate him for rescue. As I learn later in Russia, he and his son will spend two days sipping warm orange Fanta and nibbling severely rationed crackers before a local truck drives by and rescues them, after which they complete a superhuman 72-hour drive, without sleep, to catch up to us. A tiny Fiat has disappeared. No one knows where they are or even how to find them, let alone make contact. I figure it's only a matter of time before Roxanne has a catastrophic breakdown in some lonely corner of a lonely corner. I'll be left there to ration lemon Luna bars, while Bernard's tiny figure disappears over the far tawny hills to seek help.

The organizers are forever on their radios, trying to find other lost crews, organizing trucks to haul wrecked Rolls Royces. The last time there was a general mood of euphoria was over the champagne in Kharkorin. Tension grips the camp. Day runs into night runs into day. Many teams don't pull in till midnight; others depart at midnight, fraught with concern that they won't be able to complete the next day's distance. The mechanics are inundated with demands for repairs, welds, tows, spares. They catnap in half-hour stretches, running on caffeine and nicotine and nerves. As for their lighthearted promise of taking care of cars in the order signed in? Never happens. Whoever whines loudest gets their attention. Everyone is zombie-like with exhaustion. People quickly gulp a few bites of food and then return to working on their crippled cars. When someone learns of a good mechanic or a well-equipped repair shop in town they guard it like classified information, a national secret not to be revealed.

There's other bad news. Someone's had their entire tool bag stolen while working under their car on a village side street. During the day people of course have to work on their car wherever it breaks down. In Mongolia that means a sand pit, a gravely track, a rocky slope. If a Rally mechanic's van happens by, they stop to ask if you need help. If you do, they give it. If you think you can manage on your own, you give the classic OK sign, tip of thumb and index finger pinched together in a circle, remaining three fingers sticking up in the air. They continue on, looking for someone in worse trouble. I have no worries about things getting stolen while driving the desert. There's no one around to take anything. At day's end, when we're near a village, it's another story. In villages, people flock to our cars like thirsty goats to a stream. In the case of the stolen tool bag, everyone assumes it was a local, though I'm not above suspecting one of those Rally crews who came equipped with only a screwdriver and a wrench. I find it easy to understand how a satchel full of tools would make a tempting target. People are so poor here that even one tool would be worth a relative fortune. When Bernard works on Roxanne in a town I'm always standing guard while he's underneath. This job pleases me to no end. I've finally found a way to have some face time with the locals.

My outsiderness is engraved on everything about me, from my clothes and shoes, to the quantity of pens stashed in Roxanne's glove compartment. Even the soft layer of fat around my hips speaks to my well-being and thereby my otherness, though that layer is slowly shrinking thanks to my diet of gorp, jerky, and worry. Then, there's the small matter of Roxanne. She's hard not to notice. All this makes me an object of magnetic allure, and when we reach a town and try to accomplish repairs, I instantly draw a crowd. People swarm around like kids to a traveling circus. I'm the three rings and the elephant in a pink tutu combined.

It's flattering, in an awkward way. I'm not above a few minutes of preening, until I realize the crowds aren't the least bit interested in me. What they want to see, touch, sit in, is Roxanne. They jostle four deep around her. Every bit of car minutiae is a fabulous novelty that thrills them. Seat belts are tried on, windshield visors flapped up and down, the chunky plastic clips on them unclipped and pinched onto fingers and noses, wipers plucked like stiff guitar strings, plastic storage boxes popped open and snapped shut. Roxanne's tail lights, fenders, steering wheel, and tires are knocked on, marveled at, twisted, caressed. As I stand aside like a proud mother, happy that Roxanne is able to offer such pleasure, I can't help keeping a surreptitious eye on the movable belongings in the car. We need them all.

The towns that we pass through, or where we stop in hopes of more accommodating repair options, are plain and impoverished. I see row upon row of squat concrete houses, many with rebar sticking from the roof like a scraggly mohawk, walls gaping with holes where windows would be. Still, a village bespeaks humanity, and I'll take a brief sojourn among even the most derelict of buildings when the alternative is fourteen more hours on desert gravel, cresting washboards the size of storm waves, heading straight into the afternoon sun. By culture and custom, Mongolians are a nomadic people, kind and generous when they're not conquering neighboring countries. They have a fine decorative sense, lining their mobile *gers* with exquisitely colored and carved interiors. Unfortunately, they've been beset by mining interests from China, with its insatiable need for all the minerals that exist under Mongolia's parched lands. Rich in copper, coal, and gold, the issuance of mining licenses has turned Mongolia's economy into the fastest growing in the world in 2011, and prompted some citizens to start calling their homeland "Minegolia." Formerly open grazing lands have been fenced off to protect the new mines, leaving families without enough land on which to sustain their herds. Selling their animals in hopes of securing a job in town, they wind up with neither. Without animals, they can't return to the countryside as they'd have nothing to live on if they did.

While the move to town may have cost them their livelihoods, they haven't lost their sense of hospitality. The people who jostle around all welcome me. Broad, gap-toothed smiles crinkle deeply lined walnut-brown faces. Some extend their calloused hands to clasp one of mine in both of theirs, in a long and hearty shake. So I'm doubly happy that I at least have a chance to contribute a little novelty to the hard lives of these displaced people. They've become town dwellers by circumstance, not by desire. Without jobs, they wander the streets, cluster around shops with bare shelves, share a hand-rolled cigarette to pass the time.

In one town, we find a handy repair spot. It's a chipped and stained concrete ramp that someone built by the side of a street in the middle of town. It slants upward at a 45 degree angle clearly meant to elevate a car and has a gap running down the middle so you can stand underneath your car to work on it. Better yet, it's open to the air, not housed in someone's shop, which means that it's free for anyone to use. We feel very fortunate indeed that, when we drive by, the ramp is clear of other vehicles. That there's a mound of garbage in the gap between the two slanted slabs of concrete, where street dogs are nosing around for breakfast, is only a momentary deterrence.

As the usual crowd starts to mass, Bernard backs Roxanne up the ramp. Their collective intake of breath seems to suck the oxygen out of the atmosphere, as everyone waits for him to make a mistake, toppling Roxanne off the incline into the garbage below. Bernard is masterful, and when he cuts the engine and jumps heedlessly into the trash heap, the crowd does a collective hop of glee and surges forward. I stand high on the ramp, handing down tools for the usual shock absorber removal. From up there I notice a small girl, on the outskirts of the crowd, holding her mother's hand. They both look curious, but too shy to force their way forward.

Politely pushing aside the men intently knocking on Roxanne's fenders, I manage to open the trunk. I'm looking for something in my sack of giveaways that would please a child. I find it: a six-inch high stuffed brown and white teddy bear. By the time I make my way through the crowd, the mother and child are gone. I scan about, finally picking them out near the end of the street, the mother striding purposefully away, clutching her daughter's arm, the child trotting along beside her in a ragged red dress, her head turned back toward me. I run to them and hold the toy out for the child to take. She stands stock still. Instead of reaching out a hand she looks at her mother. Her mother is impassive, not encouraging. I feel ridiculous. In the world of what these two need, a stuffed animal is not high on the list. Then again, a toy is a toy. I squat down, take the child's hand, and close it around the little bear. She clutches it tight, her eyes fixed on my face. The two of them walk away.

Morning Rituals

The entire camp is asleep when Bernard crawls out of his sleeping bag near daylight, throwing on clothes and a vest to ward off the predawn chill. Bernard and I have the same rhythm on this rally, without ever talking about it. It's one of those things that two decades of marriage has done for us, and I'm grateful for it. Through our years of building a company, we've figured out how to be together twenty-four hours a day without shredding each other's nerves. Perhaps the most stressful thing we've done together, until now, was to build our own home. Pundits claim that's the ultimate recipe for divorce. I find that hard to believe. I'd spent hours picking out those bathroom tiles myself. Why on earth would I want to let someone else enjoy the shower?

One of the things we agree on during the Rally, without even needing to talk about it, is that we want to sleep at the route book destination each night, that we would feel depressed and unhappy if we had to bunk in the desert alone and with a correspondingly even longer drive to complete the next day. Both of us shudder at the thought of falling further and further behind. We also agree that sleep is nearly as important to us as food. For all of our married lives we've both preferred to go to bed by 10:30 and rise early. On the Rally, it's no different, though I find we're loners in this respect. We turn in after dinner, so Bernard can inspect things with daylight rather than a flashlight. When we crawl into our sleeping bags, sounds of laughter are spilling from the dining tent. Most of the teams work on their cars late into the night. There are plenty of people on the Rally who can drink more wine in an evening than I drink in a year and still mend their cars before sleeping, or so they believe. My opinion is that, because of all the wine, their repairs may not be as precise as they imagine. Then again, because of the wine, they probably don't care.

Our morning routine is pleasant. Having it saves us from constant discussion of who's going to do what. I don't like to chat in the morning, and I'd just as soon know my job and set about doing it in silence. An added bonus: the early day is peaceful, dew glistening, an occasional bird wheeling in the updraft as the sun rises. When Bernard slides under the car, tool bag at hand, the only people stirring are the camp staff, busy preparing a thousand fried eggs, a ton of hashed potatoes, swimming pools of coffee, and buckets of sliced fruit.

While Bernard tightens something here and lubricates something there, I pack up our belongings and organize the car. Given how continually dusty it's been through Mongolia, I also try to clean it, but my grimy cloth only shifts dirt from one part of the car to another, and then onto me. Next comes the tricky and sometimes humiliating task of wrestling our self-erecting tent into submission. That marvel of French ingenuity on which I practiced so diligently at home, has become nearly as dear to me as Bernard. When we arrive at a camp after hours on the road, I am barely able to move my joints enough to turn my knees to the right and exit the car. The first time I stand up is a mix of divine pain, as my bones realign themselves from seated to upright. It is a great consolation to know that I need merely slip our tent from its sack, fling it in the air, and our room for the night will float back to earth fully formed. That I can stand fully upright in it after hours sitting in the car is an unmitigated pleasure.

Collapsing the tent is again a struggle, and shades of that first day in our entryway come back to haunt me. My practice sessions at home resulted in a near-flawless ability to do so correctly, but that was months ago. The muscle memory I developed to do this task correctly seems to be suffering from early dementia. Each morning, I stand outside our tent, chewing my lip, rehearsing in my mind the sequence of moves to follow, like a high-diver about to execute a triple twist, jackknife, somersault from the fifty-meter platform. More often than not, the support poles rebel. I wind up in a pitched battle, my arms and legs contorted like a Chinese acrobat, holding multiple sections of the writhing tent in place as I try to subdue it. On the first try the tent always wins, ultimately evading my grasp and popping into the air, to settle smugly on the ground some feet from where we'd first set it up.

In matters of dismantling, I am all about perseverance. I have no choice. It's personally important to me to pass through the MTC looking sleek and in charge. Having a fully erect tent bulging out of our car windows as we drive by is an embarrassment I must avoid. It just would not do. So even though the game might go to the tent, ultimately the match will go to me.

Eventually though, even my self-consciousness about how we look while driving no longer matters. We've given up any semblance of being in a competition. We're up so early that at the hour we steal out of camp the MTC isn't even open. We wave to the few bleary-eyed revelers stretching outside their tents as we leave. Roxanne has no problems besides her damaged suspension, and there's nothing more we can do about that. Only the drivers who have left at 3 AM are on the road in front of us. They're so far ahead that we're alone on the road, and we follow no one. In the distance I can see snow-covered peaks. We're heading right toward them. Once we get there, we'll be in Siberia.

A New Country

KHOVD-TSAGAANNUUR-SIBERIA

Our last night in Mongolia, we camp in a hummocky green field. A babbling brook runs along the perimeter, a few sheep with matted white coats and doleful eyes graze across the road. By Mongolian standards, it's positively bucolic. It refreshes me like watermelon on a summer day.

To get there, we've traversed high passes, bringing us close to the year-round snowfields I'd been seeing in the distance since yesterday. The closer we get, the bigger the mountains seem. For the first time, we are driving *upward* on steep gravel roads, with the horizon above us. There's a wonderful mystery to this, no clue what we'll see when we finally crest a ridge and look down the other side. There have been midnight-blue rivers to ford, glacially cold. On one crossing, I loll my arm out the window for the water to splash it. As the tires gain a purchase on the firmer ground of the river bank, I am again grateful that Bernard knows how to finesse Roxanne forward, not so fast as to flood her engine, nor so slow that we get stuck. Because it would have been me who'd have to clamber out of the door, tow rope in hand, and wade to the far shore through what I know would be skin-numbing water. We see more *gers* now, sitting in the shadow of towering, snowcapped peaks or next to a glittering alpine lake. Evidently this is summer pasture, because there are small herds of goats everywhere. Best of all, the organizers announce that the final time trial of Mongolia was cancelled. All the drivers are exhausted, and none of the cars are in condition to do it. No one complains. Besides, for the first time in eight days, we are in stunningly beautiful country. I'd hate to miss a minute of it staring at the route book instead of what's around me.

It's not just Bernard and me who are relieved to leave the tortures of Mongolia behind. When we coax Roxanne the final yards into camp, the general euphoria is visible everywhere. Relief is palpable. Who would ever have thought that entering Siberia would signify a good thing? Drivers skip toward the port-a-potties, navigators bubble over with enthusiasm. Everyone seems to be digging out carefully wrapped articles of clean clothes. For the first time in days, people stroll around chatting. A dozen cars have arrived on trucks, including Matthieu's. I'm feeling very upbeat, because we are now within half an hour's drive of the border, so when I see Matthieu as I wander around the camp, I stop. "What's up with your car?" I ask him in a spirit of general friendship and commiseration. He gives me his usual hug, which always makes me feel like we *are* friends, even though in between hugs he still doesn't much speak to me.

"It's still the radiator. We thought we fixed it in UB, but it gives me trouble. I hope I can get it to Novosibirsk," the city two days from now where we'll again have a rest day and where James's planeload of spares should be waiting. I can't help it. I gloat. Roxanne is still moving under her own steam, and that's nothing short of miraculous.

I set to cleaning the car again. It seems important to me to leave as much Mongolian dust behind as I can. In hauling our copious supplies out of the trunk, I discover a dusty, sealed, tube-like carton. It's a distinguished dark green, and even though the gold lettering on it is obscured by dirt I know exactly what it is: an authentic bottle of The Glenlivet single malt Scotch whisky. What seems like a lifetime ago, Bernard and I wandered through a Beijing supermarket, refusing the Chinese-made whisky, searching out something that would lift our spirits down the road, wherever that might be. We stuffed the carton under the spare exhaust pipe to keep it safe, then forgot all about it. "Hey Bernard, want a shot?" I shout, waving the bottle in his direction. When he shakes his head ruefully, I'm not disappointed. The truth is, neither of us is much of a drinker, and besides, we're both too fatigued. "I know someone who'd love this," I say and set it aside for the dinner hour.

For the last couple of nights, we've been too tired to seek out Robert, he of the jokes and constant laugh. I feel guilty about that. I'm beholden to Robert for being my first friend. Though we're only eleven days into the Rally, the memory of our first meeting in the Beijing hotel lounge is still vivid. During the first week of the Rally, just knowing he was out there, cheerfully fixing another flat, was a crutch that propped me up when I was especially down. So it surprised me that, as I sank further into exhaustion, his nonstop cheerful banter, knockout joke after knockout joke, seemed to weigh me down like cement boots. What I know about Robert is that he thrives on reaction and the more tired I get, the less I'm able to give him the satisfying audience he craves. The one person with whom it's restful to be is Bernard. With each passing day there's less and less I need to prove. Around Bernard I can be who I am.

That evening we enter the dining tent, which after its beating in the sandstorm no longer stands square and upright. It's easy to spot Robert. He's with Nick, Sybil, and others, and they're all laughing. I ceremoniously present him with the Scotch. "For you," I say. "Because I like you. And you need this. And you're my friend."

"Well, you're not going to let a man drink alone are you?" he booms. Maddy looks at me and winks. Sybil scoots over and pats the seat beside her. Over my protests, Robert slops some Scotch into my plastic cup, passes another to Bernard, then doles it out all around. We raise our glasses. "To Mongolia," someone shouts. "Long may we be rid of her!" We drink. Someone else bellows, "And to Siberia. May her pavement be smooth!" We drink again. Bernard, sitting across from me, drains his cup, snatches mine, drains it too, then leans across and kisses me. "Stop it now, you two love-birds," Robert shouts, before giving Maddy a long hard kiss on the mouth.

Already more penetratingly tired than I've ever been, I nudge Bernard to leave the dining tent early. Outside is a moonless night, inky black and so still I can hear the tearing of grass blades by sheep across the way. Grass mounds form a minefield of ankle-twisting obstacles across the field to our tent. It's the first time I've needed my mini-Maglite, and I wave it around, CSI-style. "Look Bernard, a weapon!" I exclaim, shaking the wrench someone left outside their car.

He bends to the grass with his own CSI-style light. "And hair!" showing me a tuft of sheep fleece. I squat next to him to pore over the evidence. Then we blind ourselves by shining our flashlights in each other's eyes. "I'd like to take you to my tent for questioning."

Later, as I lie naked in my sleeping bag, the Altai's cold sharp fingers clutch at me through the seams and zipper. The sack is for summer, which is what I thought it would be in Mongolia. It's much too lightweight for the freezing temperature of the high mountains. My wool sweater and watch cap are somewhere, but rustling around to find them would wake Bernard. I resolve to bear it, forcing my body to lie rigid. The featureless dark presses its smothering nothingness on my face. Soon I'm shivering miserably.

At dinner that evening the organizers warned we could be subjected to hours of petty paperwork the next morning. The Mongolians have never let so many strange cars out of their country in one day, and the Russians have never let so many strange cars in. What will happen is anyone's guess. Once through the border, it's 450 miles to the next night's stop, a drive that in the best of circumstances would take seven hours. We've yet to encounter the best of anything on the P2P, and there's no reason to believe that happy times will start now. Like demented djinns, all manner of time-wasting situations now leap about my brain: missing documents, Roxanne's engine overheating from standing in line too long, flat tires that will occur simply because we are due. Outside an owl hoots; Bernard snores beside me. Instead of kicking him as I sometimes do, I let him snuffle on undisturbed. But not before wrapping my sleeping bag tightly around my goose-pimpled skin and scooting close enough to spoon around his body.

When a pale freezing dawn glows weakly through the tent walls, I pull on the woolens and jacket that I now can see were next to me all along and crawl outside, sleeping bag wrapped around my shoulders. The air is so sharp and clear it freezes my nose when I inhale and reemerges from my mouth in clouds of icy steam. There's a lovely calm in camp before others are up, and I stand still, savoring my last day in Mongolia. The sun has barely taken the chill off the air. All the beautiful cars look perfect, and it's easy to believe for a moment that all's well on the Rally.

Over in the dining tent, there's a quiet bustle of breakfast preparations. I can smell the coffee's ready. I fill a mug and bring it back to our tent. "Bernard, coffee," and hand him the steaming mug. "Oh, merci ma cherie," he says and gives me the drowsy morning smile I love.

I have to marvel at what we've accomplished so far. True, I'm still not reconciled to the fact that none of the P2P measures up to my expectation. Nevertheless, a year and a half ago, we were so hopelessly mired in refashioning Roxanne that it seemed unlikely we'd be ready for the Rally, let alone that we'd remain civil in the close quarters of a rally car. Now look at us. Eight of the longest days on the most unforgiving dirt roads I'd ever experienced, and we are still smiling. Sometimes. Not only that, I'd just brought him the Rally equivalent of breakfast in bed.

Back at the dining tent, I fix two mugs of sweet black tea and carry them to Robert and Maddy's tent. I scratch on the flap, forgetting that they've probably been up late finishing that Scotch. From inside comes a muffled "What the hell . . . ," then the flap is unzipped and Robert's tousled head emerges. His eyes are puffy and he looks like an angry bull. "Tea, monsieur," I say and offer him a steaming mug.

"Well, aren't you a wonder!"

"That's for Maddy. This one's for you."

He retreats back into the tent and I hear him say, "Tea, my love, from our dear friend Dina."

Our Private Heaven

TSAGAANNUUR-BIYSK-NOVOSIBIRSK

Though Russia will soon make us crafty, like starving wolves on the prowl, in our first few hours in Siberia we're lost in wonder at the flourishing green hills and bountiful farms of this isolated corner of Russia. I have a connection with Russia, part ordinary, part personal. I visited Moscow and St. Petersburg briefly thirty years ago, before *glasnost*, before the fall of the Berlin Wall. Back then, the country was still the USSR, and it was a severe country with a political fist clamped down on the populace as tightly as a lid on a canning jar. I remember walking Moscow's streets on those late November days, cottony snowflakes building a white blanket on my shoulders. By four in the afternoon it was already dark. My recollection is of store fronts through whose plate glass windows I saw nothing but empty shelves, and of women bundled in coarse black wool coats scurrying down the sidewalk, heads bowed, stout legs beating through the slush in calf-high rubber boots. During that visit I had the pleasure of meeting secretly with some Russian citizens, sitting in their apartment drinking tea and eating strawberry jam from tiny spoons. "Dina," they said. "That's a Russian name."

"Yes," I told them. "My grandparents were from Russia."

"Ah! Wonderful. That is why you look the way you do! Where were they from, your grandparents?"

"Near Kiev. Kremenchug. They left a hundred years ago though. I don't think we have any relatives left here." I'm more abrupt than I should be, but I don't want to go into details. In fact, as my grandparents and their four children loaded bundles on a train, Prince Borghese was preparing to drive his Itala from Peking to Paris. To put it bluntly, my Jewish grandparents fled Russia to stay alive. They had survived the bloody wave of pogroms against the Jews that broke out in 1903, affecting towns throughout Ukraine and Bessarabia. Finally, in 1906, they gathered what they could and left for France. I don't tell my hosts any of this. Our friendship feels fragile, something miraculous given the enmity of our two countries. It's too precious to rupture with unpleasant family facts.

Even without knowing my own family history, my high cheekbones and olive skin betray my ancestry to those inclined to pay attention to such signs. In the Rockies, the questions come from Native Americans curious about what tribe I belong to, rather than what part of Russia I stem from. Apart from how I look, my taste buds also are a dead giveaway of my heritage. My food vocabulary happily contains words like blinis and caviar, beets and potatoes, vodka and vodka. And then there's the sound of the Russian language, which makes me dreamy in a way Mongolian or Chinese never did.

Despite this natural affinity for things Russian, I know little about the country beyond recent history. It comes as a shock to me that we're literally only on the other side of the Greater Altai range, which separates Mongolia from southern Siberia, yet the people here are completely different from Mongolia. Instead of flat faces with a broad nose, oriental eyes, and black hair, they have faces with high cheekbones, pale skin, and sharp features. Barely into Siberia I can hardly contain myself. "Bernard, have you noticed the people here? They're tall."

"I know. And their houses. They're made of wood."

I finish his sentence with, "Which means they're not nomadic. There's something else completely different here. Look at that river!"

We both drink in the great rushing river along which we're driving, its water pearly gray flecked with ivory foam, its banks rising to slopes covered in towering trees. Even this close to the border, every house has a vegetable garden. How can life be so vastly different just the other side of a ridge? Here, it's like a century ago, but then Mongolia was like three centuries ago, so this seems to me to be a good sign of progress.

We fall into ecstatic fits about cafes. They exist here.

We pull in next to another Rally car parked in front of what at any other time I would describe as a slovenly loser of a roadside diner. It's a low wood building, graced with some wretched geraniums struggling to survive in broken plastic flower boxes. It also has a fountain, left over from more prosperous or more hopeful times. In its present forlorn state, the blue and green mosaic that once decorated the fountain's concrete rim is mostly a memory, or an enthusiastic entry in a Lonely Planet guidebook. Perhaps there used to be a charming statue in its center, burbling water from pursed, cherubic lips. Now there's only a stubby black pipe spouting a thin stream into the algae-laden few inches of water in the bottom. To me, it's a fairy tale wonder, the cafe is a palace, and I can't wait to be served.

The cafe door, springless, slams shut behind us. The other crew is already inside. I recognize them but, even though we've been traveling the same route for eleven days, I don't know their names. Still, we wave a friendly hello to each other and trade a few wry comments about what a novelty it is to order food in a restaurant. Shafts of daylight filter through dingy small windows. I squint around. It's probably fortunate that I can't see into the dark recess of the cramped room. What I can see is a man's head, framed by an opening in the wall. He's holding a small note pad, to take our order. On a slate board above him is a handwritten menu. It's in Cyrillic, which I can't read. Bernard, who relies on me to get food on the table, whether at home or traveling, stands behind me, hands in pockets, shuffling his feet about like an impatient school boy. I know what to do in this situation. "Go outside," I command. "Sit in the sun, get some color on your face. I'll take care of this."

Knocking on the kitchen door, I head in. There's one person in the kitchen, a short buxom woman. She's standing at a steel sink, her hair covered by a pink scarf tied at the back. A dingy apron which might once have been a matching color barely makes it around her portly waist. She straightens, startled, not sure what to think. I pat my stomach, gesture toward the pots, and then mime lifting lids and sniffing. At this she relaxes. We're fellow foodies. "Sure, sure," she gestures expansively. "Take a look."

"Goulash?" I ask, pointing at one pot. She nods. "Soup? Soopa? Soupski?" I say, hoping to sound vaguely Slavic while pointing at a tub of lumpy, pale green matter that looks and smells like split pea. Carrots and cucumbers sit in a chipped ceramic bowl on a grimy steel counter. The flies feasting on everything not covered by a lid or cloth are disconcerting, but I forge ahead, unwilling to be denied a meal simply because of a misplaced spate of fussiness. I make a chopping motion. "Salad?"

"Da."

I see a crusty loaf on a cutting board and point to that, too. She beams. Not knowing how to end this session, I put my hands together at my heart and make a little bow, then back out of her domain. Bernard has followed my instructions and is sitting outside on the cafe patio in the sunshine. When the steaming soup bowls and plates of crisp vinegary vegetables arrive at our rickety table, accompanied by thick slabs of rye bread, Bernard's radiant smile is all the thanks I need.

We feed bread crumbs to some sparrows and soak up the warm rays of sun. As we're sopping up the last of the goulash sauce, another Rally car pulls in. In a display of wanton joy, the driver leaps over the low door of his convertible roadster and bounds into the fountain, clothes, goggles, and all, cackling and making general mayhem with the few inches of water in the bottom. Even the putrid toilet stall, a long drop over the river, cannot dampen our delight. I know some things about Siberia. That it holds the 400-mile-long Lake Baikal, the largest freshwater lake in the world. That the Trans-Siberian Railroad has transported cargo and migrants across Siberia's immensity since the turn of the last century. That its emptiness made it the perfect place for Stalin to construct his network of inhuman prison camps known as *gulags*. Now, for this one short span of time, I also know that Siberia is heaven.

After lunch, we feel so optimistic that we indulge in another guilty pleasure: taking a break that has nothing to do with fixing the car. Bernard pulls off the road into a meadow of tall grass, so deeply emerald it hurts my eyes. In the cool shade of a thick-trunked tree, a couple of drowsy black and white cows barely lift their heads when we parallel park next to them. Their warm breath fills the air with the scent of new-mown hay. "Ahh," sighs Bernard, as he stretches his back. "This is the life."

"Yeah. If only . . . ." I don't have to elaborate my longing to experience what Russia has to offer, and my wistfulness at what we have missed in Mongolia and China. Bernard knows exactly what I mean. Flies buzz industriously around the fresh cow patties. I love this smell, speaking as it does of everything earthy, of rich pasture, blossoming meadows, frothy fresh milk. The cow next to me flicks her tail back and forth, steady as a metronome. It's hypnotizing. Intoxicating. I contemplate stretching out in the grass, that is if I can find a spot not already occupied by those pudding-y droppings. Just then several Rally cars whizz by, honking their horns as they pass. "Oh, yes, I almost forgot. We're supposed to be driving," Bernard says.

"Amazing what a ten minute break can do," I reply, feigning a get-up-and-go attitude I do not feel. "You realize we didn't even have *one* of these in Mongolia? I love Siberia, don't you?" We are both trying hard to be cheerful, but there's no mistaking the tinge of sadness we each feel. Because it's taken only a few minutes in this lovely, peaceful field to highlight how few such opportunities we had in China and Mongolia. The cars driving inexorably onward, despite the natural beauty around us, are a clear reminder that this trip is all about driving and not about the journey.

The great traveler Robert Byron said it perfectly: "[One] can know the world only when [one] sees, hears and smells it." (*First Russia, Then Tibet* 1933). It's a bitter pill for me to swallow that I'm going to have so few of those magical meetings or impromptu conversations that make a journey rich and rewarding. This Rally is about one thing only: getting to the day's end. Every day. If I think about this too much it'll be unbearable, so I turn my mind to something infinitely more amusing: my propensity to get sick when I read too long in a swiftly moving car. I hadn't thought about this at all in Mongolia, because we were moving so slowly it was more like we were sitting still. Now that we're on pavement, our speed has tripled. I have to keep my focus on the route book, despite the rattling of the road. Things don't bode well for me.

We bump back across the field and set out on the 450 miles of winding, undulating pavement we need to cover to reach our night's stop in Biysk. Looking up from the route book, everything I see delights me. On all sides are steep, forest-clad hills, broken now and then by granite cliffs. Through these thread white cascades, tumbling in free fall into the waiting arms of a frothing river. Fat pigs roam the roadside; now and then a tethered cow mows the grass on a quiet side lane. Occasionally, we slow to share the road with a filigreed, painted cart. The jauntily trotting horse pulling it down the highway is decorated, too, with jangling harness bells and a crocheted cap to whisk flies from its eyes. At an eddy among the rapids, a housewife dips two buckets into the river, then walks up to her house, buckets suspended from a long pole bridging her shoulders. Petunias display their pinks and purples to the sun. Sheets flap dry in the breeze. It's so lovely I can taste it.

After several hours, I turn to Bernard. "Have you noticed something's missing?"

He peers at me in alarm. "What? Did we leave something back there? What's missing? What?!"

The notion that we might have to drive three hours back is too distressing, and I'm immediately apologetic. "No, no. Nothing like that. It's just that, well, usually by this time I'd have been complaining about something. No?"

"You're thirsty? I'm sure we have plenty of water in the back."

I'm toying with him now, but my pleasure is so great that I want to draw things out, revel in the marvelous feeling like a puppy rolling in a cow patty. "No, no. I'm fine. Get it? I'm *fine*!!!"

"You're fine? Me, too. This countryside is so beautiful."

I've got to love Bernard for this. The man is so literal, so straightforward, that he doesn't get it. "Yes, I'm fine, as in, I'm not carsick. I've been reading through the route book for hours now, and I haven't gotten carsick! Can you believe it?" I'm giddy, crazed with happiness, as if announcing I've won the Nobel Prize.

"That's true! Dina, cherie, it's a miracle!" He swerves onto the grassy shoulder. By the time I'm out of the car he's already to my side, sweeping me up in his arms. "You're cured. You're cured," he shouts, swinging me around. We laugh and dance a jig by the roadside. A crow in a nearby tree caws in alarm at our antics. Who can say for sure how I lost my carsickness affliction. I like to think I just let myself get better.

Fixers

BIYSK

This is the Rally, after all, and one can't be optimistic for long. Somewhere along those miles of pavement, Roxanne's latest shock absorber mounts prove too fragile even for asphalt. The shock absorbers break again, and Roxanne is reduced to dragging her sagging trunk the rest of the way to our first night's stop in Siberia. By the time we arrive it's mid-evening, which is weirdly appropriate since the organizer staff are being housed in a brothel. I can see the place is hopping with business, and it's not just Rally business. We're eager to finally get to a room, but the buses hired to take us from the fenced, guarded car park to the several hotels in which we'll be housed haven't arrived, and those hotels are a further hour away.

I'm for trying to scrounge a room in the brothel, where at least we'll be next to Roxanne and have the best chance of organizing repair assistance for her the next morning. It is, after all, a bustling center of commerce. Bernard's having none of it. "Come on Dina, let's just go to our hotel and figure it out there."

It takes some effort to curtail my urge to snap at him severely. I would have preferred Bernard's support on this, mainly because I am fatigued enough I want to be coddled and told "Don't worry; I'll take care of everything." That I know he's right makes it worse. Of course the hotel is the place to be, especially since it'll have things we're unlikely to find in the brothel. There'll be showers, food, and all manner of modern conveniences, which, after eight days camping in Mongolia, are things to which I'm looking forward with more than ordinary longing. Still, I can't stop myself from grousing a little. "Sure," I say. "Let's go to the hotel. What's one more hour when we've already been on the road for twelve?"

Our first hotel in Russia is a welcome sight only because it's not a tent. The hotel, both outside and in, is illuminated by what must be 25-watt light bulbs, all two of them. So dim is the lighting and so dark are the recesses that I feel I'm in a John Le Carré spy story. The shower stall I've been dreaming of turns out to be a doorless, curtainless tiled pad tilted in the wrong direction so it discharges all its water toward the bedroom. The shower head is screwed to a rubber hose attached to a spigot on the wall. The hose is only two feet long. To get water on me, I have to squat. If I pull on the hose, hoping to get it to stretch, it separates from the spigot altogether. None of this diminishes the profound rapture I feel as a trickle of hot water splashes onto my head.

An hour later when we enter the dining room, Gustav sees us. Too late we notice that he's waved us over to join him and Laure for dinner. Not only that. We see that he's seen us see him. After such a long day I can barely manage civil words in English, let alone in French. What I want is to sit quietly with Bernard, with whom I don't have to converse if I don't want to. Laure adds a weak wiggle of her fingers to echo Gustav's invitation. She looks so frumpy and unhappy I don't have the heart to say no.

"Let me buy the wine, to thank you for your help," Gustav says, almost with reluctance, as if he wished he really didn't have to. Our dinner together is bleak, Bernard chatting valiantly, while I struggle to find *bon mots* to contribute. Laure sits silently. I can't stop myself from thinking longingly, "Oh, where is Robert in my time of need." As we walk back to the elevator after dessert, Gustav takes me by the elbow and whispers conspiratorially, "I hope on our day off in Novosibirsk that you will go around with Laure. You will be able to explain things to her in French! Otherwise, you know . . ." and here he waves an arm around vaguely, " . . . she will just sit in the room all day."

I'm as flabbergasted that he's roping me into being his wife's travel companion, and undoubtedly her psychotherapist, as I am desperate to avoid it. "Thank you, Gustav. But I normally help Bernard on rest days."

"Oh, Bernard doesn't need you there," he guffaws. "Go out and have some fun!"

"Well, I have to tell you, we're a team. So we like to be together." Thankfully the elevator arrives, absolving me from having to say a pointed "No."

Breakfast next morning is in a room that must double as a ballroom dancing arena, our tables huddled like wallflowers in one drafty corner. Charming young girls in green micro-minis and yellow shirts waltz in, balancing four plates apiece. They set breakfast in front of us: two green peas adorning half a sliced hardboiled egg. How thoughtful to have wait-staff that match the food.

Back at the car park, we confront a horde of desperate Rally crews trying to secure transport to Novosibirsk for their crippled vehicles. It makes me think of pictures I've seen of the fall of Saigon in 1973. Of course, we're all here by choice, and nobody's shooting at us, but the air fairly crackles with urgency and desperation. Not only are there twelve crippled Rally cars coming in on trucks, but none of those trucks will be available to help others, like us, whose cars didn't fare well on the drive from the border. They're Mongolian trucks, and they don't do Siberia any more than they can help it. So leery are some of the Mongolian drivers of even being in Russia that one of them, in his impatience to turn around and get back to Mongolia, does the unthinkable. He pushes the Rally car he's been hauling off his truck bed without ramps, while the owner dashes frantically around, waving his arms and shouting "Noooo. Stopppppp." I could read the driver's mind: "Why the worry? What's an eight-foot drop to the ground to a car that's already broken?"

People crowd around a grizzled man. His floppy jowls are stubbled with a charcoal smudge, his black button eyes deeply embedded in bruised flesh. This is the agent for the one local empty truck, whose driver right now is slumped behind the steering wheel getting some much-needed sleep, or nursing a terrible hangover. I can see the truck bed is big enough to hold Roxanne, and I'm determined to get it for us. The agent stands, legs apart, in an ill-fitting gray serge suit, jacket straining its buttons, belly spilling over his belt, the frayed cuffs of his ill-fitting pants mopping the pavement. From his pocket he withdraws a packet of tobacco, and I stare in fascination as his sausage-like fingers, stained yellow with nicotine, roll a cigarette with the delicacy and precision of a surgeon doing a quadruple bypass. The cigarette is pinched in his surprisingly sensuous lips as he drags and exhales, drags once more. Spellbound, I focus on the coarse pores of his broad nose and start counting. At ten, two streams of smoke billow from his nostrils. His eyes disappear as he squints into the smoke and rubs his ham-like palms together in anticipation. He knows he's standing in front of a gold mine.

The agent can't conceal his delight at being surrounded by men owning valuable cars, willing and able to pay anything. I, however, have something they don't: I'm a woman, and we are, after all, standing next to a brothel. Two hours pass during which I come and go, flirting, haggling, and finally flashing a wad of U.S. dollars. I win. The truck is ours for the day.

As I heave myself up into the cab I feel a flash of guilt at leaving so many needy drivers behind. If this is treason, then I'm a pleasantly relieved traitor. Plenty of others will manhandle their vehicles the next 270 miles. We won't be one of them. We'll be chauffeured and I won't have to deal with a GPS or Tripmeter or route book to get us there. We can take this truck and ignore all the Rally controls, because we're no longer competing for any medals. It feels fabulous.

Six hours later, when our driver is the one who gets us lost on the outskirts of Novosibirsk, I heave such a deep sigh of pleasure that this isn't my fault, that Bernard thinks I've fainted. We're searching for the Ford dealership, to which we have access thanks, again, to Matthieu. He's offered us his place there, which I take as a sign of repentance for his shameful behavior back at the Kharkorin *ger* camp, when he could have invited me to join his party, but didn't. It's a mob scene to get into these dealerships, and only a few manage. We, however, have an actual invitation, since Matthieu & Co. have decided instead to use Novosibirsk's Mercedes dealership for their repairs.

It's getting on toward dusk. Our driver is muscling his truck through the confined alleys of a dilapidated Novosibirsk housing development in search of the dealership, when a shiny black SUV with deeply tinted windows cuts us off and motions us to the side. At first, I think it's the secret police, and I spend a fretful sixty seconds before I see a trim man wearing tight black jeans and a fitted leather jacket hop up onto the truck steps and shove his head in the window. I look for a gun. If he has one, it's not visible. "Beautiful car," he says, grinning. "Very beautiful car." It appears we've been pulled over by a minor oligarch.

"Thank you." We're studiedly gracious, not to risk offending anyone with possible connections. Especially if he might be able to cut short our search and direct us to Ford. He sticks his hand through the window, and we each shake it.

"Why are you here? In Novosibirsk?"

"We're on a rally. From Beijing to Paris. That's why there's a number on the car. And those special license plates," Bernard says, motioning back toward Roxanne.

"I see. Very interesting. So. How much?"

Now it's dawning on me he wants to buy Roxanne. No, that can't be. He must be asking what we paid for her.

"Very expensive," Bernard says, answering any number of possible questions.

"Yes, I'm sure. How much?"

I nudge Bernard and whisper, "Here's our chance. Let's sell Roxanne. She'll have a good home here, be this man's cosseted plaything. Plus . . . we'll be able to leave without disgrace. It'll make a great story. Come on!"

"We can't," Bernard hisses back. "There's a carnet on her. Whatever car we entered the country with leaves with us, remember? It's stamped on our passports! If she doesn't leave Russia, neither do we." Of course I remember. The Rally has posted a monetary bond for every car, insuring that every one of us will take the same car out of each country that we bring into it. That does not change my desire. It's testimony to how frayed I am that even an illegal, black market deal appeals to me. That is, as long as it results in a good home for Roxanne. And no prison time for me.

"Not for sale," Bernard says.

I wonder if, thwarted, the man will now pull the gun he's surely hiding and say, "Not for sale? Well then, I'll just take her!" He doesn't. He smiles ruefully and says, "Ah, I understand. She's very beautiful. Of course you want to keep her." He gives the truck door a good wallop. "Well, good luck with her." Just like that, the man in black goes back to his black car with the blackened windows and drives off. As if a curtain has lifted, we turn a corner and there is the dealership. In short order, we have off-loaded Roxanne and driven her into a sparkling clean repair shop where she will wait for us to return the following day.

In the hotel lobby next morning, I'm astonished to see Ralph and his son, who've been AWOL since midway through Mongolia. I figured they had retired, but now here they are, fatigued, deeply bronzed, and broadly pleased with themselves. I grab Ralph and gush about how happy I am to see him. "Well done, Ralph. And my god, you made it. What exactly happened? And how did you get here?" I could have chattered on in this vein, but it dawned on me I was holding him hostage with my questions. Probably it would be more supportive of me if I let him go take a shower. He hugs me back and gives me his big snaggletooth grin. "Quite an adventure," he says. "Which I will tell you all about. But first I must get this leaf spring fixed." He shows me the tiny suspension part that keeps his tiny car from scraping the ground, a piece of metal about the heft of a fork tine. A bubble of envy rises, that he can get his car part replaced in minutes in the hotel kitchen while ours requires deconstructing a tank. On the other hand, we've already slept two nights in a hotel, while his bed has been either his cramped car seat or the sand.

For our rest day in Novosibirsk, the route book gushes "With our two-night stay here, you will have the opportunity to explore the city." I see nothing of Siberia's capital, but I do get on intimate terms with the dealership staff. These particular Russians are kissy folks. Irina and Mikael, dealership employees who are put in charge of our satisfaction, greet us with six kisses, three per cheek. That's just for me. Each time they wander into the service area, whether to bring us tea or inspect our progress, we get six more. When their friends arrive to see all the Rally cars, the time spent exchanging kisses grows extreme. I like being on a par, kiss-wise, with everyone else. It makes me feel like family.

Novosibirsk also is memorable for Siberian pizza, which we agree is far superior to that in Mongolia. As for the beauty of the dealership, Ford has spared no expense. The complex is stunningly modern, like a gleaming high-tech park in Silicon Valley, only brighter and cleaner. More important as far as we're concerned, it runs a 24/7 repair operation. They are bursting with pride to host us in their facility and spare no effort to help us out. Even the cleaning women, who circulate hourly through the repair area to mop up crumbs and errant splats of oil, take a break to be photographed with the vintage cars and shabby-looking crews.

We spend several peaceful hours alongside other teams. Roxanne is lifted on a hydraulic hoist so Bernard can easily stand underneath her. A skilled mechanic is assigned to us for the day. He doesn't speak English, but by now Bernard is fluent in drawing. The two of them pore over sketches on scraps of paper while other mechanics bring parts and spares. Together, Bernard and the mechanic change Roxanne's oil, lube parts, begin welding new shock absorber mounts. Whenever Roxanne is lowered for work on the engine I have a chance to continue cleaning the interior, an endless task that never fails to reveal more areas in which Gobi dust still hides.

Suddenly, there's a commotion at the garage entrance. Looking up, we see Matthieu, James, and their teams silhouetted in the open door. I can see them looking around at the service bays, each occupied by a Rally car in the middle of time-consuming repairs. What they see displeases them. James's rage erupts like a volcano, and soon he's spewing his dissatisfaction in a loud voice, publicly chastising the dealership manager. I don't understand why they're here. They were supposed to be working at their own private dealership. I overhear snatches of the monologue like, " . . . paid for this months ago," and " . . . haven't heard the last of this," phrases I thought were only spoken in bad movies. James strides about the service area in a fury, and I'm scared to death. Any moment I expect him to come over to us and bellow, "Get your car out of there! This is MY spot."

Bernard, though, walks over to James and quite calmly says the obvious, "Please, take our space. We can finish our car elsewhere." My heart leaps into my mouth. "What are you doing?!" I want to scream. "Haven't we had enough trouble as it is? We need this space as much as he does. No, we need it more. For god's sake, the man's driving with his own mechanic!" There's no camaraderie in me whatsoever, and I am so different from Bernard at this moment I can hardly believe we're married. I glance toward Matthieu, who shoots me a tight, placating smile and shakes his head.

James, who's a strapping six feet, stops his tirade and looks down at Bernard. It's like one of Tolkien's orcs noticing a hobbit. I expect him to grab Bernard and fling him across the shining service area floor. Perhaps it's Bernard's politeness, perhaps his shorter stature, which combine to create the opposite effect. "Thank you, Bernard," James says. "So kind of you." That's it. Bernard's made a friend. I don't think that friendship extends to me.

Siberian Cartoons

OMSK

Having nursed Roxanne over Chinese tarmac and the rutted despair of Mongolia's Gobi Desert and Asian Steppes, we just may be undone by the Trans-Siberian Highway. Even worse, we can't find our friends. When we were in China, everyone stayed in the same huge hotel each night. Once into Mongolia, the only hotel available to us was in Ulaanbaatar; other than that, we had all camped together outside small towns. One way or the other, we knew where everyone would be at nightfall. They were either working on their car or eating in the dining tent. There was no other place to be. In a bizarrely contradictory way, that was reassuring. Here in the belly of Russia's vast interior we are again in hotels, except that none are big enough to house the entire Rally, so we're split among three or four lodges every night. With people so scattered, sometimes we don't see our friends for days.

Since we're now driving mainly on the highway, and my navigation job requires me giving Bernard a direction about every thirty miles, I have ample time to gaze at the Siberian scene outside my window. We've left behind the bucolic greenery of Siberia's southern borderlands and are entering the heart of Solzhenitsyn's gulag archipelago. *Gulag* is an acronym for the agency that was officially created under the auspices of the secret police on April 25, 1930 and dissolved on January 13, 1960. It stands for *Chief Administration of Corrective Labour Camps and Colonies.* According to official Soviet estimates, more than 14 million people passed through the gulag from 1929 to 1953. Some were political prisoners. Others were imprisoned in a gulag camp for crimes such as petty theft, unexcused absences from work, and antigovernment jokes. In 1940, the year Roxanne was built, there were 53 separate camps and 423 labor colonies in the USSR.

The scenery around me gives no clue to that history. Day in and day out there's a continuous field of growing wheat, the green flatness relieved only now and then by a copse of green birch trees. In its monotone texture and color it feels much like Mongolia, though I'm still grateful to see green instead of brown. It's early summer and the air is fresh, moistened each day with several hours of drizzle. It all seems benign and cultivated, but I can see how this flat landscape, when whipped by winds during Siberia's subarctic winters, would be a more impenetrable barrier than anything man made. In areas such as this, more than a quarter of the gulag population died of cold and starvation during World War II. Today, in this massive monoculture landscape, there's no animal life to see, no shaggy Mongolian goats chased by skittering motor bikes, no shedding Bactrian camels pacing toward greener pastures. The only life along the road is an occasional black and tan raven scavenging road-killed bunnies. For all the greenery, this landscape feels more empty than Mongolia.

Occasionally, we whiz by a tired Russian hamlet, just a huddle of low, bedraggled wood cottages with filigreed shutters whose blue or green paint is cracked and peeling. Overgrown weedy yards line each narrow dirt lane. No general store, no personable fuel station, no family run cafes, dilapidated or otherwise. Sometimes I glimpse a round babushka, tight black wool dress hugging her hunched back, black kerchief over her hair. As she shambles slowly up the lane, she reminds me of a tiny, earthbound dirigible. These are places that the twentieth century forgot. If they're any indication of the might of Russia, we have nothing to fear.

Russia is huge, and we have correspondingly vast distances to cover each day if we're to get out of the country in the allotted two weeks. There are no amusing distractions like time trials planned for Russia. The organizers guessed rightly that no one would be in the mood. The only times we stop are to register our existence at a passage control and to fuel up at one of the many brightly lit, modern Yukos gas stations that dot the Trans-Siberian Highway.

Even with keeping our out-of-car time to a minimum, it's all many of us can do to complete each day's route in time for a late dinner. Still, I am pleased to be in Russia. In a sense, it's my birth right to feel like I belong here. Even though Roxanne is continually in need of suspension repairs and I'm sagging with fatigue, I still want to smile, look that gas station attendant in the eye, and say, "Spaseba," thank you, as much like a native as I can manage.

The Trans-Siberian stays well away from towns, but I sometimes see one on the horizon. From a distance, they look like a set from Dr. Zhivago, with whitewashed houses and the gold-clad onion domes of a Russian Orthodox church glittering in the sun. One day, though, our route takes us through the center of one such town, and I see something I'm not prepared for, not because I didn't believe such a thing still existed, but because I never expected to see one myself. It's a prison, whether a gulag relic or not I couldn't say. I don't implore Bernard to stop so I can ask. This is one place I want to get away from. Fast. The rot I see on the outside speaks of the conditions in which those who are inside live. Nothing about the structure tries to disguise its intent. I see guard towers jutting up from the inner courtyard and small blackened windows piercing the long building behind, like vacant, beseeching eyes. A skin of graying paint peels off concrete walls stained with black mold and topped with tangles of rusting razor wire. The concrete may be crumbling and the whole thing may speak of decay, but the armed guard at the gate makes it clear that once you go through those menacing doors, you're not getting out without their say-so. He's alert, at attention, and fierce in his gaze. Usually the sight of Roxanne makes people smile, but this guard's mouth doesn't even twitch.

We have three more weeks of intense driving to complete before we reach Paris. Roxanne's formerly roomy quarters are starting to feel cramped, though I'm certain she has not changed physical dimensions. When we reach our hotel each night, Bernard and I become two dogs fighting over a bone. I want to look around whatever city we're in, if only to stretch my legs and move about in a space wider than five feet, after which I want to flop on the bed in our room and not move. The main thing on Bernard's mind is checking Roxanne, and then he wants to have a beer at the bar.

These days I carry with me a wish that our car problems could be someone else's, so I wouldn't have to worry about them myself. Better yet, I wish to become a person who simply didn't worry. Though I'm beginning to feel resigned that I'm the worrying sort, I'm also discovering the benefits of being an active, helpful worrier. Now, when Bernard makes trenchant pronouncements about the state of Roxanne's underbelly, I say, "Guess I'll start checking around for a truck to haul us tomorrow." This simple statement makes me feel amazingly good, far out of proportion to what any twelve words should. It seems to lift Bernard's spirits, too, because when I say it, he grabs my waist, gives me a little whirl and a kiss, and says, "Don't worry about it. I'll take care of things later. Let's go check in." His arm snugging me tight, we head for the lobby together, walking hip to hip like Siamese twins.

Early evening, after reaching Omsk, I sit next to a majestic white marble stairway in our hotel lobby, happily alone in the swirl of Rally check in, while Bernard gets the key to our room. Sybil walks by and gives me a high five. It delights us both to see that the other has made it in for the day. "Doing all right?" she asks.

"Fine. Just sitting still for a few minutes. You know. Not moving."

"Sounds lovely. I'd join you, but my hair has been screaming 'wash me' for days. I better get to it."

Perched on my marble step, doing a fair imitation of a gargoyle, I zone out, not daydreaming, but not paying attention to anything. I'm pleasantly sated with caffeine and sugar, courtesy of the wife of an auto parts shop owner.

We'd pulled up to their shop before dusk, in search of the usual. While the owner and Bernard discussed shock absorbers, she invited me into the back room to relax. Like many Russian women below the oligarch class, she was portly, her rotund body squeezed into beige polyester slacks, the short sleeves of a size-too-small apricot sweater pinching her arms and stretching across a chest made pointy by a 1950s-style push-up bra. Her broad face was full of friendship, and after setting the omnipresent kettle to boil, she motioned me to sit on a dark brown love seat pushed against the wall, its cushions stained and misshapen from too many heavy buttocks resting on it. A small color TV was on, with a talking head delivering what I assumed was the evening news. Handing me a cup of tea, she sat down, then jumped back up and began changing channels. Even in Russia, the news isn't very entertaining. At each station, she turned to look at me. I shook my head. Finally something I recognized, something truly international made me nod. "Pinocchio," I said, smiling broadly to show how much I love cartoons.

"Pinocchio!" she replied and clapped her hands together with pleasure.

Even as a child I couldn't understand what Geppetto was saying, so it was no loss to me that he now was speaking Russian. My hostess grabbed her own plastic mug and plopped down next to me, the couch sagging noticeably as she settled her plump self on the cushions. Immediately she was up again, bustling around her desk, tugging open drawers. I thought maybe she'd make popcorn, but no. It was even better. Extracting a large, flat box from the bottom drawer, she lifted off the lid, rustled aside gold tissue paper, peered inside with obvious relish, then offered me first pick from the precious box of chocolates. She took one herself and we both bit in at the same time. Then we both laughed with delight when, like old friends, we simultaneously held up our half-eaten chocolate to show each other what was inside. We passed the time eating candy, sipping tea, and laughing as Donald and Daffy, then Bugs, followed Pinocchio on the screen. For once, I hoped the repair to Roxanne's suspension problems would take longer. This was one half-hour that had gone by too fast.

Brought back to the present when Bernard hands me our room key, I look around for something to do while he heads back out to check something on Roxanne. Instead of going to our room, I walk to the bar, where a sharply dressed young bartender is busy pouring draught beers and mixing cocktails. When we entered Russia, each hotel's bar became the Rally's home, the place where everyone would go at some point, to find a willing ear to bend or a friend to regale with the events of their day. I recognize Nick's tall body draped at the counter. "Hey good lookin'," I say, tapping him on the shoulder.

"Well, aren't you a sight for sore eyes. Bartender, a gin and tonic for this lovely lady."

I don't really want a gin and tonic, but I want to be a person who has a gin and tonic ordered for her.

"Where's your handsome French husband?" he asks me.

"With the car, of course."

"C'est bien. Then you can keep me company."

At this point, Hans, who's been driving the most unsightly, bedraggled Bentley on the Rally, lopes our way. His wispy blond hair glows like a halo, backlit by a ray of late afternoon light streaming through the bar window. The two of them put their heads together for a moment, and then Nick turns to me.

"We've decided to tell you something," Nick says. I know what's coming. It's about our car, and it's not going to be good.

"We've been watching you," says Bert. Oh god, it's not about the car. It's about me, and they've seen I've been faking it, that I don't know how to be a proper navigator.

"We have been discussing this for some time, and now, we must tell you, we agree you have the best ass on the Rally." They both blush slightly, broadly pleased with themselves.

This is the sort of sexist compliment that normally I'd never tolerate. I'm a woman who says no to the supermarket clerk when he offers to carry my grocery bags out, because it implies I'm too weak to do it myself. Forget about letting any guy call me "babe" or "sweetheart" or "hon" unless he's my husband. Here, in the insular world of the Rally, this statement has a different meaning entirely. It's a badge of merit, a declaration that we've been through so much together, barriers are down. The feminist in me does a discreet withdrawal. I gulp down my drink and order another. I explain to them the merits of Disney cartoons in Russian, they tell me about strange people they've met on other rallies, we do a communal gripe about how difficult this Rally is. By the time Bernard returns, I'm feeling that my mission to improve my social abilities is definitely showing promise. So much so that when James, who's ensconced with his mates at the back of the lounge, sees Bernard and hails him over, I toss away resentments and join them. I even manage to say a few words before my uncertainty about where I stand with this group turns me into someone with a need to inspect in detail the shape of the ice cube in my drink.

A gin and tonic and a half later, we cluster at the door to an immense private dining hall, where the guard glares at my chest under the guise of scrutinizing my P2P badge. It's been this way ever since we entered Russia. Each hall is the same, floors padded in gray carpet, tables covered with stained white tablecloths, walls and windows obscured by heavy wool drapes that puddle on the floor. My hopes of eating local meals each day are now but a dim fantastical memory. The last, in fact the only, truly Russian meal we've had was lunch that first day in Siberia, at the tumble-down roadside cafe. Since then we haven't even stopped for lunch, making do with chips and soda in the car, our gorp having run out and bottled water no longer quenching our thirst quite as much as a Russian Coke.

Our dinner that night is a vast buffet. On order of the organizers, every hotel has one. This is great for those crews who arrive well after dark. If you're exhausted and famished, there's nothing like being able to dig right into your food. There are always at least eight hot dishes, offering Continental preparations of pork, chicken, beef, and fish. One night the fish is sautéed with onions and the pork is sliced. The next night green peppers adorn the nameless white filets and the pork is cubed. The fish always sports a white sauce, the pork a thick brown one. Then there's a table with platters of roasted, boiled, mashed, or sautéed vegetables. The potatoes, carrots, and beets that have nourished centuries of hungry Russians have pride of place. I'm happiest at the table that holds bowls of pickled, briny, or sour-cream slathered salads, which at least seem of Slavic origin. There's always a dessert table heaped with tiered glass trays of chocolate cakes, marzipan-iced petit fours, whipped cream confections, jelly rolls with mysterious neon whorls, packaged cookies, and more. So we are not going hungry. Yet each hotel buffet is so similar to the next that the food alone, normally a beacon of my locale, gives no clue as to where we are. We could as easily be eating a mayonnaise-y pea and carrot macédoine in Paris as in Nizhny Novgorod or Des Moines. Every once in a while, I wish we were.

Police Procedural

TYUMEN

It's our anniversary. Our twenty-fourth, to be exact. As a special early morning treat, the roadblock police are waiting for us. These are aimless officials in smart olive uniforms with plenty of gold braid, whose typical day is spent stopping transport trucks so they can finagle bribes from hapless drivers. They've been on the road ever since we entered Russia. Indeed, the route book has advised us of every police barrier we will pass, so we can be sure to slow to the legal speed limit well before reaching one. At each checkpoint we see a raised barrier, next to which are policemen in clusters of twos and threes, generally just smoking and chatting. When they see a vehicle they want to inspect, one of them parts from the group and raises his baton, then swipes it down and to the side indicating "Pull over!" Police cars and motorbikes are parked at the ready next to each official police barrier, evidence that if you dared to ignore their dictate, they'd catch up to you in a flash.

In China, the police were placed along our path by the state. They never stopped us, never tried to speak to us. Their sole aim was to keep us moving. Here, it's the opposite. From the moment I see my first Russian police checkpoint, they make me nervous. They're an unknown quantity, being the law, but somehow also outside the law. We are too obviously foreign, too clearly a source of merriment in an otherwise long, dull, monetarily unfulfilling day. Giving ourselves up to the pecuniary tortures of a bored cop makes me uneasy. They have all day to play with us and no place else to go, whereas we have no time to waste and miles to cover before we sleep.

I know it is only a matter of time before they stop us. Whenever we approach a police barrier, which is several times a day, Bernard slows Roxanne to a crawl, challenging them to take him up on his offer to stop. I study the route book to avoid making eye contact. By this I hope to indicate "we're so innocent I don't even notice you, so please just ignore us." Over the past many days, we've passed more than twenty police barriers; each time they've waved us through. Not this one. Today, with the Rally coming through, the officer in charge has rewarding game to go after. He stops us by placing himself squarely in Roxanne's path, arm raised. With a swift downward swing of his baton, he motions us to get out. He and his taller underling, who's dressed in a similar long wool coat, but without even a stripe on his shoulder, escort us into their shack. There they commence to shout at us in Russian. I can see through the shack's one window that the sun is still shining brightly outside, but inside, standing in front of the policeman's desk, it feels like I've fallen into the clutches of the dark side.

"I think they expect money," I stage whisper to Bernard. "I have a few hundred dollars with me." I show him my fist, curled tight to hide the dollar bills inside.

'No!" he says, slapping at my hand. "Put that away."

"Yes. They seem to like you better. You hand it to them."

"No! Absolutely not. They'll be insulted and then we'll never get out of here." Who knows what a bored, offended Russian policeman might do.

"Documentzhi!" snaps the shorter of the two officers, his voice making up for what he lacks in height. He's a bulldog, but right now he's slouched back in his swivel chair, legs splayed open in the classic pose that says, "I have all day and I know you don't." Bernard hands him his driver's license. The officer tosses it on the table dismissively. "Nyet!! Passaport!"

One thing I've sworn never to do is hand over my passport, but I cave in the face of the officer's fierce gaze. His eyes are so pale as to be almost colorless, which makes them even more creepy. Plus, I can't run. His colleague blocks the door. We hand over the passports, and I feel strange shivers run down my legs. It's not that I fear for my life, it's more that I know this is not a situation in which any of my usual devices, like shouting or crying, are going to help.

Riffling through all the pages, the officer then slams the passports onto his desk alongside the driver's license. Perhaps he's toying with us. If so, it's effective, because I'm feeling exactly the loss of control that he wants. He harangues us in Russian. Bernard has no idea what he's saying, but speaks to him in English, using his happy tones, to show he's compliant and willing. This goes on for an hour, during which the door guard is ordered to abandon his post to prepare us chai. This is not a cordial gesture. It's meant to show us what a personage the officer really is, that he can order another to do the work of a minion.

Finally, the policeman motions us to follow him back outside. I walk several steps behind, head down, intent on displaying that I'm truly an abject and subservient female. I'm so relieved he's escorting us back to Roxanne I'd walk anywhere. Unfortunately, he stops right outside the shack, plants his bulbous-toed black boots on the sidewalk and points down the road from where we came. He's sending us back on a trumped up mission, to fill paperwork that his sign language explains is required in this particular city. He'll be pleased to hold onto our documentzhi till we return. "No, Bernard," I hiss. "We're not going. If we do, we're sunk. We'll never get our passports back."

Maybe it's the caffeine in the chai, but finally my brain reminds me of something useful: the organizers have hired Russian fixers to help with just this sort of situation. One of them, Natalya, has given everyone her cell phone number. Until now, we've been proudly taking care of ourselves, so I've never tried to use it. I'm not even sure my phone will work. Still, if ever there were a time to get outside assistance, this is it. I dial, and when Natalya answers, I stifle a whoop, executing a modest fist pump of joy instead. When I hand my cell phone to the officer, he's so reluctant to take it, it's as if I'm handing a slab of raw, rotten meat. Natalya's voice blasts Russian recriminations in his ear. He crumples slowly, deflating like a gray serge party balloon. Call over, he flicks the phone closed. I can see the light has gone out of his rheumy eyes, but he puts a good front on, straightens his back, and claps Bernard on the shoulders. It's a new day, one in which he hands back our passports and driver's license as if it were his idea. And when Bernard says "Thank you," he replies with "You are welcome. Where do you go from here?" He's understood English all along.

Bernard now relaxes into boisterous commiseration of a manly sort. With a shrug of his shoulders and a well-timed "Heh, heh, heh," he manages to express sympathy with the soldier's tough job and characteristic interest in his rifle. I want a souvenir, and what I long for is the soldier's high-peaked cap with the gold braid and black patent-leather brim. Perhaps it's fortunate that I can't figure out how to convey that with my shoulders and that I suppress my own impulse to chuckle.

Our morning police break isn't the only thing that slows us. Roxanne's failing shock absorbers merit care and vigilance of the sort usually reserved for savoring a fine meal. It's late afternoon before we reach the city of Tyumen. Like Omsk before and as I'll soon see, Yekaterinburg and Perm after, it exudes a grimness that even its broad, straight avenues can't hide. The heavy Stalinist architecture is ominous, big concrete, blocky apartment buildings pressing down on the saplings lining the road. It's sunny, but there's no lightness in the air. Electric wires span the streets like so much spaghetti, tangled evidence that the city's infrastructure hasn't kept up with recent growth. Store windows are drab, no thought given to displaying merchandise in a colorful or attractive way. There's something disturbing about how people walk through the streets. Sidewalks are packed, but there's no air of relaxation. Instead, pedestrians seem bunched tight into themselves, scuttling toward their destination, tight posture implying "better move along before someone sees me." Even I have a hard time mustering enthusiasm for a stroll down these streets.

Early in the Rally I had visions of celebrating our anniversary with friends. I imagined popping champagne corks, hosting a wonderful dinner surrounded by people who knew exactly what we'd been going through and had shared it all with us. As with most things on the P2P, my fantasy does not match reality. On arriving in Tyumen, we register our presence as required at the finish time control. It's set up in the lobby of one of the two hotels reserved for the Rally. Standing in an atrium of red velvet, black marble, and gold chandeliers, I chat with the Control staff and express the hope that we can just stay put in this hotel, that we won't have to get back in our car and drive to the other one. "Sorry, dear," one says. "You are booked over there. Don't worry though, love. It's not more than half an hour to get there. Really, it's not far." This is easy for her to say, since her room is right upstairs. The notion of getting back in Roxanne for more creeping along in rush hour traffic is more than I wish to bear on this particular day. "Let's just stay here," I entreat Bernard. "It's lovely, velvety, shiny. Maybe they have an extra room."

Bernard goes to the reception desk. My hopes are not high. With 300 people on the Rally, any hotel that takes even a portion of the participants tends to be full just with their allocation. At first it seems we'll have to get back in Roxanne after all. No rooms are available. Perhaps sensing my disappointment, or maybe discerning an opportunity to make more money, the reception clerk asks whether we might like to use their presidential suite. Bernard turns to me. "We need a presidential suite, don't we?" Not even waiting for my response, Bernard then books us a table for two in the hotel's private dining room. Growing up in France, Bernard never has become accustomed to the celebrations surrounding American holidays like Thanksgiving. But the man does know how to treat me right on our anniversary. Visions of ordering from a menu and having a plate with food brought to me fills me with pleasure. First I get to spend a lazy couple of hours enjoying our deluxe accommodations. We lounge together in the tub under white pillows of bubbles, use fluffy towels, then swan about in our plush terry cloth bathrobes. The clothes in my duffel are still filthy, but for this one night at least, I feel clean, special, and certainly loved. That evening, we raise our champagne glasses to each other. We're just about half way to Paris.

Truckin'

P E R M - K A Z A N -

N I Z H N Y   N O V G O R O D - M O S C O W

Svetlana and Alex, Irina and Mikael's counterparts, are waiting for us at the Volvo dealership in Yekaterinburg, capital city of the Urals, founded in 1723 by Tzar Peter the Great and named for his wife Catherine. Since I have to forego Yekaterinburg's sights, her monuments and museums, beautiful churches, elegant estates, I'm glad I have these two for compensation. Svetlana is petite, pert, and white blonde. In her tight, flattering beige suit, she's dressed more like a model than a sales clerk. Alex, an amiable schlumpf, does not match her for looks, but outshines her in his eagerness to practice English. The two are equals when it comes to physical contact though, enclosing us in embraces, smacking our cheeks with more kisses, holding each door open and then, with a hand on the small of our backs, escorting us into their facility as if we're royalty. Considering what happened to Tsar Nicholas II and his family, the last royals to pass through this city, I'm not convinced this is a good thing. Regardless, the Romanov murders happened in 1918 and this is 2007, so surely enough time has passed that Russian antipathy toward non-proletariats has dissipated. Besides, wandering around yet another car repair shop, I feel anything but noble.

Alex is all about self-improvement, imparting over the course of another long day in a dealership his hopes for a future in upper management. Meanwhile, though, he's happy to order chicken sandwiches for us for lunch, to find a mechanic to do some spot welding under Roxanne, and to introduce us to Vladimir, his colleague in the parts department, from whom we decide to buy a new jack.

We have an excellent jack with us. To be accurate, we have two. One is the usual sort, designed to lift a car up by pumping up and down on a lever. It's heavy, though, robust enough to jack up a vehicle even weightier than Roxanne. The other isn't an ordinary jack at all. It's a balloon of heavy plastic, which Bernard ordered from Taiwan, which inflates with hot air from the exhaust pipe. The idea of it is that, if Roxanne were ever stuck in soft sand, where a normal jack would sink into the ground, the balloon would spread over the soft surface and not sink in at all. As it filled, Roxanne would rise, pressed upward by the inflating mattress underneath her. The idea did not come through in practice, as the one time we tried to inflate the gadget, Roxanne's heft won out and the inflation device gave one last gasp when the balloon was barely half full.

Given the fragile state of Roxanne's suspension, Bernard wants to cut weight wherever we can. Despite the failure of the Taiwanese balloon jack, Bernard loves the concept and won't part with it. Anyway, though two jacks might be overkill, there's no question that a folded piece of plastic weighs much less than a collection of steel parts. He's decided to ditch the heavy jack in exchange for one of more modest size, scope, and weight.

Vladimir offers us several options, each smaller and lighter than the last. Bernard selects a medium jack, one which Alexander's translation assures us will extend to a height appropriate for Bernard to ease himself under Roxanne whenever he needs to. We stow our new, bright red, bottle jack in the trunk. Who knows? Having five pounds less in weight could be all the difference between breaking down on the Trans-Siberian and making it to Paris. Bernard gives the super-jack to Alex who appears over-joyed to be the recipient of such a strong, well-made, useful American item. Neither of us thinks to ask whether he owns a car.

Next morning, ready to drive on to Perm, the true brutal heart of the gulag, I carry satchels and bags down from our room to stash in Roxanne. I've perused the map of Russia, and despite having covered nearly 1,400 miles, it looks like we've barely made any progress at all. Russia just goes on and on and on. It's daunting and demoralizing. No matter how much effort we put into completing a day's drive, one look at the map shows we've barely made a dent in the huge distance that must be crossed before we reach the border with Estonia. The weird Russian potholes aren't helping. They're unlike anything I've seen.

First off, like the country itself, they're vast, though that's not the worst thing about them. While other countries put effort into filling potholes, Russia makes them bigger. What surely starts as a modest, shapely pothole with slightly sloped edges is sculpted by a road crew into a shallow trench, sometimes several feet across and as much as five or six feet long, with sharp edges and vertical sides. They're meant to be temporary, filled in and smoothed over when an asphalt truck arrives. The problem is, there are no asphalt trucks on the highway, at least not that have made themselves apparent to me. The potholes seem to have taken on their own separate existence, and the longer they're left open, the wider they get. They appear out of nowhere and can churn sturdy tires into mincemeat or shatter leaf springs as if they were made of balsa wood rather than quarter-inch-thick steel. Drivers have been known to risk death by swerving into oncoming traffic rather than to take a Russian pothole head on.

For a while that morning, we drive through pleasant countryside. The smell of new-mown hay fills the car. Looking for tractors pulling hay rakes and balers like at home, instead I see people in the meadows raking hay by hand. The villages we pass are prosperous. I know this because there are solid brick houses, with pots of red geraniums inside lace-curtained windows. It's a lovely day, sunny and cool. When I close my eyes I can sift out the sweet, vanilla scent of the purple lupine and Queen Anne's lace blooming along the road.

Without warning, Roxanne lurches. My eyelids fly open just in time to notice the largest, sheerest pothole I've seen. The truck we would have hit if Bernard had tried to avoid the pothole thunders past. Roxanne gamely jolts through, up, and out the other side. No tires explode. Her gas tank doesn't erupt. Sadly, like many a mature woman, her backside now is drooping worse than ever. Even the slightest divot in the road is enough for her rear to swing wildly up and down. Bernard tightens his grip on the steering wheel to manage the bucking bronco we're now riding in. Tension simmers between us. We each mull over the possibilities and consequences of what may have broken.

Bernard appears to calm himself by planning how he'll address what his experience tells him is likely to be wrong. I don't want to believe that the shocks are gone again, but don't know what else could be causing Roxanne to want to drag her behind on the pavement. My imagination gallops through the valley of infinite disasters with me in tow.

We arrive early at the first passage control, thankful it's a parking lot with plenty of flat surfaces for jacking up a car. Out comes the cheerful, cherry-red, new jack from the trunk. Bernard sets it up in front of Roxanne's right rear tire. He starts pumping. The jack's handle is flimsy and immediately bends. Roxanne rises centimeter by centimeter. Bernard glances up at me. It's hot in the parking lot and beads of sweat are already dripping down his cheeks and neck. Finally, the jack has reached full extension, and it becomes clear that, regardless of the blithe promises on the packaging, this jack does not have the reach it's supposed to have. Our lovely, lightweight jack is stretched to capacity, yet it barely creates enough clearance for Bernard to slide under the chassis on his back. There's no room for him to lift his arms when under there, let alone wield any tools.

I stand next to him. Though I look for all the world like a relaxed navigator guarding the tool bag as usual, I can feel my teeth grinding and inside my pockets my hands are balled into fists. I just know that whatever's wrong won't be simple to fix, not here in the middle of nowhere. That, plus the thought that the flimsy Russian jack might collapse, sending our overloaded car smashing onto Bernard's head, is making me anxious. Not wanting to add my unconstructive agitation to Bernard's cares, I keep my mouth shut and paste a grimace on it that I hope will fool people into thinking I'm smiling.

Bernard wriggles back out from under the car, sweat pouring from his face, his collar soaked, his shirt pitted by gravel. "Broke the shock absorber mount again," he tells me. It's the sixth time it's happened. In a sense, I'm relieved that this will be just another routine repair. On the other hand, I can feel aggravation building, as the loss of the shock absorber yet again makes a long day even longer. Even more irritating, while other crews have managed to execute complicated repairs to their engines out of nothing, mending major breakages like blown head gaskets and bent tie rods, we have failed to secure a proper fix for something far more simple.

Bernard heaves a sigh of frustration. "We need to find a ramp or a pit. Something I can drive the car onto and get underneath to remove it." We give the surrounding dirt lot a quick once-over. It's a simple affair, just a large parking area where long-haul truck drivers can pull off for a rest or refreshment. There's no fuel here, no service bay, no mechanic.

So we leave, hoping to find a place down the road where Bernard can work on the car. To our surprise, within ten kilometers we do indeed spy a ramp, just like the one we found in Khovd, Mongolia. This one's at the back of what appears to be a deserted auto repair shop. All the windows in what used to be the shop are broken, lethal fragments jutting from the window frames, shards scattered on the ground. Trash wafts through weeds choking for sunlight among the pavement cracks. There are no crowds here. There's no one here at all. By now we have so much experience with shock absorbers that we make quick work of removing this one. Then Bernard turns to me and says what I've been dreading to hear for the past two weeks: "I couldn't see this back at the checkpoint, but here it's obvious."

"No, no, no," I beg silently. "I don't want to hear this."

"I don't think the leaf spring will hold up much longer."

I can tell you now that a leaf spring is part of what keeps a car's rear end from bouncing uncontrollably up and down and sideways. It keeps the car straight, and gives the passengers that comfy feeling that they and their vehicle are all going in the same direction. Back then I didn't exactly know what would happen if the leaf spring gave up, but I'd faked knowing for so long that I couldn't bring myself to ask for details. Ignorance had been bliss. Until now.

Inching the car down off the ramp, we bump over the lip of the deserted lot onto the highway. That's all it takes. After 4,400 miles on washboards, through sand bogs, down outrageous inclines, over rocks and holes, after whatever the world's roads could throw at us, the leaf spring gives out on a simple curb. There's nothing dramatic about it. One second Roxanne handles normally, the next she acts like two halves crabbing down the highway, with her front and back ends wanting to go in separate directions.

Instead of heading down the road toward the day's destination of Kazan, Bernard turns back toward the passage control. Gone is any pretense of things being OK. The gravity of our situation is painfully apparent. Despite his relentless optimism, the best he can muster now is, "I think we can make it back. Then we'll see."

Bernard has a bottomless well of positivity to draw from. He's Mr. Can-Do. If he of all people is unsure about the future, where does that leave me? Absorbing the possibilities, my eyes expand like sponges while my lungs constrict to the size of a pea. Even though I have felt variations on a theme of pity and disdain for those who have quit or whose cars have broken beyond repair, I have also, secretly, longed to be one of them. Now I'm gasping and staring, realizing my wishful thinking may be about to come true. Except that with an early end a real possibility, I find that more than anything, I don't want it. That what's starting to matter more is to finish what I started.

Within the fifteen minutes it takes us to retrace those ten kilometers, while I simmer in my nauseating anxiety, Bernard formulates a plan. "Look over there," he points toward the row of empty big rigs parked behind the Rally checkpoint. "Maybe one of them's going our way. Go get us some ice cream." Bernard's in his element now. When calamity strikes, he gets stronger and more assured, and somehow he finds a little space for me in that, a little job that gives me a necessary place in the ultimate success of his plans. I love having a worthwhile task on which the success of the whole depends. Right now, the success of the whole depends upon ice cream. I'm delighted to be in charge of getting it.

I emerge from the sweltering, sour-smelling restaurant across from the passage control, lime green and cherry red Popsicles already starting to melt. Squinting in the sun's glare, I see Bernard standing by a new-looking vehicle transport truck, one that typically has ten new cars strapped double-decker fashion on its bed. Only this one is empty. A glimmer of hope appears amid my glowering thoughts. Waving me over, he points to the stocky blond driver in oddly short shorts, who's standing proudly next to the truck cab. "Mikhail here is going to Moscow."

"Moscow? Really?" I squeak, handing Bernard the cherry Popsicle so it drips all over his fingers rather than mine.

An hour later, our car is strapped securely on the transport frame and we are cozily ensconced with Mikhail, me on the passenger seat, Bernard hunched over on the sleeper bed behind us. Our outrageous good fortune continues as we discover that Mikhail runs a no-smoking vehicle. What looked to be a disaster has turned into a proper adventure. Never mind that the truck seat has no suspension and that my back is aching within an hour of our start. Who cares that Mikhail and I have exhausted our meager vocabulary in each other's language after four minutes. We're on our way to Moscow, and we don't have to do the driving.

Several hours pass before we stop at a roadside stand for a Russian fast food lunch of shashlik: tiny hunks of lamb succulently barbecued on a small coal brazier, served on a heap of stewed onions and peppers. The juices drip down my chin and seep through the flimsy paper plate. It's the best meal I've had in Russia since we entered Siberia seven days and 2,300 miles ago. Later that afternoon, Mikhail pulls over near a group of women squatting next to little baskets of berries. He buys us a sack of the jewel-like strawberries picked in the nearby woods, waves off our attempts to repay him, and says with his limited English that the harvest won't last much longer. They're so rarely available he always stops for some. Back on the road, the three of us snack on berries, our fingertips staining red, and I toss our last pack of biscuits on top of the glove box to add to the feast.

Ten hours after leaving the passage control, Mikhail turns into a magnificent truck stop, complete with a new motel, a large self-service restaurant, and at least one hundred darkened trucks parked like tinned sardines in the lot behind the motel. Bernard and I stumble down from the cab, two rag dolls stupefied from the long, bouncing drive. Mikhail, who's as sprightly now as he was when we started, and who does not seem to react to the chilly air despite his tiny shorts and skimpy T-shirt, leads us into the motel foyer, a stark, efficient affair from which room keys are dispensed but little else. He chats up the concierge, motioning at us with his head. It seems he tells the concierge we are honored travelers and must have their best room, because when she shoves a gray rate sheet across the desk and points, her finger reveals that ours is the highest priced accommodation they have.

Somewhat slumped with relief that we're no longer in the truck, we signal that any old bed will do, as long as it's not moving; that we really don't need their most expensive suite. Mikhail stiffens and shakes his head. We offer to pay for his room, too, but he indicates that he will be sleeping in his truck, end of discussion. The set of his shoulders is indication enough that he will take offense if we don't treat ourselves to the best the place can offer, so we stagger up two flights of stairs and down a long hallway lined with black and purple carpet. Our accommodation turns out to be the truck stop honeymoon suite, a room so large, with such voluminous blood red velvet brocade curtains, that we burst out laughing. Velvet paintings of Russian monuments adorn the walls, an onion dome here, a triumphal arch there. On the bed is a plush burgundy coverlet, which, when flung back, reveals a fleece tiger print quilt. Two table lamps complete the Victorian safari brothel effect, managing to cast a meager buttery glow through their dense maroon fringed lampshades, leaving much of the cavernous red room in darkness. No matter. This is better than we ever expected.

We break open a bottle of warm juice, toast our unexpected good fortune, and share a handful of smashed cookie crumbs. Then we pull back the tiger spread and collapse into bed. Tomorrow we'll be in Moscow.

Ballet

MOSCOW

We have a rest day in Moscow, one which I expect to spend as usual, getting oil on the soles of my shoes and lending moral support to Bernard in the begrimed bay of another repair shop. Much to our surprise and my personal joy, the mechanic and the shop owner where Roxanne will undergo major suspension surgery refuse to let us do any of the work. "No, no, you go rest, enjoy Moscow," they say. Like fussing babushkas, they hustle us out of the shop with promises to call if they have questions. That's how, on Day 23, having driven through China, Mongolia, and all of Siberia, a miracle occurs. We finally have a day together to wander around.

It feels like a first date. We amble through Red Square arm in arm, admiring the jewel-like onion domes of Vasily Cathedral, now so garishly painted it reminds me of its copy at Disneyland. We stand rapt inside a Russian Orthodox church listening to a mass sung in rich, ancient harmonies. Overcome with the beauty of the singing, I succumb to one of my spiritual moments, lighting slender beeswax tapers for each member of my family. Since I don't pray, I make a wish that each should get whatever his or her heart desires, and hope that will suffice. I also make a wish for Bernard and me, that this new level of trust and companionship we're finding in each other will continue to grow. That seems a worthy outcome for this deeply exhausting, difficult journey.

"We're in Moscow, Bernard, home of the Bolshoi Ballet! I can hardly believe it," I exclaim. "Let's see if they're performing." Bernard isn't into cultural performances. He didn't grow up going to ballet, concerts, and theatre the way I did. In all our years of marriage, I don't even need one finger to count the number of times he's suggested we go to a play or concert, though he's usually agreed to accompany me when I've bought tickets for an event. We've developed an unspoken agreement that we each get to have our likes and dislikes, and that feels mature and proper to me. This is an unusual circumstance, though: a day free in Moscow in the middle of an epic trip. More than ever I want to go out. I imagine that more than ever Bernard will want to stay in and be peaceful. My glimmer of hope fades almost as soon as it appears. What am I thinking? This is the Rally, where magic does not happen. Just as I know that he will say no, I also know I am too fatigued to put up an argument. I sigh to myself at the inevitable, just as he says, "Of course, ma cherie, if it'll make you happy."

I hadn't realized candle lighting would work so fast.

In further tribute to the power of candles, our hotel concierge secures us two tickets for the ballet. Realizing we will be exposing ourselves to a world beyond similarly dirty Rally crews, we both go through some ugly duckling moments, clawing through our duffels for something proper to wear for the occasion. I wish I had a dress and high heels with me, something appropriate for a hall as storied as the Bolshoi Theatre. There's a limit to what candles can do though, so I settle for one of my least wrinkled slacks and a reasonably clean shirt. The bathroom washcloth serves to push the dust back into the crevices of my walking shoes, but not even a magic wand can transform them into Manolo Blahniks. It'll have to suffice.

On our way to the Bolshoi, we stop for a drink and pre-ballet snack at a small, elegant hotel. We're feeling special, giddy about finding a place where the two of us can be alone. Just as our bill is brought to us, we hear a man's voice calling "Bernard." It's James, who bounds up the steps to where we're sitting, seeming uncommonly pleased to see us. "Have a drink with me," he enthuses.

"Yes," Bernard says. "Yes, we'd love to. Come, join me. Tell us, what are you doing here?"

"I'm staying here."

"You mean you're not at the Rally hotel?" I blurt, as nonplussed as I was when I heard his plane was bringing in spare parts. In thinking about it, I realize there's no rule that states it's a requirement to stay in Rally organized lodging. It's just simpler that way. Our hotel in Moscow is a relic from the Intourist age, that travel agency founded in 1929 by Stalin and staffed by KGB agents. It's designed to house 3,000 guests a night and is so faded it clearly accomplished that mission for decades without respite or renovation. Though the KGB provenance makes bugs in the phone a possibility, the place is such that it feels more probable we'd find bugs—the biting sort—in the mattress.

"No," James says. "Those hotels are fine. I just prefer this one. Why don't you stay here, too?" It's easy to see why James has chosen this place. A clue to its exclusivity are the Maybachs and Maseratis parked in front, half-million dollar cars that are the property of oligarchs who exit the hotel wearing Raybans, regardless that it's nighttime. Every one of them sports an oligarchess on his arm, slim, strikingly beautiful, and fabulously dressed. The staff here is discreet, polite, there when you need them, vanished when you don't. At the Rally hotel, the laundry operation is so inefficient that, when garments haven't been returned the night before our departure, security guards break into the room of one team and yank the driver out of his bed, enraged by his earlier demands for his clothes. They then slam him up against the wall and, while he's dangling from the fist encircling his neck, explain to him the niceties of Russian laundry. Other teams on that floor, hearing the commotion, stage a protest in the lobby in the wee hours of the morning, with one Rally driver stripping naked and parading around the lobby to emphasize the need for clean clothing and its speedy return.

I'm dazzled at the plethora of good things coming my way. First, ballet tickets. Now an invitation from James. It hasn't escaped me that, ever since Novosibirsk, James has been seeking out Bernard's company. I've seen the two of them together many evenings, engrossed in conversation. When I join them I wind up talking to one of James's teammates, but I can still overhear smatterings of politics, helicopters, airplanes, wine, and cars coming from their direction. Bernard and I are now torn as to which group to sit with: the first group of Robert, Maddy, Sybil, and the rest with whom we're comfortable, or the second group of James, Matthieu, and cohorts, whom we're just getting to know. It's a dilemma I never expected to find myself in.

Explaining to James that we have ballet tickets, we stroll to the famous hall through a cold drizzle, the bubbling murmur of voices from an excited crowd crescendoing as we approach. Entering the warm glow of lobby lights, I see a delicate misty shawl of water droplets spread over my shoulders, sparkling like diamonds.

Russia is all about officialdom, and at the Bolshoi the aisle ushers take their jobs seriously. One of these stout ladies scrutinizes our ticket as if it's a counterfeit hundred dollar bill, wrinkles her nose at it and at us, and escorts us to our perfect seats in a dress circle box.

The lights have dimmed and the orchestra taken up the first few notes of the overture to the first ballet, *Carmen*, when the usher brings in two more people. The first is a portly matron in a dress meant for someone half her size. The other seems to be her daughter, who, coincidentally enough, is half her size. The box, though, is already full. As they look around for somewhere to sit, others in the box seem to recognize them and a polite whisper rustles behind us, like dry leaves in the fall wind.

Bernard, gentleman that he is, immediately offers the matron his seat. She misunderstands his gesture and stands like a stout tree, rooted in place. He then misunderstands her stolid refusal as a preference to stand. Only after he sits again does she make herself comfy—on his lap. There she nestles for the entire performance, her massive bosom obscuring most of the ballet, unless Bernard wishes to lean his cheek against the sofa cushion of her left breast. Not to be outdone, I offer the half-size woman a corner of my seat, which she is small enough to squeeze into without overwhelming me.

After the last curtain call, everyone stands, including Bernard, much to my relief. Toward the end I'd been fearing that two hours of unbudging Russian heft might have flattened him like Road Runner on a bad day.

Handshakes and hugs all around, and the two women depart. Only then does my seat neighbor explain they are the mother and daughter of the orchestra conductor, and they're off to congratulate him backstage. Everyone around us exudes pleasure that we behaved so well with two such honored guests. Bernard is relieved not to have any pressure from me to discuss the performance. After all, he really couldn't see a thing.

Going Solo

ST. PETERSBURG

When we arrive at our immense hotel in St. Petersburg, towering above the shores of the Gulf of Finland, we're immediately confronted by Gustav. He sees me and grabs me. "Tomorrow, on our rest day, I would like you to take Laure around the city." He's not even bothering to ask. I look to Bernard for help and say, loud enough for Bernard to hear, "I'm so sorry Gustav. We need to work on our car tomorrow."

Gustav's having none of it. "She'll be waiting for you in our room."

Bernard, ignoring my beseeching eyes, thinking he's supporting my ususal desire to see what's around, takes his side. "Yes, Dina. You're going out anyway. You'll enjoy the company." As Gustav walks away, I say to Bernard, "I can't do this. I can't speak French all day to someone who's depressed. It's Gustav who should go around the city with his wife. You've got to get me out of this."

My long hours in repair shops have given me more than just an opportunity to study the fine print embossed on each wrench. I've also discerned the patterns of other Rally crews. Who helps out, who works alone. I've had plenty of time to ponder what I see.

There's an interesting distinction between male teams and couples. With the former, the pair arrives at the repair shop, works on the car together, and drives out (usually) at day's end. With the latter, the husband appears at the repair shop, digs around for his tools in lonesome solemnity all day, perks up happily when someone—usually me—brings him a bite to eat, and returns to the hotel to find his wife refreshed and invigorated from a day out with the girls. Except, that is, for Gustav's wife. She seems so out of her element, so isolated, that she can't find her way toward human contact.

Then there's me. Call it loyalty, call it stupidity, I cannot abandon Bernard and the weakened Roxanne. I surprise myself by this, because in our past life, in the period pre-Rally, this was not my way at all. Back then, I easily did what I liked, figuring if Bernard needed me, he'd say so. That was my approach when the Rally began. I was all about the journey, and Bernard was all about the day's goal. Now, the Dina who'd ditch Bernard seems like another person. When it comes to doing what's necessary to keep Roxanne moving, I'm with Bernard all the way. Bernard, too, is morphing. He's seeing the benefits of changing his mind from car matters, even if it only happens once he's parked the car and even if it's only for an hour.

I've been developing a new philosophy these past weeks, which I haven't been able to articulate very well. It's something like, if we are to enjoy the good times together, then we have to go through the bad together. It strikes me as unsportsmanlike to be along for the ride and then leave Bernard alone to put in hard labor trying to keep Roxanne going. Though I'm still no star mechanic, I am good, and getting better, at extracting the right tools, offering moral support, persuading the boss to assign us a mechanic or a welder. I'm also accomplished at ordering lunch. I'm ready to stake a claim that this has importance and meaning beyond the mere actions.

Bernard has had a chance to see me try hard to change myself, while accepting that some of my worst personality traits are here for good. Take, for instance, a few days ago at a hotel, where I spent a half-hour in loud confrontation with a desk clerk. As I argued for a different room, tears of frustration turned my eyes red and my cheeks splotchy. Bernard, meanwhile, took refuge in the bar, hoping that mere distance would dissociate him from the strident complaining person that was me at that moment. We don't talk about this side of me. What I am learning, though, is that it's OK to forgive myself, even when I've embarrassed us both. Because while Bernard's been drinking, I've gotten us a better room. Yes, I'm still keeping score.

Despite all this, St. Petersburg's my last chance to see something of Russia, because our next stop will be Tallinn, the capital of Estonia. Bernard and I discussed this in friendly fashion during the interminable 455-mile drive north to St. Petersburg from Moscow. Because Bernard does rational, not emotional, I extracted the following from my play book. "I need a break," I tell him. "I just don't think I can spend another rest day with the car. Of course I will if it'll really help, but it seems to me nothing much is wrong with Roxanne now, at least nothing that we can fix." This sounds clear and objective to me. I know it's also a tad defensive, but after twenty-four days on the road, we've made it through more dicey situations than this.

"Sure. You should see St. Petersburg. I'll check Roxanne. Don't worry about it."

When he gives me permission to go, I reverse course. "I don't have to, though," I dither. "Or maybe you'd come with me?" I look at him, imploring him to connect with me telepathically and read what my mind's saying: "Please, just ONCE reject the responsible course and come be irresponsible with me."

Bernard's no mind-reader. Rational doesn't allow for that. "No, I want to check a few things. You go ahead. Take the whole day. I'll be fine here."

Spending my one free day shepherding a distressed woman around St. Petersburg is beyond my ability. If I'm going to have freedom, it'll have to be on my own terms. I sneak out of the hotel, Bernard having agreed that, if he sees Gustav, he will tell him I'm off on an errand for the car. Nevertheless, when I leave the hotel my shoulders are not swinging with insouciance. It's more like toting a hundred-pound sack of potatoes on my back, so burdened am I by guilt. Nevertheless, I set out, determined to enjoy my day wandering St. Petersburg.

My plan is to romp around the Hermitage Museum and other parts of the Winter Palace, afterward inspecting whatever Russian Orthodox churches I come across. With no time to spare, I bypass the snaking line at the museum entrance by melding into a French tour group. I find myself wandering the museum aimlessly, the heavy antiquity on display making me feel ever more dark and gloomy. I decide eating will lift my spirits. The cafe in the museum's basement is filled with tables groaning under delectable gooey salads, ceramic platters of jewel-like beets and carrots, glass bowls of salty herring and smoked fishes with their attendant loaves of rye and pumpernickel bread, and of course the full array of goulashes, soups, potatoes (both latkes and mashed), and desserts. Even this appetizing spread can't stifle the needling voice of dismay that's been whining its mantra of "Shame on you," ever since I left the hotel. Innocent enjoyment is what I'm supposed to be experiencing, not this sense of delinquency that's dogging me.

Ditching the museum for the bright sunshine, I wait for the bustle of the city streets to work their usual magic, because the energy of any city is something I've always enjoyed. Now, it's all rather disorienting, too many tourists swarming about, everything big and vacuous. Really, what am I doing out here by myself? Isn't the whole point of this trip to stand shoulder to shoulder with Bernard against whatever comes?

Rooted amidst the hubbub, I seem to rise above the busy clamor, seeing myself far below, silhouetted starkly, like the martial statues in the Winter Palace courtyard. A ray of warm sun shines down, as if a brain-based janitor has stopped dusting inside my skull to pull back a corner of curtain to let more light in. Exactly what she hopes to illuminate I can't yet say, but I do feel a change, at best a modest permutation of my normal way of thinking. It's not an earthquake, more like a slight shifting of ground that alters my perspective. What I realize is that "Is Bernard with me?" or "Am I with Bernard?" aren't the right questions. Nor is it about "Is he better than me?" or "Am I better than him?" These questions aren't even relevant.

Stretching out my arm, I signal a cab to stop. A much dented, rusty jalopy pulls over. Though it's a shabby affair, I instantly feel more at home inside this vehicle than I did on the street. My enthusiasm on discovering Bernard in the car park is made all the warmer by the happiness of his smile when he sees me get out of the cab well ahead of my proposed late-afternoon return time. He's let me go. I've come back.

As fate would have it, Gustav wanders over shortly after I've returned. "What did you do today?" I ask him, to distract him from asking me the same thing.

"Laure and I went on a tour of the city," he says smugly. I couldn't be happier. I have no doubt that an afternoon enjoying St. Petersburg with her husband was exactly what Laure needed. "So now I will go work on my car. Perhaps we will see you at dinner," and he strides off in the direction of the car park on the other side of the hotel.

We nod noncommittally and, as soon as he's far enough away, we grab satchels from Roxanne and duck into a cab, peering behind to make sure no one's seen us. We've learned a quick lesson from James and have booked a room for ourselves in a hotel near the Hermitage. Emerging from the taxi with our little overnight bags, we hand them to a doorman who's more elegantly dressed than we are. For dinner, we indulge in a sampling of Russia's rarest caviars and small-batch vodka. I eat more black fish eggs and drink more fine liquor than I should, but I can't help myself. The two go together as naturally as chips and beer. Bernard matches me shot for shot, spoonful for spoonful. We finish off with a glass of champagne. It feels like vacation. It feels like we're just married.

Borders: Take Two

By the time we learned that the rest of the Rally was held up at Ivangorod, Russia's border with Estonia, we were already cruising Estonia's gorgeous coastline. The air was fresh, tangy with salt from the Baltic Sea. While the rest of the Rally set up tents in the border parking area, took out sleeping pads, and, as Sybil reported later, did yoga on the tarmac, alternately meditating and shouting at scandalized Russian border officials, we breathed the air of the free. Russia was behind us. We swept down a sunflower-lined Estonian byway, rounding a bend to discover fields of deep blue cornflowers. A winding dirt lane crooked a finger and beckoned us past Hansel-and-Gretel cottages with brick chimneys. Some chimneys sported large nests, a bristling collection of branches in the middle of which stood a stork, often with its long bill pointed into the nest where perhaps chicks were feeding. We were so filled with nameless joy that we giggled like embarrassed school kids. Whisked along as if Roxanne were a magic carpet, we slid from buttery sunlight through deep, peaceful shade under a gothic archway of trees. It was enough to give us religion, so starved were we for ease and beauty.

We had time. Time to park in a simple village and stroll, hand in hand, to the pebbly seashore. I gazed across midnight blue waters to the infinite horizon, the sun warming my skin, its heat slowly, resolutely, thawing my spirit. It felt like I'd been holding my breath for weeks, and now, finally, I allowed myself to exhale. "Look Dina, we can buy a sandwich," Bernard said, pointing out a nearby kiosk. "And a drink, too!" Under other circumstances, we'd have turned our nose up at the cellophane-encased, dry sliced bread assemblage on display. Now it struck me as a veritable smorgasbord of possibilities. Ham? Cheese? Salami? With tomato and lettuce? Even a citrusy Orangina? Nothing could be more exquisitely savory. We shared sips and bites, sitting on a triangle of green grass in front of the local World War II memorial. We were blissfully unaware of how truly fortunate we were.

It began as an ordinary day. After two weeks hard driving we are almost through with Russia. Not interested in dallying, Bernard and I head for the border post as early as our need for a good night's sleep will allow. Happily dispensing the last of our rubles to gas up, we follow signs down a narrow, sloping road designed to funnel cars single file into the immigration control area of the border between Russia and Estonia.

We're not the only ones with this plan. The organizers are in front of us. We spy them just as they're making a rapid U-turn, spurting dust from their tires in their haste back up the hill. Words fly out their window like shreds of litter as they tear past. I grab at scraps which I think are "closed," "guard," "back," plus curses. These are words that might make an intriguing haiku on the refrigerator door, but with a schedule that spells out that a hundred-plus cars will cross the border that morning, and with Russian facilitators to handle the bureaucracy, they make no sense at all.

So we disregard them, continuing our sedate roll toward the checkpoint in question. "If need be we'll just crash the barrier and continue on," the brave, new, desperate-to-be-gone-from-here me says.

"Or we could claim faulty brakes," Bernard offers, in a tone that conveys he's checked them and knows they're perfect.

Generally I leave it to Bernard to do the innocent and friendly bit. Today, the guard is on my side of the car. I can see him peeking at us through the smudged window of his flimsy wood shack. He doesn't do any of the things that a guard bent on turning us back would do, like jump to his feet, shout at us, or point threateningly up the hill. If this is a sign, I'm going to take it as a good one.

I thrust my arm out the window, passports in hand, offering him access to our most precious documents. Tentatively, he steps out and peers at what I hold, as if it were a Faberge egg. Then he stares like he's seeing men from the moon. Perhaps he's thinking, "*Nyet, nyet, nyet.* Boris not raise bar. Supervisor very angry for use personal judgment." I wonder fleetingly whether what we're doing could be a shooting offense, then dismiss that as the product of one too many spy movies, not present-day reality. Besides, this guard is dressed in his warm weather uniform, just a buttoned-up shirt tucked into his stiff, pressed army trousers. I can see he has no gun on him. I shout "*Dobroye utra,*" which is "Good morning" in Russian, followed by "Passports," which I waggle at him for illustration, and "Border?" which I embellish by pointing at the gate. My very pores ooze compliance.

With a sharp jerk he pulls his beaked cap tighter onto his close-cropped head, does an about face and strides officiously away from me, back to the sanctuary of his ticky-tacky bunker. "We're sunk," I think. Just before he gets there, he jabs an electric button and the barrier floats up. Then he slumps into the old chair that's against the shack wall, relic of someone's once-fancy dining room, his face impassive, gloved hand raised in a curt wave.

Turning a blind corner we find ourselves at the actual border checkpoint, facing four glass booths in which passport control officials should be perched. They're empty. Our decision to arrive at the border early has been fortunate. There are no other cars around. Leaving Bernard to keep Roxanne company, I trudge the twenty yards to a building signed Immigration Control. One of the things I dread about border crossings is the endless queueing. The shuffling forward foot by foot drives me crazy, as does the stern official who won't make eye contact with anything that can talk back. Like me.

Inside, it looks like I'm first in line. In fact, empty desks show no sign of having been used recently for anything, official or otherwise. Conversation will be at a minimum here. It's so deeply deserted that my Vibram-soled shoes make loud squeaking echoey sounds on the highly polished floor. On the one hand, I'd like someone to know I'm here. On the other, I'd prefer it weren't my shoes that gave me away. I flinch when a door slams; a harsh voice shouts at me. A man has come in, clearly an official by virtue of his agitated voice and his uniform, and he's flinging Russian words at me in a tone sharper than I'm used to. I'm in trouble, I think. I hope Bernard got a good look at my back, because that may be the last he sees of me.

I scurry toward the official in a slight crouch that's meant to convey an agreeable disposition. He doesn't haul me away; instead of handcuffing me, he holds open the door and shoos me back to the car. Following me a few steps, he gives a tightlipped smile, points to a side door, and says, "Chai." To which I am about to give the polite response, "Yes, I'd love a cup of tea," when Bernard interjects—discreetly of course—"Dina, they're on tea break."

Within ten minutes, we're in business, with four uniformed officers, energized by chai and biscuits, ready to give us their full attention. Which we hope will be a good thing. First, we must get through the dance of where exactly to park Roxanne while we do paperwork. Bernard drives forward, a guard prances around on a white line, others stomp about behind us flailing arms in some ancient Cossack signaling ritual. Bernard reverses till Roxanne is behind the line and then gets out of the car. More prancing and flailing. Finally, everyone's satisfied with Roxanne's and Bernard's position relative to the magic stripe, and I am permitted to approach the booth.

A good-looking woman in her forties glances up at me. Her blonde hair is swept into a fashionable French twist, and she wears her military uniform with flair, collar turned up, white shirt open at the neck, small gold cross visible at her throat. If I have the option, I always choose a woman official over a man. My rationale is there'll be some element of empathy from which to negotiate. The opposite usually is true. In most countries, women still have to outdo men when upholding the letter of the law and their position. They're tougher and stricter, less inclined to cut you slack. Still, I can't suppress my inner "You go, girl!" when this woman stretches her manicured hand through the window for passports, car registration, car insurance, and Russian permits. She's got my business.

On the cubicle desk in front of her are an old computer and a pad of forms. The forms themselves are in Cyrillic, which I can't read, but in the long months before the Rally, I have at least taught myself how to count to one hundred in Russian, how to say the niceties of civil society such as hello, yes, no, good morning, thank you. I also know a few helpful words like eggs, soup, and goulash, but I don't expect I'll find a use for those here.

"*Dobroye utra*," I say encouragingly. This startles her to such an extent that she appears to wonder whether her pre-work pick-me-up really was just chai. She considers my smile, flushing from below the collar of her official white blouse, then drops her head to return to the endeavor confronting her. I'm heartened whenever I see her write on the form, which happens twice. After an hour, most of the form is still worrisomely blank. I practice my breathing lessons and tell the angry, impatient side of me to go back to bed.

By now, about a quarter of the Rally has entered the border parking area behind us. It's jammed to capacity, with more cars in a growing line that stretches up the hill. The officials are not delighted about this, especially the one in charge of all things sidewalk. He's bounding off in different directions, sweat stains visible as he flings his arms like a traffic cop getting electric shocks, trying to persuade people to park properly and respect his white line. His agitation doesn't bode well for those to come. Since I've already said good morning and smiled at him, the job of soothing seems to be mine.

"Is there a problem?"

"Da!" he says. "People. Too many. Must wait in cars. You tell them, please." I convey this to the first crews to relay to the cars behind. They ignore me. It doesn't take a religious revelation to know this border crossing is not going to go smoothly. Irritation is spreading through the ranks like a sniffle in a kindergarten.

Something must be done to break the impasse between documentation and officialdom. At the risk of revealing the obvious, I stick my hand through the window to point at my passport number and do the one thing I can: repeat my passport number to her in Russian. "*Dva, chitire, dva, shest, vosem . . .*"Jackpot! Finding what's what on my US passport has been her sole hang-up. She graces me with a warm "*Spaseba*," followed by asking if I speak Russian.

"Nyet," I have to reply, and I mime that I know only a few words, such as numbers. She steps her finger down the lines of the form, and at first hesitating, then with encouragement, I guess at what needs to be filled in, pointing it out to her on my passport. In short order, she's finished. A few slams of her inked stamp and we're cleared to go. A further cursory survey of the tightly packed goods in our trunk follows. Fifty yards separate us from Estonia. I am so eager to be there, that as I return to the car I unconsciously tilt forward, like a runner chesting toward the finish line. Bernard puts Roxanne in first gear, and we creep away from Russia to where Estonian guards lean against their barriers smoking. They are nonchalance personified. As we approach, they flick ash on the ground, give the barrier a lethargic swing upward, and wave us through without interrupting their conversation.

Behind us we've left 250 people on the wrong side of the border, hot, cramped, impatient, and most of them not knowing Russian numbers. The Russian facilitators, who should be helping sort out the difficulties, seem to have taken their money and run. The organizers have been released right after us, and they, too, head into Estonia without a backward glance.

The 125 other Rally cars are log-jammed for eleven hours inside the Russian border. Most get to Tallinn, Estonia's capital, so late in the evening that I don't hear the stories about the border delay till the following night. I can just imagine the scene. When you've been doing the lotus position in a parking lot for that long, the niceties of benign acceptance can understandably give way not just to sore knees, but to fury of epic proportions. However, as the peaceful sun of post-Iron Curtain Europe shines on us in flowery Estonia, I know none of this. What I do know is that the day's control points are strangely empty. That for once we make them on time. That there are more time trials on the day's route. It's time to have some fun.

Race Bunny

TALLINN-RIGA-VILNIUS

Bernard slams on the brakes, and Roxanne, who loves momentum, slows to a halt in a cloud of silver powdery dust. She doesn't stop on the proverbial dime, but it'll do. My window is already open, so I can fling my arm out, timecard in hand, without losing a precious second. Holding it to his computer timer, the marshal reports, "Two minutes, thirty-nine seconds. Well done, you two. Ready to have another go?" A lithe Estonian girl, her blond hair wreathed in blue and pink wildflowers, hands me a bouquet. "Welcome to Estonia. Did you enjoy our rally course?"

"Loved it!" I tell her, cackling so hard I can barely speak. "Absolutely loved it. So, yes, YES," I turn to the marshal. "We're definitely doing another tour." I don't hesitate when I say this, because on an endurance rally noted for its particularly long, often monotonous days, time trials are the burst of fireworks at a picnic, the spicy bite of jalapeño in a bland bean burrito. This is the most fun I've had in weeks, and I'm not going to miss a one. I feel alive and in the moment, car damage be damned.

I've come to love time trials. In part, this is because they are so well-defined, with their designated start, short, specific route, and defined end. Just the notion that we can let loose for a few minutes fills me with the same feeling of reckless abandon I felt when I first tried magic mushrooms in college. I did a lot of laughing on that occasion, too. After weeks of ultra-cautious driving over terrain so vast it seems without end, taking blind curves or hairpin turns at top speed is a thrill, and the straightaways on which Bernard presses Roxanne's gas pedal to the floor make me want to shriek with joy. Time trials are furiously fast, and, as far as I'm concerned, always over too soon.

Bernard is passionate about time trials, cramming as they do a banquet of skill tests into a tiny package. They also remind him of his younger days as an automotive hell-raiser. All this is to be expected. The shocker is me. The fact that I'm his equal in getting addicted to the thrill is a morale boost of the best kind. It includes both of us. If there's an option to run a course a second time, I am all for it.

Estonia, Latvia, Lithuania, and Poland are time-trial heaven, their curvy country byways and quaint scenery a driving nirvana. Each national auto club closes a network of lanes for our private enjoyment. Locals staff the entry points to explain to their neighbors that, sorry, it's not possible to get eggs at Farmer Sikorski's until after 3 o'clock. At the speeds we're moving, it'd be suicide for anyone or anything to be caught on the same roads as us.

By now, even my modest acumen in math has understood the time trial's simple formula: difficult terrain multiplied by maximum speed equals winner. I'm Terminator Ten, a fearsome navigating machine, my gaze swiveling from the Tripmeter, which displays incremental distance, to the route book, which gives details of each turn on the course. The changes are so close together, and maintaining speed is of such importance, that I am working as hard as Bernard to keep up with what's coming, and I'm as wrung out as he when we reach the finish line.

One day in Poland's Lake District, we wend our way down a shaded lane. The leafy branches of magnificent trees, whose stout trunks would take three sets of my arms to circle, form a cathedral ceiling above us. Crossing quaint villages, we traverse undulating farmland, past neat limestone houses where horses peer at us from behind trimly fenced hedgerows. Gardens are immaculate, happy vegetables and flourishing flowers bursting from chocolate brown soil. It's hard to believe this, too, was so recently under Communist domination.

Near the starting line for that day's time trial, I see a roadside shrine, one of those memorials that marks a spot where someone's died in a car accident. This one's small and has been there a long time. The pale blue paint on its stucco sides is peeling. Faded plastic flowers offered by the bereaved adorn the ground in front. Bernard slows enough that I can see a votive candle flickering inside as we drive by. I've noticed many such shrines along the way, a sign that either Poland's a staunchly Catholic country, or they're really bad drivers, or both.

On our first circuit, we make a respectable showing. It's a beautiful course, with the Gulf of Finland playing hide and seek between flaming yellow sunflowers. At one dramatic zigzag, we see another Rally car, rear wheels off the course, nose nuzzling the shrubbery like a hungry cow. For a nanosecond I'm dismayed, then I see the teammates sitting in the shade well away from the road. One lofts the OK sign above her head as we lunge by. A tow truck will have to extricate them. Till then they'll enjoy the best seats in the house. From there, we enter a pine forest, the dirt lane dappled in shadow, the air pungent with resin. As we fly by another competitor whose distraction ended their time trial before the finish line, I briefly loosen my grip on the handle to offer an apologetic wave. Then it's over.

Now that he knows the ins and outs of this track, Bernard is eager to do better the second time. We pull to the starting line, where I smile at the photographer from the village newspaper before handing over my time card. "Three, two, one, you're off!" Bernard mashes the accelerator pedal, I grab the door handle, my head flies backward, for all the world as if it wanted to wait for me at the starting line. Roxanne nearly snarls as she charges forward down the straight sandy track. On either side of us tall measured rows of green grass straitjacket the lane. We have 900 yards at top speed before our first turn.

We're at 70 mph when a hare darts out from the field and takes off down the road in front of us. "Rabbit on the course!" I shout. "Bernard, the route book says *nothing* about this!" Despite my navigator job, which I do take utterly seriously, I start chuckling. Soon we're both engulfed in full blown laughter, the deep bellyaching kind that brings tears to our eyes.

The richly planted fields leave no room to get around the bounding bunny. This is one panicked hare, and a panicked hare knows only one thing: keep going. His furry paws slap the ground, kicking up spurts of dust as he bounds down the track, trying to dodge the gargantuan blue bullet bearing down on him. For him it's hundred yard dash after hundred yard dash. Bernard downshifts to second gear; at maximum bunny pace we're constrained to 45 miles per hour, well below our top speed the first time around.

Not soon enough, the hare makes a desperate bid for safety, plunging off the lane into the tall grass. I imagine him lying on his back, panting and wiping his furry brow as Roxanne roars past. Within minutes we pull up to the finish, which is when the oh-shit handle above my door falls into my lap, victim of too many crazy turns. The marshal eyes us a bit suspiciously when our time comes in at double our first run.

"Have a spot of trouble on that one?" he inquires. My cheeks are streaked with tears, which the marshal thinks illustrate the agony of defeat. Bernard's face turns red as he wheezes with laughter. The marshal doesn't know what to make of this, but being a good sport, starts scrounging for reassurances for what he takes to be our devastation. "Good for you," he says, patting me on the shoulder. "It's all fun, isn't it? Time doesn't matter so much, does it?"

"Hare-raising, no?" I say to Bernard. I don't dare turn around as we drive off, howls of laughter wafting from our open windows.

Bonds

RIGA-VILNIUS-MIKOLAJKI-GDANSK

"Bernard," says James, when we arrive at our hotel in Mikolajki, Poland's Lake District. "I've found a delightful small hotel outside Gdansk for tomorrow. It's not the official Rally hotel. Much nicer. Charming. Lovely gardens. Good parking for the cars. We're all staying there. Join us. We'll relax. Do a celebration dinner. Perhaps you'd like to? Of course, no pressure. You and Dina talk about it. Think it over. But we'd love to have you." Is the man I now hear offering this flustered invitation the same one who so officiously chastised the Novosibirsk service manager three weeks ago?

"I'd love to go there, Bernard," I say. "Let's do it. James is right. We *do* deserve this." Ever since we abandoned the Rally hotel for our private delight in St. Petersburg, we've seemed to be on a different path from Nick, Sybil, Robert, and the others. While I'd been thinking our presence didn't much matter to anyone, in fact our absence was noticed. "Where were you guys in St. Petersburg?" Sybil asks me when we finally meet up in Tallinn after her harrowing hours at the Russian border. I detect a faint ring of accusation in her tone, which makes me feel a tad embarrassed to reveal what until that moment I'd considered our brilliant move.

"We treated ourselves to a little hotel, near those beautiful churches downtown," I tell her. I don't go into details, don't want to make too much of it.

She looks at me oddly. "With the James contingent?" she asks, trying hard to mask the incredulity in her voice.

"No, no. We didn't go *there*," I say, though I have no idea where "there" is. "We just wanted to have some time to ourselves. To reward ourselves a little . . ."

Sybil, being a genuinely kind person, looks at me with comprehension and says, "Oh, I get it. The two lovebirds!" Is it just me feeling self-conscious or is there a bit of a chill in the hug she gives me as she walks away? That day we drive to Riga, the capital of Latvia. When we see Robert and Maddy already at a table at dinner that evening, I go over to exchange our usual evening pleasantries. "So," Maddy says. "I hear you ditched us for better digs." Word travels fast in Rally circles.

"We're not good enough for you, eh?" Robert chimes in, with his big laugh, then clowns to Maddy, "Will you continue slumming it with me, darling?" Their voices are lighthearted, but when they don't ask us to join them I detect that it's not all in jest. It seems by making ourselves comfortable we've broken an unwritten Rally code, something they know about and we don't. And when, the next few evenings, we come upon Nick and Sybil with their old friends, though they do urge us to sit and we do take them up on it, we don't stay long. The sense of belonging that I had through Mongolia and most of Russia is gone. At first I'm saddened by this. I'm also perplexed, because if someone told me they'd found a wonderful hotel for a special night, I'd say, "Oooh, sounds great. Next time, tell me where it is so we can go there, too!"

By the time we're through Lithuania and into Poland, though, I've observed that the growing distance isn't directed at me; everyone seems to be going through the same metamorphosis. For weeks now it's seemed to be us against the world. Anyone who was on the Rally belonged; whoever was not on the Rally could not relate to the depth and breadth of our tribulations. That alone was enough to bind us even to Rally crews with whom we had rarely spoken. Now we're less than a week from Paris and it's becoming clear that everyone who's made it this far will make it to the end. People don't feel so dependent on, so bound to each other anymore. We're on good roads now, and though distances are correspondingly longer, because of the easy pavement driving, there are few breakdowns to contend with. When people work on their car at all it's to reapply whatever patches are holding their car together, rather than fixing a new problem. Now I no longer feel like a ship-wrecked soul, tossed by rogue waves, desperate for a hand to reach out and pull me to safety. Or if I do, then my life preserver, the thing that circles me and holds me up when I need saving, is Bernard. And me, him.

As distance grows between us and our earlier mates, the group that receives us with welcoming arms is Matthieu & Co., which is why when James issues his invitation, I'm more than pleased to accept. My response seems to gratify James. "Good. It's settled. We'll see you there." He seems happy to have us. I feel happy that he's happy.

The crunch of gravel under our tires as we approach the inn the next afternoon speaks volumes. It tells me of gracious living, rich foods served on delicate porcelain, wines in fine crystal, and soft white sheets of infinitely high thread count. Also, a massage. The gravel speaks the truth and the inn doesn't disappoint. I spend an hour on my stomach, having my rigid back muscles pummeled from a hard, board-like mass into a somewhat softer, board-like mass. Probably a hundred hours of massage is what'll be needed to return my tense shoulders and stiff neck to some semblance of normalcy. An ultra-long hot shower follows, and turning the faucet off is almost more than I can bear, so mesmerized am I by the continuous press of hot water on my scalp. When Bernard and I arrive on the flowered terrace, James bounds over with a hearty handshake. He's still formal with us, no hugs yet, but I understand that now and don't mistake it for brusqueness as I used to.

"Welcome, welcome," he says, as gracious a host as if we've arrived at his private residence. "Have champagne!" indicating with Coke in hand the perspiring ice bucket that chills a bottle of Dom Perignon. We do, and raise our glasses for the first of many toasts. "To us all," we say. "And to Paris."

True to his word, James has organized a feast for that evening. Ten of us sit round a damask-clothed table set with several tiers of Polish crystal and Dresden china. The center of the table is resplendent with a flower centerpiece dense with pink roses and sprays of orange and red lilies. I'm on James's right, Bernard his left. Though I'd always rather be seated next to Bernard, table chat not being my forte, I am honored. Wine flows. Platters heaped with roast vegetables, succulent lamb chops, fresh poached fish, and more are passed around. There's the clink of cutlery on china, the modest laugh of someone acknowledging a bon mot. It's all so dreamlike, the familiar faces scrubbed, shaved, and shining, women with pretty earrings and sparkling necklaces, men in wrinkled but clean, open-necked shirts. I have extracted my one white blouse, and Bernard has on one of his relatively unworn shirts. But the others seem to have opened a new suitcase or else raided the hotel's shop. Everyone looks refreshed. Though we all have permanent dark smudges under our eyes now, the expressions around the table are relaxed. As I sit, quietly savoring the exceptional meal, I look around the table and note Americans, Swiss, French, Dutch, Greek. And the one nationality we now all have in common: Rally.

Replete with a more sumptuous meal than any of us have eaten in a month, we waddle from dining room to terrace after dinner. The air is balmy and as we install ourselves on the deck chairs, frogs chirp in the trees around the garden. Espresso arrives in translucent porcelain cups, accompanied by crystal decanters of cognac, slivovitz, and Grand Marnier. Between the shivering leaves above, I can see Venus bright in the sky. James passes around Cuban cigars. I haven't seen him without one since we left Beijing, and still he has enough to share. Clearly the man has his priorities straight. Among my special secret pleasures is a love of smoking a cigar under the stars. I happily snip the one offered me, lifting it toward Bernard for a light.

That lull that some say is an angel passing over, when everyone is sated with a good meal and all conversation suddenly ceases, happens now. In the hush, I watch musky cigar smoke swirl about my head, as intoxicating as any liqueur. Without preamble, one of James' mates walks over and taps Hans on the shoulder. "Come," he says. He starts to whistle, a lilting, poignant tune of such ineffable longing I can barely keep from crying. Hans smiles and joins him on the patio. The two men, one handsome, swarthy with a shock of black hair, the other with his trademark frizzy blond halo and beatific grin, each sling an arm around the other's shoulder. Joined this way, they start to sway, then slowly, each raises his free arm to the side and snaps his fingers. They dip down on bent knee, rising on the other side with another rhythmic snap. It's Zorba-like, but not so. It's heartbreaking, passionate, joyous, and I know we all feel it. We band of brothers.

Finished?

POTSDAM-KOBLENZ-REIMS-PARIS

The warm midday air of Paris offers me its special mix of exhaust and perfume, wine dregs and baked bread. I struggle to inhale, can't get a deep breath, feel like I'm suffocating. It seems impossible to me that we are here, 400 yards from the end of the Rally.

The past few days have been idyllic. Firmly following our own route, checking in with the organizers only to confirm each evening that we're still alive, we've woven our way through the sparkling vineyards of the Moselle Valley, surprised an army guard at the camp where Bernard was stationed as a young artillery lieutenant decades ago, and spent a somber afternoon at World War I trenches around Verdun. There, acres of tall trees grow on moss-covered moguls, mute reminders of the bombardment that shattered lives and twisted smooth ground into a scarred and disfigured landscape.

As we drive, Bernard and I are largely silent, each caught in our own thoughts. It's not unpleasant, this being separate but together. I used to feel that if we weren't actively doing something together, then we were apart. I don't feel that anymore. I'm exhausted, yes. But that word doesn't begin to access the depths of mysterious mental numbness in which I exist, as if my brain were swaddled in thick, cushy strips of cotton. When I dig into it, I find the tight, twisty feeling that tied my stomach in knots for so much of the trip has faded. In its place is something else, like a melding of me with Bernard, that I haven't ever felt before.

Every evening we've shared a meal, either with Robert and Maddy, or Nick and Sybil, or James, Matthieu, and their group. The mood alternates from somber to euphoric. Everyone's edgy and worn. I can see how each person's mind has turned toward the wife, children, friends waiting to be reunited with them in Paris. Mine certainly has. We all know that we are now so close to the end that, even if a car breaks down it can still be trucked to Paris for the finale. As for us, unless we have an accident, we know we'll be driving into Paris on our own four wheels. Roxanne is in good shape, only thirsty, drinking more oil than normal. Bernard does a perfunctory check of the car at the end of each day, but he doesn't need me for that. I have a smidge of time for myself now. With an hour free one afternoon, I buy scarlet polish and paint my toenails. I find a pair of pointy soft leather flats in a simple shop. The nail lacquer is too bright, the shoes fashionable two years ago. Together, they make me feel peppier than I have in weeks.

On the morning of the final day of the Rally, I cradle the route book on my lap one last time, but I don't really need to use it. Bernard lived in Paris. He knows exactly where we are and how to get to the finish line. When we drive out of Reims around 9 AM, I imagine our personal cheering section having a nervous breakfast of croissant, soft-boiled eggs, and coffee at their Paris hotels. A couple hours later, as we cruise on the highway past smooth green hills, I see them making their way on foot to rue de la Paix. My cousins, with great foresight and some judicious greasing of palms, reserved the front section of an entire café for our forty-odd family and friends, so they'd all have front row seats for our arrival. At the first checkpoint in the 20th Arrondisement, we pull up behind James. Just like the entrance to Mongolia a lifetime ago, the organizer has us in a holding tank. He's going for maximum drama, releasing the more unusual old cars first so they can enter the finish area alone. He's proud of these cars, proud that his organization enabled all but eight of the cars that started at the Great Wall to reach Paris. He wants each of the seventy-, eighty-, and ninety-year-old cars to have its solo moment. That means we have a long wait ahead, since, as we have for the past 35 days, we're ready to go well before our appointed time. Bernard dashes to a bakery and returns with a carton full of savory pastries. We pass the quiches and baked brioche sandwiches, all still warm from the oven, from car to car.

Usually food soothes me, but I can't calm down. Waiting is excruciating and I'm jittery with anticipation, thinking about what those awaiting us at Place Vendome must be thinking. Matthieu has already left, then James is flagged through, and now, of the group, it's just Bernard and me standing curbside. We have so much longer to wait that I know by the time we get to Place Vendome they'll be gone, already off celebrating with their own families. We haven't even said goodbye.

Finally, it's our turn. The course marshal holds his radio close to his lips and says, "Car 84 is on its way." He turns to us with a smile. "Off you go, you two." Bernard steers Roxanne through afternoon traffic on Boulevard de la Madeleine. Shoppers and tourists swivel their heads to stare as we drive by. Already there's been a veritable parade of elegant old Bentleys, Lagondas, and Mercedes, enough to draw people out of the stores to stand gawking on the sidewalk. They know something's up. Perhaps they notice the battered, but still bright, yellow and red "Peking to Paris" license plate strapped to our front fender. Maybe this reminds them of an article they read that morning, about those who drove out of Beijing thirty-five days ago, following a 7,800-mile route last undertaken by cars in 1907.

We are less than five minutes from the finish. Bernard makes a right turn onto rue Daunou. Three more blocks to go. My skin feels tight, my eyes nervously restless. I want to have time somewhere in silence, to face the question that's been pulling at the corner of my mind for the past few days, like a new scab on fragile skin: What next?

Somewhere in this crowd is our personal cheering section of sisters, nephews, grandchildren, and friends from both sides of the Atlantic, here to wave us to the finish line. They have followed our trials through the organizer's daily reports, put pins in maps to mark our progress, been frantic on reading that our car was seen strapped to an otherwise empty long-distance hauler on its way to Moscow and then lost from contact for two days.

Bernard drives slowly, but even at a stately pace it doesn't take more than a minute to reach rue de la Paix. This is it, the last turn we will make on the Rally. Though he needs no instruction, I have to say it: "Turn right at the corner and straight on from there." Bernard turns the steering wheel, and Roxanne glides down the last stretch like she was born to it. One long block followed by a stubby one and we'll be in the broad, elegant plaza.

The hubbub subsides to slow motion. After thousands of rights and lefts, there are no more directions for me to give. I have nothing to do. For an eternal second I sit, quiet, waiting. Suddenly, I hear a joyous laugh, a French greeting hollered: "Eh voila! Ils sont la! Bravo, Bernard! Bravo, Dina!" More cheers and yells: "Voiture 84! Bravo, bravo!" In a daze I see Bernard's son running alongside our car, clutching his seven-year-old daughter by one hand, filming us with the other. She's still small enough to fit through the window and he lifts her up so I can pull her, legs first, onto my lap. My nephew zooms in, sticks his head in the open window to plant a kiss on my cheek. He's thoughtfully penned Car 84 all over his T-shirt, in case anyone might question his allegiance. My sister is running behind him, video camera trained on him, me, us, waving, cheering, her cheeks flushed with happiness that I am here and I am safe. Bernard's sisters dash to his side and clutch warmly at his shoulder.

Then it's over. A dense crowd jostles around the flag standard announcing PEKING TO PARIS FINISH LINE. The Rally secretary is on tiptoes, waving us forward. Her clipped British accent breaks through, instructing us to step out of the car, stretch across the top to shake hands. We do, grabbing at each other hard and not wanting to let go. We stand there a minute, dazed, smiling for the cameras. My sunglasses hide my tears. "We did it," I mouth to Bernard. "My god, we did it!" Then we're back in the car, bronze medal in hand. "Take your victory lap," the secretary tells us.

Bernard looks at me. "Where do we go?" he says.

"I don't know," I say. We drive slowly once around Place Vendome, Roxanne leaving her personal signature in the form of oil splotches on the historic cobblestones.

Suddenly, we're mobbed. I try to reach my sister for a hug. Others intrude between us, each eager to be recognized, to let me know they're thrilled to be here, to see me. They're smiling, happy, bursting with questions and congratulations. They grab at me, pull me close, and I can't get to her until I've gone through them.

In a disturbing way, our familiars feel like strangers. They're not of the Rally galaxy in which we've been living. There's now a yawning gulf between us and the rest of the world, even family. I feel like the Little Prince, stranded on my own strange planet, unable to comprehend what's happening elsewhere, wanting only to retreat to what I know. I go through the motions expected of me, squeal with delight, offer appropriately warm expressions of surprise or happiness or thanks to each. I imagine everyone wants to get close enough to touch the marvelous car that we've driven halfway around the globe. I invite them to sit in my seat, explain the gadgetry I used to navigate, show them what's in the trunk.

One cousin's little boy is overwhelmed by the commotion and starts to cry. In a breach of rally etiquette, someone cuts one of our stuffed animal talismans off Roxanne's front grille and gives it to him. Secretly, I know this little brown bear is one of the reasons we made it to Paris. Now it's in the hands of an eighteen-month-old who knows nothing of its significance, nor why he's been given such a stained and distressed stuffed animal. He cries harder. I know how he feels.

Yesterday in Reims, the capital of France's champagne country, we'd bought a special bottle to contribute to what I'd imagined would be our Place Vendôme festivities. I expected a reunion scenario with everyone bringing champagne, corks popping, spumes of bubbly erupting and drenching us all. I guess even after thirty-five days of imagination failures, I still hadn't learned. Our bottle is it. We eke it out in droplets, just enough for everyone to have a sip. Disappointment, then regret washes over me. Why didn't we buy more when we had the chance?

Through the dull haze of sound one thing comes into painful focus. I can't imagine any other routine than being in the car each day. Outside of the car, I no longer fit in. I feel naked, exposed, like a worm under a freshly upturned stone. I know that the ranch, my home, waits for me, as do all the friends who could not be here today in Paris, but I can't fathom returning to pre-Rally life and can't imagine what a post-Rally life will be.

I notice Bernard on the other side of the car, surrounded by a crowd of his siblings and children. Our tight cocoon, spun over the hardships of the past thirty-five days, ruptures just like that. I wonder if he feels as I do, bewildered by the commotion, longing suddenly for the quiet certainty we had in Roxanne: that I was by his side all day every day, and he was by mine. "Look at me," I want to shout, "Remember that I'm here," as I'm drawn one way and he's drawn another. I strain to see him as hands grip his shoulders and nieces tug on his shirt. Then his head turns, he searches for me and our eyes meet, just as they did more than two years ago on the courthouse lawn. There's no need to speak, even if our voices could be heard across the clamor and tumult of the crowd. Yes, we nod to each other, we will find a way.

Post P2P Blues

Back at the ranch, weeks pass and I find myself still sifting through the detritus of the Rally. Others thrill to the glory of what I've done, but I can't seem to. The amount of worrying I've done during the past thirty-five days has had an unpleasant aftereffect. It's worn me out. I'm a well-trained worrier, but this was more than even I was in shape for. It's as if I'd run a marathon after training half an hour on a StairMaster.

Like everything else I'd imagined before the Rally, my immersion therapy seems to have resulted in the opposite effect. I am not seeking out groups and being sociably chatty. Then again, I don't have to, because everyone in town approaches me instead. It turns out that for May, June, and part of July, we were the hottest thing in town since regular mail service. It didn't even matter that I'd sent only one email, and that from Moscow. The organizer's daily reports had made up for my silence. People read them every morning, along with blogs posted by a few other crews. "Have you heard the latest from the P2P?" our friends and neighbors asked each other. "Did you notice they've slipped in the standings?" they said, when unbeknownst to them we suffered the first of our many shock absorber problems. Someone even sounded the alarm, "They don't know where Dina and Bernard's car is!" while we were enjoying our impromptu truck ride to Moscow after Roxanne's leaf spring broke.

I find myself grumpily amused that, upon our return, I have 1,400 new buddies, all huggy and happy and hungry for the backstory no one else has been told. When well-wishers greet me with, "Gosh, it must have been a blast," I find I can only relate the hardships, can only talk about how difficult it was. I burst into tears without cause, and, even though I sleep extra hours to make up for what I missed on the P2P, when I wake up I think mostly about just going back to sleep. I'm not so far gone that my behavior doesn't disappoint and mortify me. To collapse after such an accomplishment . . . wouldn't that be rather contradictory?

Bernard shows signs of being embroiled in a similar struggle. He goes his separate way during the day, getting our hay crew settled in. Evidence that he's not happily in the swing of life comes out when he grouses to me about things he knows happen every hay season: equipment breakdowns; lending his tools and getting them back filthy; too much hay cut too soon, turned to acres of brown mush in the seasonal monsoon. We sit together at meals as we always have, but there's little conversation. The general silence in our house is more brooding than companionable. It's as if, without Roxanne around us anymore, we've each landed on opposing rims of the Grand Canyon, and, instead of walking down and trying to connect somewhere in the middle, we've turned our backs on each other and are walking away.

When I look at Bernard across the table, he seems small, distant, out of focus. He's going through the motions of ranch work on autopilot. I can tell his heart isn't in it. Usually a paragon of patience, he now has little. He snaps at me over ridiculous things, like why am I taking so long to put on my shoes and how could I forget to buy his favorite juice on my weekly food run. It's obvious to Bernard, too, that something's not right with me. A month after the Rally's end, instead of being out with the horses, I drag about the house, listless and unenthused. I match him for pettiness, chiding him about not fluffing both pillows on the bed and setting a sloppy table for dinner.

For over two years, preparations for the P2P have consumed all of our waking moments, and, for me at least, too many of my sleeping moments as well. Now it's over. It feels like we've crash landed, and the peace and natural beauty of the ranch are not enough to distract us from rehashing all the what-ifs of the Rally. What if Roxanne had been ready sooner? What if we'd been able to test her? What if we hadn't packed so much? What if Bernard hadn't careened off that rock? What if we'd thought of bringing spare steel to make new parts?

After six weeks of this nonsense, we start to talk about it. "You know, I was remembering this morning about our stay in Gdansk, at that beautiful inn. With James and the rest. That was wonderful, wasn't it?"

"Um hmm. Remember that meal? And the cigars? Hey, and when we reached Tsagaannuur, just before Siberia, how exhausted we were. Little did we know . . . . And when we gave Robert that bottle of Glenlivet? How his eyes lit up?!"

"Yeah, but they weren't quite so lit the next morning. I know, because I saw him before anyone else did."

"You did?"

"Well, remember that cup of coffee I brought you? I wanted to let you hang out in the tent so I brought him and Maddy a cup of tea."

"You woke him up? I didn't know about that." We're off, reminiscing about P2P high points, surprised and delighted to rediscover there are quite a few. After a while we both sit back, smiling, ruminating on how we've finally started to shrug off the obvious disappointments that for these past weeks have laid so heavily upon us.

Though it's just a fraction, the door is now open enough to let a slim ray of light enter. I revisit that door a few days later and give it another nudge. "You're going to think I'm nuts to say this," I start out one evening at dinner, while Bernard frowns into his salad. "But I miss the Rally." This is such a shocker that Bernard jerks his head up, a leaf of salad half way into his mouth. I can see he thinks I've lost whatever remained of my mind. I fumble for clarity. "Well, that's not essentially true. Of course I don't miss the Rally overall. But you know what I do miss? I miss that surge of drama I felt, wondering how I'd cope with each day's route instructions. I miss seeing something new each day. I even miss discovering what gas stations are like in each country. I also miss the time trials. God, I really *loved* them. Hard to believe, huh?" I stop here, momentarily lost in my recollections.

"I wish we could find something like that to do here. Just a time trial. For the fun of it."

It's astonishing to both of us that either would dare broach doing anything related to a rally again, let alone that we would associate any element of the P2P with the word "fun." In one way, it feels like too soon to be reliving the intensity of that experience. Then again, what's becoming clear is that there are big parts of the Rally that we both miss profoundly. And now the flood gates open.

"So, you know," I say, "We're here, we're home, and we're doing the usual things. But it's as if we're not together anymore. I *liked* being in the car with you. It was just you and me, and we were together all day, every day, figuring things out . . . I liked that."

Bernard looks at me, listening, and for the first time in weeks I feel us starting to reconnect. "You did?" he says, reaching for my hand and squeezing it hard. "I miss that, too. I miss *you*."

"I know. I loved that part of the Rally. That the car was the only place we had to be. And we both had roles to play. We did well at them, don't you think? And we didn't fight. It was just you and me, against the world. Kind of."

"Would you do another rally?"

"Another rally? Are you crazy? No way!"

"So what would you do?"

"Well, I don't know. As far as the Rally organization and having to do everything by their rules? That I don't miss, and that I'd never do again. *Ever.* Those other things we've been talking about, like driving together somewhere new? I think I'd like that."

A week passes, during which we both tussle with a nascent idea. Bernard offers the opener, again at the dinner table, since that's the only place where neither of us is distracted by something else. "Remember my drive around the world?" he starts out. "We could do something like that."

"Drive around the world? Isn't that a bit long?" He's barely begun and already I'm hesitant, afraid he's going to propose something that I can't see myself doing.

"No, not around the world. We'd pick a place and go explore. Unplanned, sort of. We'd take it day by day, the way I did on that round-the-world drive, staying longer in places we enjoyed and moving on when we were ready.

I don't know what to make of this. I've never traveled without a plan, not knowing where I might be the next day, not having hotel reservations for each night. I want to keep this conversation going, though, so I say, "Hmmm," which strikes me as reasonably positive and properly noncommittal.

Bernard charges on, "It'd be perfect to get away from here for a couple of months in the middle of winter, don't you think? Anyway, I've had enough of plowing and shoveling every day for months on end."

"A couple of months?" I splutter. This is all moving too fast for me. I started out imagining we'd do a local drive for a week or two. Left to his own devices, Bernard's gone off on a totally different tack, and now he's proposing we go away for a period longer than the Rally, without even booking a room for the night. "Oh no, what have I started?" I think. I've barely finished the Rally that nearly did me in, and now Bernard's concocting another escapade that is so beyond the borders of my comfort zone I doubt I can even get a visa for it.

Then a strange and wonderful thing happens. The nameless dreads subside, and I move into rally mode, searching for something productive to make of Bernard's idea. When I do, what's obvious to Bernard becomes obvious to me. His suggestion isn't as far-fetched as I feared, because if there is one thing I know how to do now it's a long road trip. If I can be in a car for thirty-five days, why not forty or fifty? What's the big deal? Besides, what I said to Bernard days ago was the truth. For weeks now, I've been filled with a veritable ache, a hunger, to be in an automobile again, as long as it's with Bernard. I crave it the way I crave a juicy Angus ribeye after a hard day's work. At those times, the urge to get back in a car, close the door, and see what happens next is almost more than I can stand. The very unknowingness of being on a new road, unmasking the secret of what's around the bend, reveling in the fatigue and the exhilaration of driving and discovering, all with Bernard beside me, fill me with longing. If the man offered to drive me to the moon, I'd say "When do we go!?"

This time though, I have one imperative: I want to do it my way. "You mean just the two of us, right? On our own. Picking a region and then going there and driving through it. Right?" It feels important at that moment to make sure Bernard doesn't have another rally hidden up his sleeve.

"Never again three hundred people," he says. We grin at each other in relief.

"OK!" I say, two syllables which are so quickly said and can get me into such trouble. "No support organization because we won't need one, no ambulance crew because we don't get sick anyway, no mechanics because you're the best one there is." I want to wake up in the morning and pore over a map with Bernard, pinky finger tracing a thread of road as we decide where to go that day, free to wander as the spirit moves us. "This," I say to Bernard, "is going to be the polar opposite of the P2P in every way."

With that, we're transformed. We click back into sync, excited to find time together during days that now seem filled with too many distractions from the essential. The essential being figuring out where we're going to go on our first multi-week road trip and what we're going to use to cover all those miles. The second part comes easier than the first.

"Shall we use Roxanne?" Bernard asks, raising the obvious question. "She's ready to go." I can tell from his tone that he misses her, misses this vehicle into which he poured a year and a half of his life and so many dreams.

"I know," I tell him, and I sigh to buy more time, procrastinating, not wanting to hurt Bernard's feelings by what I say next. "Obviously, I do know just how much effort you, *we*, put into getting Roxanne ready for the Rally. Still, I don't think I can do another long car trip in her. At least not right now. I realize nothing should go wrong with her now, but theoretically nothing should have gone wrong with her on the Rally. And it did. If we use her I'll be worrying all the time about what might break next. I don't want our next trip to be about the cool car. I want it to be easy, no car worries, just us seeing what's around. Know what I mean?"

"No, no," Bernard says, which is how he expresses that he agrees with me. "You're right. We could get a different car." His eyes get that wounded puppy look, and I can tell he's stifling some disappointment, but he's not making a big deal of it. We're figuring out our next trip and we've both adopted the practice of compromise that served us so well on the P2P.

"We don't need to buy yet another car, I don't think. How about we just rent? You know what'd be great about that? Car repairs would be someone else's problem!" I feel quite triumphant about this. "We get a car from Avis or Hertz, and if it breaks down, we call them and they bring us another one." I'm in love with my new adventure, my imagination already running wild with the marvels of wherever we'll be going.

"Yes. You're right. Perfect."

Figuring out where to go takes more thought. Bernard starts. "We could go around Europe. Visit friends and family. Go skiing," he suggests. I applaud the notion of touring ski resorts and being away in February and March, the depths of our snow season. "But," I say, "if we go to Europe during ski season we're just trading one winter for another. It'd be more inspiring to get away from winter altogether, wouldn't it?"

"So that means somewhere where it's summer during our winter. How about Australia?"

"How about Patagonia?"

"Patagonia? That's a country in South America right?" Bernard's stumped. I've finally caught him out by proposing a place he doesn't know of. What he doesn't realize yet is that Patagonia's not a country at all. "It's a region at the tip of South America" I explain, "that's split between Chile and Argentina and goes all the way down to Cape Horn, in Tierra del Fuego. Remember when my father went there, about 15 years ago?"

It's an area that my father, by then in his late seventies and well past his prime mountaineering days, loved. Looking at photos in the den of his Salt Lake City home, he described to us the majestic black spires of Torres del Paine and FitzRoy, the pure sparkling rivers spilling from immense glaciers, the coastline teaming with penguins and seals, magical names like Straits of Magellan and Beagle Channel, and gauchos in black berets galloping horseback through the waving grasslands of the pampas. He loved the clarity of the air, the broad, sweeping views. Above all, he was enchanted with the start of what was projected to be a magnificent wild road called the Carretera Austral, which for the first time would permit access by car to Chile's isolated southern coastline. I'd been longing to go there ever since.

"Patagonia is the region where I wanted to do that long horseback ride through, but couldn't because of work, remember? I think I must have shown you the description of that horse trek several times." I'm nudging Bernard along, trying to jog his memory and impress on him that my suggestion isn't pure whimsy. At this point, I have no idea whether the Carretera Austral will be too scarily remote even for the new me. I do know one thing, though, which is that Bernard is not excited about a place where I would go horseback riding. To reel him in I have to hook him with something enticing. Seven hundred miles of deserted gravel road is my worm.

We go to the computer together and google "Carretera Austral." As Bernard reads the description, he's silent. He turns to me and says, half puzzled, half accusatory, "How come I've never heard of this before? Tell me again how you say it?"

Cah-rreh-teh-ra Ow-strahl" I say, rolling the r's. "It means Southern Highway." Though I'm no fisherman, I sense he's got the hook in his mouth. It's time to set it. "Hardly anyone ever drives there. Especially not driving themselves in their own car. I mean rental car." I can feel the hook dig deep and grab.

"Really? Patagonia. Hmmm. You know, maybe I have heard of this Carretera," which he says like most Frenchmen, unable to roll an "r" to save his life. "Yes, yes. I think I read something about it." Bernard loves to be the most knowledgeable about everything. Then he returns to reading the road information on the screen. "You know, I think I'll go to my office and see what else I can learn about this road. Do you think we could find a map of it?" The hook is set so hard that Bernard is going to reel himself in. I'm jubilant.

We're going to Patagonia. Our travel companions will be maps and a guidebook. We'll have three hotel reservations, one in Santiago for the day of our arrival, and one each to guarantee us the perfect locale in Torres del Paine and for access to FitzRoy. The notion of being so footloose fills me with a delicious dread. Four months later, we board a plane for Chile.

Epilogue: Are We There Yet?

APHORISMS FROM A DRIVING LIFE

Roxanne did not return with us to Colorado at the end of the P2P. One of James' friends, visiting in Reims the night before the rally ended, fell so completely under her spell that he asked if he could adopt her. "I will care for her as if she were my own," he said. From the comfort of her climate-controlled, heavily guarded garage near his home, she was outfitted with a new windshield, got her leaky parts tightened, and had proper shock absorber mounts measured and welded in place.

We had planned to drive her again, indeed we kicked around several possible jaunts, but somehow it never worked out. Finally, wishing her a chance to once more strut her stuff on the roads of the world, we sold her to an Australian couple who wanted a rally-ready car to take on a variation of the P2P being run by the same organizers in 2010. They did a shake-down rally with her in 2009, driving from London to Casablanca. She performed beautifully, but afterward her new owners decided she merited a new engine. A year later, they started the P2P with her, at the same spot in Badaling where we departed three years earlier. This time it was Day 2 when a fan bolt broke, severely damaging the radiator. Roxanne made it to Ulaanbaatar where the damage was repaired, but within an hour of the start from UB it happened again, this time destroying her radiator completely. Roxanne was withdrawn from the rally altogether and shipped back to England. The whole episode gives me the shivers. It's more than odd that on both P2Ps a fan-related incident happened within the first two days, the only difference being that, in our case, we kept Roxanne going.

Part of me likes to think my fender hugging in Greeley really did touch Roxanne's soul.

When the first P2P race was run in 1907, cars were still a novelty. It was cause for celebration when someone got one and cause for repeat celebration every time you went out in one and returned home unscathed. Since the P2P, we've driven tens of thousands of miles more. Avis supplied us with a spunky white Isuzu in Patagonia. A borrowed Mahindra Jeep I called Sexy Beast took us from the southern tip of India to the foothills of the Himalayas. Our own Land Rover Defender, whom I named Brunhilde, because she's fair and full of fortitude, squired us around a thousand hairpin turns climbing up to Peru's altiplano and from there down to Bolivia's deserts. She stood by us when we drove from Djibouti into and throughout Ethiopia and back, skirting the Somali border along the way. Brunhilde never flinched when tasked with conveying us 9,000 miles from Istanbul through Iran, more former Soviet 'stans than my passport had visa space for, onward through China, Tibet, Nepal, and finally India. Through it all, we've recaptured that euphoria that people used to feel a hundred years ago when they got in a car. They'd close the door, if there was one, sit back, and know that adventure awaited them. Now we do the same. I don't even get carsick.

The isolation within a car interior is a perfect foil for travel. It's familiar and by its familiarity, it is comforting. Yet it's that very familiarity that keeps everything that's outside, the unfamiliar, in sharp relief. I see more clearly when I'm in a car and I have time to reflect on what's around me before engaging in whatever it is that's going on. By driving ourselves, Bernard and I have the freedom to go where we wish when we wish. In a car, the very process of transit—the getting there—makes everything that much more vivid.

You'd think that after all this driving, I'd be besotted with cars. I'm not. I'm as much a babe in the woods mechanically as when we first got Roxanne. On the first day of a long road trip, I still quarrel with myself about whether I can manage to sit in the passenger seat for six to eight hours a day. I bid clean hair, regular meals, and chic shoes a reluctant farewell. I'm still my toughest critic. I still preface simple sentences with "Sorry," so if it turns out I've made a mistake, I've already apologized for it. I've had to accept how insufferably impatient I am, and how exquisitely exasperated I become when I can't control a situation. Still, I marvel how being in a car could have taught me so much.

Take, for instance, one of the times when Bernard was tightening something or other under the car. It was hot, he was dripping, and I'm sure he would have preferred to be somewhere else, especially if that somewhere involved breezy shade and an ice cold beer. I know I would have, and I wasn't even down in the gravel, copiously perspiring. I was standing by the tool box cursing the humid heat, wondering whether I couldn't somehow start the car so I could sit in it with the air conditioning on full blast, without simultaneously asphyxiating Bernard. Bernard stuck with it, of course. He finished the job, because there's no time like the present to take care of a bothersome rattle or worrying clang. After we continued that day's drive, blessedly rattle-free, I was, naturally, grateful that Bernard had dealt with the problem. I knew, also, that if he hadn't been able to fix it, he'd have stored the matter away to take care of at the next opportunity. Here's how I summed it up: *If you can fix something, do. Immediately. If you can't fix something, accept it for the moment and move on.* There's nothing inherently wise about this as it pertains to car maintenance, but apply it to the next problem in your relationship with anyone, whether boss, lover, sibling, or parent, and you'll see what a great notion it is.

There are still occasions when I enjoy a good sulk as much as the next baby. I've gotten better, though. During those long P2P days I'd tell myself: *Reject dramatizing a situation. Emotion won't improve things. Action will.* I tried so hard to take this to heart on the P2P, with only middling success. I still struggle with the rationale that *if sulking equals exhaustion, and exhaustion can only result from action, then sulking must be action, too.*

Locking two prisoners in a five by five cell would be considered cruel and unusual punishment. I still don't know what possessed me to voluntarily commit myself to join my husband in that size space. I do know that when we hit a rough patch, which on road trips can sometimes be daily, I need only think of the Russia/Estonia border or the one between Mongolia and China. Because *borders exist to be crossed, boundaries respected.* It helps me remember the distinction between seizing an opportunity to push beyond my natural limits and pushing myself so hard I become dysfunctional. Or between harping at Bernard to do something I want versus backing off because I've invaded Bernard's space and letting him arrive at what I want in his own time. On the road, Bernard has adjusted to my fervent desire to go out and walk around the streets, any streets, as soon as we've reached our day's destination. Now, though, I can wait until he's had a shower, changed, and drunk a beer before we do so.

Momentum: have it and you'll get through the rough spots. Lose it and you're going nowhere. This came to me during a time trial, when we plowed slowly through deep sand, which had already trapped another car. Bernard looked at them and said, "Typical error. People think they have to speed up to get through sand. It's the opposite. Go as slowly as you can while still moving forward. That way you won't spin your wheels and carve ruts." It came up again when Bernard and I were struggling to excavate ourselves from the morass we were stuck in following the P2P. Each tentative opener of conversation meant movement. The way forward was slow, and neither of us knew quite where that way was leading, but even baby steps were better than no steps at all.

I'm at ease with my follower position now. And I've decided it doesn't matter whether you're the follower or the leader. One is not inherently better than the other, and each needs the other simply to exist. In fact, it's the ultimate symbiotic relationship. Think of it. Where would Genghis Khan have gotten if he hadn't had an excellent horde behind him? Here's a truth I now know: *It takes a great follower to make an accomplished leader.* I'm happiest that, when we search our atlas for a likely candidate for our next trip, and I suggest to Bernard that he might go with someone else, because that particular place scares me, he says, "But I don't want to go with someone else. I want to go with you." This despite the fact that I still confuse west with east and have trouble believing that the direction ahead of me cannot always be north. These are the limitations of a dashboard devotee. I've come to terms with them, as has Bernard. That's why he's installed a permanent GPS on *his* side of the dashboard, the screen tilted toward him so I can't even see it.

Oh, one last thought, which is perhaps the most important of all. It's seen me through many a dark moment on the road, become my guiding light at home, and I want to share it with you: *When in doubt, get a pedicure. Things are always clearer when you have polish on your toenails..*

Acknowledgments

Behind every writer is an avid reader. Or many. For company and insight on the reading journey, I am in debt to the women of my Colorado book clubs: the Never Summer Readers of Walden and the Magnolia Blossoms of Nederland. Every month you gave me a chance to play with words and refine what it is in books that captivates me. I hope I've managed to capture some of that in my own.

The marvelous Iowa Summer Writing Festival provided the forum for a much-needed writing tune-up. I am ever grateful to Lon Otto, my superb instructor at ISWF, for looking me in the eye and telling me just to get on with it. Thanks to his referral, the wonderful Michele Hodgson took my collection of anecdotes and helped me craft them into a real story.

For believing in me, keeping me laughing when times were tough, and finding a publisher for my work, I thank Ken Wright. Landing on Planet Wright was one of the luckiest days of my life. Michele Rubin stepped in and with extraordinary flair and passion took over the reins. I cannot imagine how I became so fortunate as to have such a kindred soul as my agent.

Marjorie Braman inspired me and left an indelible imprint on this book. Thanks for tips on where to buy the best French mustard, for insight on how to dress for the horse races, and for great taste in restaurants.

The impressively talented Lindsey Breuer, my editor at Skyhorse, brought this book to fruition, applying a discerning eye and an ineffable sense of the rightness of phrasing and teaching me lessons about poise under pressure. Thank you for your enthusiasm, your hard work, and most of all for going the extra mile on my behalf, even when that extra mile was actually ten.

My spirit is supported by the love of very special friends. For countless hours playing Scrabble and Bananagrams, joining me on horseback adventures, bike rides, hikes, and walks, patiently listening to my dreams, reading drafts of this book, and sharing priceless feedback, I thank Peg Brocker, Betsy Kates, Vivian Long, and Annie Sjoberg. Thank you to Donna Meitus for opening your home to me and showing me the joys of Zumba, planking, and pho lunches. I am deeply, humbly grateful to Janine Brownstone and Pat Heiber for ignoring my uncoolness and becoming life-long friends with whom I can still resume a conversation started so many years ago. To all of you: You lift me up; you make me smile; my life is immeasurably richer for your presence.

The readers of my travel newsletter shared my amazement and laughed along with me at the odd things I encountered on my road trips. At the risk of leaving out many, I extend heartfelt thanks to Heinz and Heidi Löber, the many-numbered Gateau family, Michael O'Malley, Laura Border, the late Carl Trick, Sr., Marie Thomas, Bob Tointon, Tessa Wardlaw, Marian Cramer Wood, BJ Holmes, Phil Teeter, Inga Schalburg, Rosalie Culver, Dani and Yvonne Bernstein, Cherie Long, Bob and Audrey Williams, and Bruce Blythe. Your feedback while I was on the road was like high-octane fuel, and your insistence that I put it into a book is the reason why this one exists.

I can never repay the boundless welcome and no-strings-attached love of Nina, Izzy, Kate, Chloe, and Skip. Special thanks to Magic, Bridger, Scout, and Beau, who took me over fields, through willows, and into the hills, never questioning where I wanted to go, knowing simply that I needed to get gone.

I clearly won the lottery in my sister Vivienne, who contributed in countless ways to this book. She is confidante and advisor, playmate and admirer, editorial coach and my biggest cheerleader. She laughs at my jokes, will forever be tall and blonde to my not so tall and brown, grounds me when I get carried away, then lets me fly. Given the extent to which I tormented her as a child, I am thrilled she is still willing to accept me as her sibling. I have only one sister and that's all I need.

Everyone thanks their family in their acknowledgements. For me, the issue runs deeper, as this story would never have happened if not for my husband, Bernard. That he helped me step into his dream and let me make it mine was an act of the purest generosity and faith. Without you, my life would be a poorer thing.

Appendix 1

1940 LASALLE 52 COUPE
RALLY PREPARATION September 2005– March 2007
CHASSIS 4330056

Mileage when purchased: 29,651

Body and Interior

Provision for tow-bar attachment
Replace front seats with Sparco high-end rally seats
Install 3-point harness
Insulation on fire wall
New paint, correct to model year
Install electric windshield wipers
Install safe under copilot seat
Install new carpet, headliner, and door panels
Install special compartment behind seats to hold all spares

Electrical Instrumentation

Change from 6 volts to 12 volts
Replace dynamo with 50 Amp alternator
Install map lamp for copilot
Install accessories plugs for GPS and Tripmeter
Install wheel probe and universal cable probe for Tripmeter

Add instrument cluster with oil/water temp and tachometer

Replace all electrical wiring with waterproof wiring

Install two 925 Amp dry-cell batteries with metal jacket

Suspension, Chassis, and Tires

Replace king pins

Add telescopic shock absorbers front and rear

Install new set of leaf springs

Raise rear suspension 3 inches

Replace helical springs with heavy-duty ones

Replace bushings with Polygraphite ones

Change wheel bearings

Check chassis welds and redo as needed

Sand blast and powder coat chassis

Install aluminum, multisegment under-body protection

Replace wheels

Install radial tires

Brake System

Replace brake lines with stainless steel lines

Replace master cylinder

Replace all wheel cylinders

New brake linings

Arcing all brake shoes

Engine and Power Train

Overhaul engine, new pistons, valves, lifters

Install oil filter

Replace engine mounts

New radiator core

Manufacture 3-point radiator mounting system

Install more efficient air filtration system

Change ignition system for a solid-state one

Replace and reroute exhaust system

Change all oils to synthetic

Engine Dyno before installation: 107HP and 197lb-ft @ 3400RPM

Rebuild carburetor

Fuel System

Install 40-gallon stainless steel fuel tank

Install two Facet POSI-FLO fuel pumps with pre-filters

Run two separate, steel braided fuel lines

Install RACOR fuel filter with water separator

Appendix 2

PEKING TO PARIS MOTOR CHALLENGE 2007 ROUTE

DAILY DESTINATION	KILOMETERS
Day 1 May 27 Sunday Beijing to Datong	363
Day 2 May 28 Monday Datong to Siziwang Qi	368
Day 3 May 29 Tuesday Siziwang Qi to Erenhot	248
Day 4 May 30 Wednesday Erenhot to Saynshand (+Border)	223
Day 5 May 31 Thursday Saynshand to Ulaanbaatar	436
Day 6 Jun 1 Friday Rest Day Ulaanbaatar	REST DAY
Day 7 Jun 2 Saturday Ulaanbaatar to Kharkorin	365

DAILY DESTINATION	KILOMETERS
Day 8 Jun 3 Sunday Kharkorin to Bayankhongor	428
Day 9 Jun 4 Monday Bayankhongor to Altay	388
Day 10 Jun 5 Tuesday Altay to Khovd	433
Day 11 Jun 6 Wednesday Khovd to Border Camp	295
Day 12 Jun 7 Thursday Border to Biysk (+Border)	635
Day 13 Jun 8 Friday Biysk to Novosibirsk	437
Day 14 Jun 9 Saturday Rest Day Novosibirsk	REST DAY
Day 15 Jun 10 Sunday Novosibirsk to Omsk	668
Day 16 Jun 11 Monday Omsk to Tyumen	632
Day 17 Jun 12 Tuesday Tyumen to Yekaterinburg	315

DAILY DESTINATION	KILOMETERS
Day 18 Jun 13 Wednesday Rest Day Yekaterinburg	REST DAY
Day 19 Jun 14 Thursday Yekaterinburg to Perm	379
Day 20 Jun 15 Friday Perm to Kazan	688
Day 21 Jun 16 Saturday Kazan to Niz. Novgorod	392
Day 22 Jun 17 Sunday Niz. Novgorod to Moscow	439
Day 23 Jun 18 Monday Rest Day Moscow	REST DAY
Day 24 Jun 19 Tuesday Moscow to St. Petersburg	730
Day 25 Jun 20 Wednesday Rest Day St. Petersburg	REST DAY
Day 26 Jun 21 Thursday St. Petersburg to Tallinn (+Border)	450
Day 27 Jun 22 Friday Tallinn to Riga (+Border)	406

DAILY DESTINATION	KILOMETERS
Day 28 Jun 23 Saturday Riga to Vilnius (+Border)	394
Day 29 Jun 24 Sunday Vilnius to Mikolajki (+Border)	403 GMT+3 (UK+2)
Day 30 Jun 25 Monday Mikolajki to Gdansk	351
Day 31 Jun 26 Tuesday Rest Day Gdansk	REST DAY
Day 32 Jun 27 Wednesday Gdansk to Potsdam (+Border)	598
Day 33 Jun 28 Thursday Potsdam to Koblenz	556
Day 34 Jun 29 Friday Koblenz to Reims (+Border)	461
Day 35 Jun 30 Saturday Reims to Paris	161
Total kilometers	12642
Total miles	7901

Appendix 3

Type	Year	Engine
Itala 40	1907	6500
Itala 40	1907	3000
Brasier 22/30 Torpedo	1911	3700
Knox Type R	1911	7166
Talbot 35HP	1908	5300
Ford Model T	1909	2859
Lancia Theta	1916	4700
Itala 51B	1924	2813
Packard Twin Six	1917	6900
La France Roadster	1918	14500
Essex 6A	1919	2800
La France Roadster	1919	14500
Rolls Royce Silver Ghost	1922	7500
Rolls Royce Silver Ghost	1923	7500
Rolls Royce Silver Ghost	1926	7428
Vauxhall 30/98	1923	4398
Mercedes 60HP	1903	9236
Singer Le Mans	1934	933
Bugatti Type 44	1927	3000

Type	Year	Engine
Buick Pickup Roadster	1925	2550
Rover 12 Six Light Saloon	1938	1496
Alvis 12/50 Beetleback	1930	1635
Sunbeam 16	1932	2200
Chevrolet Roadster	1929	3500
Rolls Royce 20/25	1933	3669
Chrysler 65	1928	3200
Chevrolet AB Roadster	1928	2700
Chrysler 72	1928	3000
Lagonda High Chassis T1	1927	4500
Bentley	1926	3000
MG SA	1938	2288
Chevrolet Coupe	1930	3180
Alvis Speed 20	1933	2655
Rolls Royce Coupe	1936	7340
Lagonda M45 Tourer	1933	4453
Lagonda T7	1934	3000
Lagonda M45 Tourer	1934	4553
Talbot 95	1934	2687
Lagonda M45 Tourer	1935	4500
Ford Model A	1931	3300
Ford Model A Roadster	1931	3225
Lancia Lambda	1929	2570
Rolls Royce 20 Tourer	1927	3000
Bentley 4.5 Le Mans	1927	4398
Delage D6L	1930	3075
Delage D7S	1930	4050
Bentley Open Tourer	1937	4398

Type	Year	Engine
Mercedes 630 K Sport	1927	6300
Mercedes 630K	1927	6240
Bentley 4.5 Le Mans	1928	4398
Bentley 4.5 Le Mans	1928	4398
Jaguar 3.5 litre Saloon	1948	3500
Bentley 4.5	1929	4398
Bentley 6.5 Tourer	1929	8000
Chrysler 75 Roadster	1929	4078
Bentley 3.5 Tourer	1935	3500
Bentley 4.5 Le Mans	1929	4398
Chrysler 75 Roadster	1929	4600
Ford Pilot V8	1936	3622
Bentley 6.5 Tourer	1929	6493
Bentley 6.5 Tourer	1929	6597
Bentley 6.5 Tourer	1927	6597
Riley 16	1937	2443
Derby Bentley	1936	4250
LaSalle Cadillac Roadster	1936	4098
Derby Bentley	1939	4259
LaSalle Cabriolet Sedan	1937	5280
Derby Bentley	1937	4250
LaSalle Coupe Cabriolet	1940	5280
Citroen Traction Avant	1939	2867
Ford 01A	1940	3622
Chrysler 77	1929	4275
Bentley 6.5 Tourer	1926	6500
Chevrolet Coupe	1940	3501
Buick Coupe	1937	2480

Type	Year	Engine
Bentley Speed Six	1927	6500
Buick Sedan Saloon	1938	2480
Cadillac 70 Fleetwood	1936	5700
LaSalle Coupe	1940	5277
Chevrolet Roadster	1937	4000
Packard Coupe 120	1938	4625
Chevrolet Fangio Coupe	1938	3540
Chevrolet Fangio Coupe	1938	3500
Chevrolet Fangio Coupe	1941	4250
Chevrolet Fangio Coupe	1940	2998
Alvis Silver Eagle	1934	3571
Buick Convertible	1940	8000
Buick 4L straight-eight	1940	4000
Ford Coupe TC	1940	4000
Ford Convertible	1937	3600
Buick Convertible	1941	3900
Chevrolet Coupe TC	1939	4000
Austin 16	1948	2199
MG Magnette ZA	1956	1798
Volkswagen Beetle	1959	1300
Volkswagen Cabriolet	1959	1500
Bentley R Saloon	1953	4566
Land Rover Series I	1955	1997
Citroen Traction Avant	1954	1911
Sunbeam Alpine	1954	2267
Citroen Roadster	1950	1911
Riley RMB	1951	2443
Chevrolet Bel Air	1950	3550

Type	Year	Engine
Ford Pilot V8	1950	3622
Studebaker Starlite Coupe	1951	3785
Alfa Romeo Giuletta TI	1957	1290
Citroen 2CV6	1965	602
Rover P4 80	1960	2286
Holden FC	1958	2250
Lancia Aurelia B20S	1954	2400
Sunbeam Rapier Saloon	1960	1592
Triumph TR3A	1958	2188
Morgan plus 4	1953	1991
Porsche 356A	1959	1600
Bentley Drophead	1952	4500
Aston Martin DB6	1969	3995
Mercedes 220S	1958	2195
Ford Coupe TC	1950	4000
Aston Martin DB4	1960	4000
Volvo 1800S	1967	1800
Jaguar MkII	1961	3794
Volvo PV544	1964	1780
Aston Martin DB6	1965	3995
Mercedes 200 Saloon	1966	1988
Bentley Special	1936	6554
Bentley Special	1953	5675

Appendix 4

WHAT ROXANNE CARRIED WITH HER

INSIDE BAY

U-joints
Alternator
Shocks x 4
Water pump
Exhaust pipe section
Spring compressor
Terratrip rally computer
Fire extinguisher
Rear cylinders x 2
Mounted tires x 2
Bungee cords

Hazard triangle
(behind driver's seat)
Brake shoes—front set
Transmission shaft
Front springs x 2
Tent
Three bags with all tools
Master cylinder
Front cylinders x 2
Headlight beams x 2

TRUNK

First-aid kit
Starter (box)
Carburetor (box)
Tow rope
Jack
Jumper cables
Gas can

Emergency blankets
Transmission oil—1 quart
Engine oil—3 quarts
Air filters x 2
Nuts and bolts
Water container
Shovel

Hitch
Skid mats
Compressor
Sleeping bags x 2

Belts and pipes
Work light
Distilled H20—1 gallon
Sleeping pads x 2

BOX ONE

Radiator sealer—yellow bottle
Radiator quick solder
Duct tape
Gasket maker—red tube
Teflon tape
Springs—various
Hose clamps—large and small
Exhaust mount
Headlight trim screw
Bulbs x 9
Racor filters x 2
Wiper blades
Double-sided tape

Gas tank repair
Exhaust bandage x 2
Velcro
JB Weld—2 sets
Loctite (medium)
Vacuum hose—silicone
Spark plug leads—grommets
Tire repair kit
Rail nuts x 2
Driving light bulbs x 2
Peterson filters
Hubcap remover tool
Ziploc bags—extras

BOX TWO

Idler arm
Rear spring bolts
Wheel nuts x 11
Spark plugs x 2 sets
Distributor cap
Dimmer switch
Elec. ignition
Rotor arms x 3
Points x 2 sets
U-joint bolts

Ball joints—steering
Lifters x 8
Exhaust nuts
Spark plug leads—full set
Vacuum advance
Terratrip 1.5 mm probe + cable
Ignition coil
Relay 30A x 2
Condenser x 2

BOX THREE

Locking washers—front and rear
Springs—heavy x 8
Brake shoe assembly—parts
Brake line fittings/lines
Posi-Flow fuel pump
Transmission mount
Rear bearings

Springs—light x 6
Rear seals x 2
Roller bearings x 2
Oil filter
Fuel line fittings

BOX FOUR

Brake fluid funnel
Fluid pump
LPS #1
Fuel lines x 2

Brake lines—front and rear
Brake fluid x 2
Grease pump

Appendix 5

RALLY TERMINOLOGY

(adapted from www.rockyroadracing.com and
How to Win a Road Rally by Alan Smith)

Driver

The person who drives the rally car. Unlike other forms of motor racing, the driver does not know the course in advance. Instead he or she must rely on their navigator to tell them where the road goes.

Navigator

The person who sits in the passenger's seat of the rally car. Using the route book for reference, he or she describes the approaching road to the driver.

Route Book

A series of pages created by the rally organizers that use mileages, written descriptions and notes, as well as schematic-like drawings to explain and describe the route. This book is used by the navigator as a basis for describing the route to the driver.

Rally Tripmeter

A special computer installed in a rally car that measures mileage to the hundredth of a mile, reads time to the hundredth of a minute, as well as a host of other things.

Route Instruction

An individual row giving the mileages, written descriptions, and notes to identify significant corners or other important things along the route. As there are far too many junctions to specify each in the route book, the rule of thumb is to continue on the road you're on until instructed to turn.

Tulip Diagram

A small line-drawing diagramming a junction where a turn must be made. The circle at one end of the diagram depicts where you arrive and the arrow on the other end depicts where you need to go. Originally used on the Dutch Tulip Rally in the 1950s, the odd thing is that the Dutch call this diagram style "Ball and Arrow."

Time Card

A special paper or booklet, carried by each rally team, where the course marshals write the rally team's time at each control point during the day, before and after any time trial, and at the end of each day.

Microchipped Time Card

Traditionally, the course marshal took a car's arrival time from his own watch, wrote it on the time card, and signed. Now, microchips are used, with a chip embedded in the time card twinned to one in the course marshal's timing gadget. The microchip provides greater accuracy and enables a computer to speedily update the standings at the end of each stage, allowing rally staff that much more time at the bar.

Main Time Control (MTC)

The manned station where, at the beginning of each day of a long-distance rally, each team clocks in to receive certified departure time for that day's stage. Cars depart the MTC at one-minute intervals.

Finish Time Control (FTC)

The manned station at the end of each day where each team books in to have their arrival time recorded on their time card.

Arrival Time Control (ATC)

A manned station just before the start of a time trial where each rally team is required to check in at an assigned time. Teams are penalized for checking in early or late, discouraging them from speeding on the transits or taking extra service time.

Time Control (TC) and Passage Control (PC)

Generally a manned stopping point used to make sure there's no cheating, such as taking unsanctioned short cuts. Each day has multiple TCs and PCs. Every car has a designated arrival time at each TC, based on their assigned departure time from the MTC. Penalties are assessed for every minute a car is late and also for every minute a car is early. At a PC, there's no particular time one needs to check in, but there will be a marshal who signs the time card as proof you've been there.

Time Trial

A flat out racing section of a rally's route. These roads are closed to the public and are generally a few miles long at most. There's no pre-assigned start time for a time trial. You just get in the queue when you reach one and must be ready to go when your car reaches the starting line.

Stage Time

The amount of time, to the hundredth of a minute, that it takes a rally team to complete each day's stage as well as any time trials. A team's final score is determined by adding up all their individual stage times. The rally team with the lowest cumulative time wins.

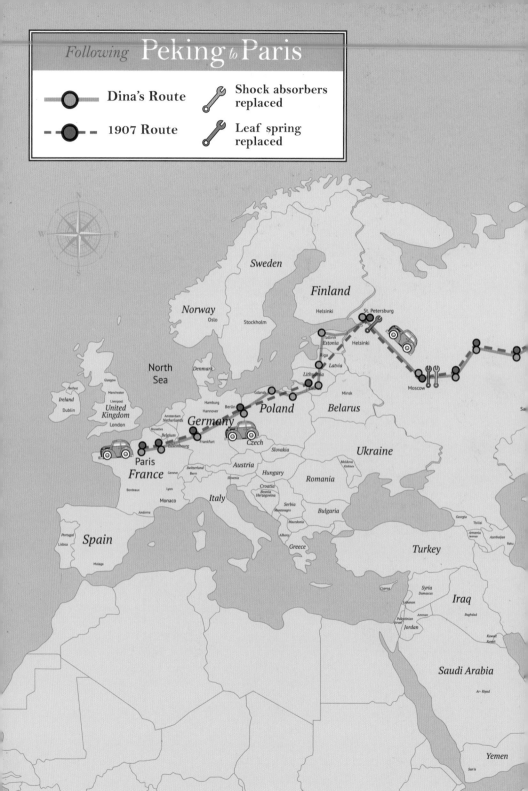